THE COMPLETE
ITALIAN
COOKBOOK

THE COMPLETE ITALIAN COOKBOOK

Over 200 Classic and Contemporary Italian Dishes Made for the Modern Kitchen

13-Digit ISBN: 978-1-64643-168-7
10-Digit ISBN: 1-64643-168-5

This book may be ordered by mail from the publisher. Please include $5.99 for postage and handling. Please support your local bookseller first!

Books published by Cider Mill Press Book Publishers are available at special discounts for bulk purchases in the United States by corporations, institutions, and other organizations. For more information, please contact the publisher.

Cider Mill Press Book Publishers
"Where Good Books Are Ready for Press"
PO Box 454
12 Spring Street
Kennebunkport, Maine 04046
Visit us online!
www.cidermillpress.com

Typography: Adobe Garamond Pro, Gotham, Farmhand, Avenir, Linotype Centennial
Image Credits: Photos on 30, 46, 65, 67, 91, 95, 103, 108, 114, 117, 119, 121, 122, 125, 133, 141, 142, 167, 172, 175, 176, 178, 183, 222, 226, 330, 338, 346, 353, 354, 357, 365, 366, 369, 381, 386, and 393 courtesy of Cider Mill Press. All other photos used under official license from Shutterstock.com

Printed in China

Front cover image: Roasted Tomato & Garlic Sauce, see page 102
Back cover image: Fig, Prosciutto & Balsamic Pizza, see page 316

3 4 5 6 7 8 9 0

THE COMPLETE
ITALIAN
COOKBOOK

Over 200 Classic and Contemporary Italian Dishes
Made for the Modern Kitchen

CIDER MILL
PRESS

BOOK
PUBLISHERS
KENNEBUNKPORT, MAINE

TABLE of CONTENTS

❉ ❉ ❉

INTRODUCTION

❃ ❃ ❃

When asked what they think of Italian food, most people will respond with a positivity and passion that is all too rare today.

Ask those same people what their favorite offering from the cuisine is, and many, maybe even an overwhelming majority, will offer up something like pizza, chicken Parmesan, penne alla vodka, pasta primavera, or tiramisu.

Purists will roll their eyes at these responses, but they do reflect an evolution that has been underway since large numbers of Italians begin to emigrate to America beginning in the early twentieth century: Italian food, though it will always bear the mark of its origin, has developed into something else entirely, with the American influence taking the cuisine increasingly toward the comforting, king-sized dishes that diners in the US tend to envision when "What about Italian?" comes up as dinner plans are being discussed.

This development, while no doubt delicious, does keep too many unaware of the emphasis on simplicity, freshness, and exceptional ingredients that drives the cuisine back in Italy, a trio so powerful that the country has come to be viewed as the world's culinary mecca by industry heavyweights like Nancy Silverton, who returns time and time again for inspiration.

This book attempts to balance that tradition and the undeniable innovation the cuisine has undergone since it arrived on America's shores. There will be plenty of pizza for those who (rightly) view it as the world's most enjoyable food. But there will also be a number of the regional focaccia enjoyed throughout Italy, as these sumptuous flatbreads are what pizza grew out of. Fans of chicken Parmesan and pasta primavera will find recipes that bring these dishes within reach at home, but they will also have plenty of chances to look beyond this well-trodden ground, and expand their palates with fresh pastas and more traditional dishes. There is a recipe for tiramisu, but those who go to pieces in its presence may be surprised to see how much more they love it when it features homemade ladyfingers instead of the dubious commercial varieties that are frequently employed.

The hope, in the end, is that this book leaves no doubt as to why Italian food has managed to conquer the world like no other cuisine. Within its pages, one will discover the reason it is able to supply such unprecedented satisfaction: every single dish tastes like home.

CHAPTER 1

APPETIZERS, SALADS & SIDES

Many conjure visions of tables and belts buckling when Italian is mentioned, but its true genius has always been the ability to do a lot with a little, using flavor and quality ingredients to satisfy, instead of quantity. These dishes celebrate that original spirit, and are versatile enough to be deployed as a series of small plates for a casual and delicious dinner in the summer, placed beside a bowl of soup or fresh pasta to round out a meal, or placed beside a good wedge of cheese and a few cured meats.

CAPONATA

YIELD: **6 SERVINGS**

ACTIVE TIME: **1 HOUR**

TOTAL TIME: **2 HOURS**

INGREDIENTS

1 LARGE EGGPLANT (ABOUT 1½ LBS.)

2 TABLESPOONS EXTRA-VIRGIN OLIVE OIL

1 ONION, CHOPPED

2 CELERY STALKS, PEELED AND CHOPPED

3 LARGE GARLIC CLOVES, MINCED

2 RED BELL PEPPERS, STEMMED, SEEDED, AND CHOPPED

SALT AND PEPPER, TO TASTE

1 LB. RIPE ROMA TOMATOES, PEELED, SEEDED, AND FINELY CHOPPED; OR 1 (14 OZ.) CAN OF CRUSHED TOMATOES, WITH THEIR LIQUID

2 TABLESPOONS SUGAR, PLUS A PINCH

3 GENEROUS TABLESPOONS CAPERS, RINSED AND DRAINED

3 TABLESPOONS CHOPPED GREEN OLIVES

3 TABLESPOONS RED WINE VINEGAR

DIRECTIONS

1. Preheat the oven to 425°F. Place the eggplant on a baking sheet, place it in the oven, and roast until it has collapsed and is starting to char, about 25 minutes. Remove from the oven and let the eggplant cool. When cool enough to handle, roughly chop the eggplant.

2. Place 1 tablespoon of the oil in a large skillet and warm it over medium heat. When the oil starts to shimmer, add the onion and celery and cook, stirring, until the onion starts to soften, about 5 minutes. Stir in the garlic, cook for 1 minute, and then add the peppers. Season with salt and cook, stirring frequently, until the peppers are tender, about 8 minutes.

3. Add the remaining olive oil and the eggplant and cook, stirring occasionally, until the eggplant begins to fall apart and the other vegetables are tender. Stir in the tomatoes and the pinch of sugar, season the mixture with salt, and cook, stirring frequently, until the tomatoes start to collapse and smell fragrant, about 7 minutes.

4. Stir in the capers, olives, remaining sugar, and vinegar. Reduce the heat to medium-low and cook, stirring often, until the mixture is quite thick, sweet, and fragrant, 20 to 30 minutes. Taste, season with salt and pepper, and remove the pan from heat. Let the caponata cool to room temperature before serving. If time allows, chill in the refrigerator overnight and let it return to room temperature before serving.

CASATIELLO

YIELD: **1 LOAF**

ACTIVE TIME: **45 MINUTES**

TOTAL TIME: **5 HOURS AND 30 MINUTES**

DIRECTIONS

1. To prepare the sponge, add the yeast, 1 teaspoon of sugar, and water to a mixing bowl, gently stir to combine, and let the mixture stand until it is foamy, about 10 minutes. Add the egg yolks and remaining sugar and stir until smooth. Stir in half of the flour and beat the mixture until it is smooth. Add the remaining flour and the salt and stir until the mixture comes together as a soft dough. Place the sponge on a flour-dusted surface and gently knead for 3 to 4 minutes. Transfer the sponge to a bowl, cover it with plastic wrap, and let the dough rise at room temperature until it has doubled in size, about 1 hour.

2. To begin preparations for the dough, beat the eggs, sugar, and salt together in a large mixing bowl until combined. Add 1 cup of flour and stir until smooth. Cut the sponge into small pieces and add them to the dough. Beat to incorporate, add the remaining flour, and work the mixture with your hands until it comes together as a shaggy ball. Add the butter and work the mixture with your hands until incorporated. Add the Pecorino and Gruyère and knead the dough to incorporate.

3. Transfer the dough to a flour-dusted work surface and knead until it is elastic, extensible, and smooth, 5 to 10 minutes. Grease a bowl with olive oil, place the dough in the bowl, and cover it with plastic wrap. Let the dough rise at room temperature until it has almost tripled in size, about 1½ hours.

4. To prepare the filling, place the dough on a flour-dusted work surface and pat and roll it until it is a large rectangle that is about ¾ inch thick. Sprinkle half of the provolone, salami, and pepper over the dough. Fold into thirds, as you would a letter in order to put it into an envelope. Roll the dough out again so that it is ¾ inch thick. Sprinkle the remaining provolone, salami, and pepper over the dough and fold it into thirds. Gently knead for 2 to 3 minutes to distribute the cheese and salami evenly. Cut the dough in half and gently knead each half into a round ball.

5. Place each ball in a buttered, 2-quart charlotte mold or souffle dish. The dough should fill about half of the container. Cover with a towel and let the dough rise to the tops of the container, about 1½ hours.

6. Preheat the oven to 400°F. Brush the top of each loaf with the lightly beaten egg white. Place in the oven and bake until the tops of the bread are very brown and shiny. Remove from the oven, remove the loaves from the molds, and let them cool on a wire rack before slicing and serving.

INGREDIENTS

FOR THE SPONGE

4½ TEASPOONS ACTIVE DRY YEAST

1 TABLESPOON SUGAR, PLUS 1 TEASPOON

1¼ CUPS WARM WATER (105°F)

4 EGG YOLKS

2½ CUPS ALL-PURPOSE FLOUR, PLUS MORE AS NEEDED

1¼ TEASPOONS FINE SEA SALT

FOR THE DOUGH

4 EGGS

½ CUP SUGAR, PLUS 1½ TABLESPOONS

1⅓ TEASPOONS FINE SEA SALT

4¼ CUPS ALL-PURPOSE FLOUR, PLUS MORE AS NEEDED

2 STICKS OF UNSALTED BUTTER, PLUS 2 TABLESPOONS, AT ROOM TEMPERATURE

2 OZ. PECORINO ROMANO CHEESE, GRATED

2 OZ. GRUYÈRE CHEESE, GRATED

EXTRA-VIRGIN OLIVE OIL, AS NEEDED

FOR THE FILLING

ALL-PURPOSE FLOUR, AS NEEDED

2 OZ. PROVOLONE CHEESE, CUT INTO SMALL CUBES

3.5 OZ. SALAMI, CHOPPED

2 TEASPOONS BLACK PEPPER

BUTTER, AS NEEDED

1 EGG WHITE, LIGHTLY BEATEN

PEPPERS STUFFED WITH TUNA

YIELD: **6 SERVINGS**

ACTIVE TIME: **15 MINUTES**

TOTAL TIME: **45 MINUTES**

INGREDIENTS

1 LB. MINIATURE BELL PEPPERS

1 GARLIC CLOVE, PEELED

1 TABLESPOON CAPERS, DRAINED AND RINSED

1 (6 OZ.) CAN OF TUNA PACKED IN OLIVE OIL, DRAINED

1 TEASPOON DIJON MUSTARD

2 TABLESPOONS EXTRA-VIRGIN OLIVE OIL

2 TEASPOONS FRESH LEMON JUICE, PLUS MORE TO TASTE

1 TEASPOON FINELY CHOPPED FRESH ROSEMARY

2 TEASPOONS FINELY CHOPPED FRESH PARSLEY

1 ANCHOVY FILLET, RINSED, BONED, AND MINCED

1 TEASPOON APPLE CIDER VINEGAR

SALT AND PEPPER, TO TASTE

DIRECTIONS

1. Preheat the oven to 425°F and line a baking sheet with aluminum foil. Place the peppers on the baking sheet, place them in the oven, and roast until soft and lightly charred, 10 to 15 minutes, turning them once or twice. As the peppers will be different sizes, there will be some variance between how quickly they cook, so make sure to keep an eye on them and remove as they become ready. After removing the peppers from the oven, let them cool.

2. Place the garlic and capers in a mortar and use a pestle to grind them into a paste.

3. Place the tuna in a mixing bowl and incorporate the mustard, olive oil, lemon juice, rosemary, parsley, anchovy, and vinegar one at a time. Taste and season with salt and pepper.

4. When the peppers have cooled, slice off the tops, remove the seeds and stems, and discard them. Fill the peppers with the tuna mixture and either serve or store in the refrigerator, letting the peppers come to room temperature before serving.

   NOTE: Make sure you purchase the best anchovies available for the preparations in this book. They should be meaty and plump, and packed in salt or olive oil. Rinse the former before using, and drain the latter.

ZUCCHINI SOTT'OLIO

YIELD: **4 SERVINGS**

ACTIVE TIME: **15 MINUTES**

TOTAL TIME: **24 HOURS**

INGREDIENTS

¼ CUP KOSHER SALT, PLUS MORE AS NEEDED

2 ZUCCHINI, TRIMMED AND SLICED

4 ANCHOVY FILLETS, RINSED AND BONED

1 GARLIC CLOVE

EXTRA-VIRGIN OLIVE OIL, AS NEEDED

DIRECTIONS

1. Bring 8 cups of water to a boil in a medium saucepan. Add the salt and the zucchini and cook until the zucchini is just tender, about 4 minutes. Drain and let the zucchini cool.

2. Taste the zucchini. It should taste too salty, which is what you want in this particular preparation. If not, season with salt until it tastes too salty.

3. Place the zucchini in a jar, add the anchovies and garlic, and cover the mixture with olive oil. Place the mixture in the refrigerator and let it sit overnight before serving over the Fett'unta (see page 35) or Crostini (see page 40).

ROASTED GRAPES

YIELD: **8 SERVINGS**

ACTIVE TIME: **10 MINUTES**

TOTAL TIME: **1 HOUR AND 30 MINUTES**

INGREDIENTS

1½ TO 2 LBS. SEEDLESS GRAPES, RINSED AND PATTED DRY

EXTRA-VIRGIN OLIVE OIL, AS NEEDED

SALT, TO TASTE

DIRECTIONS

1. Preheat the oven to 350°F. Place the grapes in a mixing bowl, drizzle olive oil generously over them, and toss to coat. Place the grapes on a baking sheet, season with salt, and place in the oven. Roast until most of the grapes have collapsed and are slightly charred, about 25 minutes.

2. Remove from the oven and let cool completely before serving—the longer you let the grapes sit, the more concentrated their flavor will become.

FRIED ARTICHOKE HEARTS

YIELD: **4 SERVINGS**

ACTIVE TIME: **20 MINUTES**

TOTAL TIME: **30 MINUTES**

INGREDIENTS

2 LARGE ARTICHOKES

1 LEMON, QUARTERED

EXTRA-VIRGIN OLIVE OIL, AS NEEDED

SALT, TO TASTE

DIRECTIONS

1. Prepare the artichokes by using a serrated knife to cut off the top half with the leaves and all but the last inch of the stem; continue whittling away the outer leaves until you see the hairy-looking choke within. Using a paring knife, peel the outer layer of the remaining part of the stem; cut the remaining artichoke into quarters and remove the hairy part in the middle. You should have the heart with a little bit of lower leaves left. Place in a bowl of water, add a squeeze of lemon juice, and set aside.

2. Bring water to a boil in a small saucepan. Add the artichokes and parboil until they begin to feel tender, about 3 to 5 minutes. Remove from the water, drain, and pat dry.

3. Place another small pot on the stove and fill with enough oil that the artichoke hearts will be submerged. Warm the oil over medium heat until it starts to sizzle.

4. Place the artichokes in the oil and fry until they are brown all over, turning occasionally, 8 to 10 minutes. Transfer to a paper towel–lined plate to drain. Season with salt and serve with the lemon wedges.

BAGNA CAUDA

YIELD: **4 SERVINGS**

ACTIVE TIME: **30 MINUTES**

TOTAL TIME: **30 MINUTES**

INGREDIENTS

½ CUP ANCHOVY FILLETS, BONED AND CHOPPED

⅔ CUP EXTRA-VIRGIN OLIVE OIL

2 TABLESPOONS UNSALTED BUTTER

4 GARLIC CLOVES, MASHED WITH A MORTAR AND PESTLE

SALT, TO TASTE

DIRECTIONS

1. Place the anchovies in a mortar and use a pestle to grind them into a paste. Set the anchovies aside.

2. Place 2 tablespoons of the olive oil and all of the butter in a small saucepan and warm over low heat. When the butter has melted, add the garlic, reduce the heat to the lowest possible setting, and cook, stirring to ensure that the garlic does not brown, for 5 minutes.

3. Add the anchovies and cook for 5 minutes, stirring occasionally. Cook until the mixture starts to darken, stir in the rest of the olive oil along with a pinch of salt, and cook at below a simmer for 15 to 20 minutes. If the mixture starts to sizzle, turn off the heat for a minute or so. Serve warm with sliced raw vegetables for dipping. If the bagna cauda cools down, return it to the stove and warm it up again.

PROSCIUTTO-WRAPPED FIGS

YIELD: **4 SERVINGS**

ACTIVE TIME: **10 MINUTES**

TOTAL TIME: **30 MINUTES**

INGREDIENTS

12 THIN SLICES OF PROSCIUTTO

6 RIPE FIGS, HALVED LENGTHWISE

AGED BALSAMIC VINEGAR, TO TASTE

DIRECTIONS

1. Preheat your gas or charcoal grill to high heat (500°F). Wrap the prosciutto tightly around the figs and place them on the grill, cut side down. Cook until browned and crispy on each side, 2 to 3 minutes per side.

2. Transfer the figs to a platter, drizzle balsamic vinegar over the top, and serve.

GRISSINI STICKS

YIELD: **6 SERVINGS**

ACTIVE TIME: **20 MINUTES**

TOTAL TIME: **1 HOUR**

INGREDIENTS

½ CUP BREAD FLOUR, PLUS 2 TABLESPOONS

1 TEASPOON FINE SEA SALT

1½ TEASPOONS ACTIVE DRY YEAST

2½ TABLESPOONS SEMOLINA FLOUR

1½ TEASPOONS EXTRA-VIRGIN OLIVE OIL

6 TABLESPOONS WARM WATER (105°F)

1½ TEASPOONS DRIED PARSLEY

1½ TEASPOONS DRIED OREGANO

1½ TEASPOONS POPPY SEEDS

½ TEASPOON CARAWAY SEEDS

DIRECTIONS

1. Preheat the oven to 375°F. Place the bread flour, salt, yeast, and semolina flour in a bowl and work the mixture with your hands until combined. Gradually add the oil and water and work the mixture until thoroughly incorporated.

2. Stir in the dried herbs and seeds, place the dough on a flour-dusted work surface, and knead it until smooth, about 5 minutes. Transfer the dough to a greased bowl, cover it with a moist kitchen towel, and let it stand for 20 minutes.

3. Place the dough on a flour-dusted work surface, cut it into 4 pieces, and cut each piece into 6 strips. Roll the strips out until they are approximately 12 inches long. Place them on a parchment-lined baking sheet and let them rest for 5 minutes.

4. Place the baking sheet in the oven and bake until the sticks are golden brown, about 20 minutes. Remove and briefly let them cool before serving.

GARLIC BREAD

YIELD: **8 SERVINGS**

ACTIVE TIME: **10 MINUTES**

TOTAL TIME: **30 MINUTES**

INGREDIENTS

2 STICKS OF UNSALTED BUTTER, SOFTENED

1½ TEASPOONS FRESH LEMON JUICE

4 GARLIC CLOVES, GRATED

3 TABLESPOONS CHOPPED FRESH PARSLEY

SALT AND PEPPER, TO TASTE

8 SLICES OF CRUSTY BREAD

DIRECTIONS

1. Preheat the oven to 425°F. Place the butter in a mixing bowl and whisk for about 2 minutes, until it is light and fluffy. Stir in the lemon juice, garlic, and parsley and season the mixture with salt and pepper.

2. Generously spread some of the butter on each slice of bread. Stack the buttered slices of bread and wrap them in aluminum foil.

3. Place in the oven and bake until the butter is melted and the edges of the bread are browned and crispy, about 15 minutes. Remove from the oven and serve immediately.

SPICY BROCCOLINI

YIELD: **4 SERVINGS**

ACTIVE TIME: **15 MINUTES**

TOTAL TIME: **15 MINUTES**

INGREDIENTS

SALT AND PEPPER, TO TASTE

½ LB. BROCCOLINI, TRIMMED

2 TABLESPOONS EXTRA-VIRGIN
OLIVE OIL

6 GARLIC CLOVES, MINCED

1½ TABLESPOONS RED WINE
VINEGAR

¼ TEASPOON RED PEPPER FLAKES, OR
TO TASTE

SLIVERED ALMONDS, TOASTED, FOR
GARNISH

DIRECTIONS

1. Bring water to a boil in a large saucepan. Add salt until the water tastes like the ocean. Add the broccolini and cook for 30 seconds. Drain and transfer the broccolini to a paper towel–lined plate.

2. Coat the skillet with olive oil and warm it over medium-high heat. When the oil starts to shimmer, add the broccolini and cook until well browned. Turn the broccolini over, season with salt and pepper, and cook until browned all over.

3. Stir in the garlic, vinegar, and red pepper flakes and cook, while tossing to combine, for another minute. Transfer to a serving platter and garnish with toasted almonds before serving.

FRIED SQUASH BLOSSOMS

YIELD: **6 SERVINGS**

ACTIVE TIME: **30 MINUTES**

TOTAL TIME: **45 MINUTES**

INGREDIENTS

CANOLA OIL, AS NEEDED

1¼ CUPS ALL-PURPOSE FLOUR

1 TEASPOON KOSHER SALT, PLUS MORE TO TASTE

12 OZ. PILSNER OR CLUB SODA

24 ZUCCHINI BLOSSOMS, STAMENS REMOVED

DIRECTIONS

1. Add canola oil to a Dutch oven until it is approximately 2 inches deep and warm to 350°F over medium heat. Place the flour and salt in a bowl, stir in the beer or club soda, and stir until the batter is almost smooth.

2. Dredge the zucchini blossoms in the batter until coated. Working in batches so as not to crowd the pot, carefully lay the zucchini blossoms in the oil and fry until golden brown, 2 to 3 minutes, turning the blossoms over once as they fry. Remove from the oil with a slotted spoon, drain on a paper towel–lined plate, and season with salt. Serve warm.

FETT'UNTA

YIELD: **4 SERVINGS**

ACTIVE TIME: **10 MINUTES**

TOTAL TIME: **30 MINUTES**

INGREDIENTS

4 SLICES FROM LOAF OF CRUSTY BREAD (EACH SLICE 1½ INCHES THICK)

¾ CUP HIGHEST QUALITY EXTRA-VIRGIN OLIVE OIL, PLUS MORE AS NEEDED

1 GARLIC CLOVE

FLAKY SEA SALT, TO TASTE

DIRECTIONS

1. Preheat your gas or charcoal grill to high heat (500°F). Brush both sides of the bread slices generously with olive oil.

2. Place the bread on the grill and cook until crisp and browned on both sides, about 2 minutes per side.

3. Remove from heat, rub the garlic clove over one side of each piece, and pour 3 tablespoons of oil over each one. Sprinkle salt over the bread and serve.

SAVORY TART SHELLS

YIELD: **2 TART SHELLS**

ACTIVE TIME: **30 MINUTES**

TOTAL TIME: **2 HOURS**

INGREDIENTS

2½ CUPS ALL-PURPOSE FLOUR, PLUS MORE AS NEEDED

⅓ CUP EXTRA-VIRGIN OLIVE OIL

½ CUP ICE WATER

1 TEASPOON FINE SEA SALT

DIRECTIONS

1. Place all of the ingredients in a bowl and work the mixture until a dough forms. Divide the dough into two pieces, flatten them into disks, wrap them in plastic, and refrigerate for 1 hour.

2. Preheat the oven to 400°F. Grease and flour two 9-inch pie plates. Place the pieces of dough on a flour-dusted work surface and roll them out into ¼-inch-thick rounds. Lay the crusts in the pan, trim any excess away, and prick the bottom of the crusts with a fork or a knife. Cover the crusts with aluminum foil, fill the foil with uncooked rice, dried beans, or pie weights, and place in the oven. Bake until firm and golden brown, about 20 minutes.

3. Remove from the oil, remove the foil and beans, and fill as desired.

   NOTE: If not using right away, store in the refrigerator for up to 1 week or in the freezer for up to 6 months.

ASPARAGUS TART

YIELD: **8 SERVINGS**

ACTIVE TIME: **15 MINUTES**

TOTAL TIME: **45 MINUTES**

INGREDIENTS

½ TEASPOON KOSHER SALT, PLUS MORE TO TASTE

1 LB. ASPARAGUS, TRIMMED

1½ CUPS RICOTTA CHEESE

¼ CUP EXTRA-VIRGIN OLIVE OIL

2 TABLESPOONS HEAVY CREAM

2 EGG YOLKS

1 TEASPOON CHOPPED FRESH ROSEMARY

1 SAVORY TART SHELL (SEE PAGE 36)

DIRECTIONS

1. Preheat the oven to 350°F. Bring a pot of water to a boil. Add salt until the water tastes just shy of seawater, add the asparagus, and cook for 2 minutes. Drain, pat dry, and set aside.

2. Place all of the remaining ingredients, aside from the tart shell, in a mixing bowl and stir to combine. Distribute the mixture evenly in the tart shell, arrange the asparagus in the custard, and place the tart in the oven. Bake until the custard is set and golden brown, about 25 minutes. Remove from the oven and serve warm or at room temperature.

NOTE: This simple custard and the recipe for the Savory Tart Shell come courtesy of the simply magnificent Tamar Adler. The pair is so reliable and versatile that any vegetable can comfortably be swapped in for the asparagus.

CROSTINI

YIELD: **6 SERVINGS**

ACTIVE TIME: **15 MINUTES**

TOTAL TIME: **30 MINUTES**

INGREDIENTS

1 BAGUETTE, SLICED

2 TABLESPOONS EXTRA-VIRGIN
OLIVE OIL, PLUS MORE TO TASTE

SALT AND PEPPER, TO TASTE

DIRECTIONS

1. Preheat the oven to 400°F. Brush the slices of baguette with the olive oil and place them on a baking sheet. Place in the oven and bake for 12 to 15 minutes, turning the slices over halfway through. When the slices are golden brown on both sides, remove from the oven.

2. Top the crostini as desired, drizzle olive oil over them, and season with salt and pepper.

   TIP: There are limitless ways you can utilize these crostini. Those pictured feature ricotta and pea shoots, but you can top them with anything you like, or just serve them on the side and let people top them as they please with a number of the other preparations in this book.

PEPERONATA

YIELD: **6 SERVINGS**

ACTIVE TIME: **30 MINUTES**

TOTAL TIME: **2 HOURS**

INGREDIENTS

½ CUP EXTRA-VIRGIN OLIVE OIL

4 LARGE GARLIC CLOVES, SLICED THIN

1 RED ONION, HALVED AND SLICED

2 TEASPOONS KOSHER SALT, PLUS MORE TO TASTE

BLACK PEPPER, TO TASTE

4 BELL PEPPERS, STEMMED, SEEDED, AND SLICED THIN

1 TABLESPOON SHERRY VINEGAR

1 TABLESPOON DRIED OREGANO

½ CUP PITTED BLACK OLIVES

CAPER BERRIES, DRAINED, FOR GARNISH (OPTIONAL)

DIRECTIONS

1. Place a rack in the middle position in the oven and preheat the oven to 400°F. Place the olive oil in a large skillet and warm it over medium-high heat. When the oil starts to shimmer, add the garlic and onion and cook, stirring frequently, until they begin to soften, about 1 minute.

2. Season with salt and pepper, add the bell peppers, and cook, stirring occasionally, until the peppers begin to soften, about 10 minutes.

3. Stir in the sherry vinegar and oregano and cook for another 2 minutes. Transfer the mixture to a large baking dish and use a wooden spoon to make sure it is distributed evenly.

4. Top with the olives, place the dish in the oven, and bake until the edges of the peperonata start to char, 1 to 1½ hours. Remove from the oven, top the peperonata with the caper berries (if desired), and serve.

BRUSSELS SPROUTS WITH SHERRY VINAIGRETTE & BREAD CRUMBS

YIELD: **4 SERVINGS**

ACTIVE TIME: **15 MINUTES**

TOTAL TIME: **25 MINUTES**

INGREDIENTS

FOR THE VINAIGRETTE

¼ CUP SHERRY VINEGAR

2 TABLESPOONS MINCED SHALLOTS

1 TEASPOON KOSHER SALT

½ TEASPOON BLACK PEPPER

2 TABLESPOONS EXTRA-VIRGIN OLIVE OIL

FOR THE BRUSSELS SPROUTS

1 LB. BRUSSELS SPROUTS, TRIMMED AND HALVED

½ CUP EXTRA-VIRGIN OLIVE OIL, PLUS MORE AS NEEDED

1 TABLESPOON KOSHER SALT

½ TEASPOON BLACK PEPPER

1 TABLESPOON FRESH LEMON JUICE

FRESH BREAD CRUMBS, TOASTED, FOR GARNISH

FRESH HERBS, FINELY CHOPPED, FOR GARNISH

DIRECTIONS

1. To prepare the vinaigrette, place the vinegar, shallots, salt, and pepper in a small bowl and whisk to combine. Let the mixture sit for 5 minutes before adding the olive oil in a slow, steady stream while whisking to incorporate it.

2. To begin preparations for the Brussels sprouts, place the Brussels sprouts in a bowl, drizzle olive oil generously over them, and sprinkle the salt and pepper on top. Toss to combine and set the Brussels sprouts aside.

3. Coat the bottom of a large skillet with some of the olive oil and warm it over medium heat. When the oil starts to shimmer, add half of the Brussels sprouts and cook until golden brown on both sides, about 3 minutes per side. Transfer the Brussels sprouts to a bowl, add more of the olive oil, and warm it. Add the remaining Brussels sprouts, cook them until browned on both sides, and then transfer them to the bowl.

4. Add the lemon juice and vinaigrette to the bowl and toss to combine. Taste, adjust the seasoning as necessary, and top with the bread crumbs and herbs such as tarragon, chives, parsley, and/or chervil.

PANZANELLA WITH WHITE BALSAMIC VINAIGRETTE

YIELD: **6 SERVINGS**

ACTIVE TIME: **25 MINUTES**

TOTAL TIME: **45 MINUTES**

INGREDIENTS

FOR THE SALAD

1 TABLESPOON KOSHER SALT, PLUS 2 TEASPOONS

6 PEARL ONIONS, TRIMMED

1 CUP CORN KERNELS

1 CUP CHOPPED GREEN BEANS

4 CUPS CHOPPED DAY-OLD BREAD

2 CUPS CHOPPED OVERRIPE TOMATOES

10 LARGE FRESH BASIL LEAVES, TORN

BLACK PEPPER, TO TASTE

FOR THE VINAIGRETTE

½ CUP WHITE BALSAMIC VINEGAR

¼ CUP EXTRA-VIRGIN OLIVE OIL

2 TABLESPOONS MINCED SHALLOT

¼ CUP SLICED SCALLIONS

2 TABLESPOONS CHOPPED FRESH PARSLEY

2 TEASPOONS KOSHER SALT

1 TEASPOON BLACK PEPPER

DIRECTIONS

1. To begin preparations for the salad, bring water to a boil in a small saucepan and prepare an ice water bath. When the water is boiling, add the 1 tablespoon of salt and the pearl onions and cook for 5 minutes. When the onions have 1 minute left to cook, add the corn and green beans to the saucepan. Transfer the vegetables to the ice water bath and let cool completely.

2. Remove the pearl onions from the water bath and squeeze to remove the bulbs from their skins. Cut the bulbs in half and break them down into individual petals. Drain the corn and green beans and pat the vegetables dry.

3. To prepare the vinaigrette, place all of the ingredients in a mixing bowl and whisk until combined.

4. Place the cooked vegetables, bread, tomatoes, and basil in a salad bowl and toss to combine. Add the remaining salt, season with pepper, and add half of the vinaigrette. Toss to coat, taste, and add more of the vinaigrette if desired.

POLENTA

YIELD: **4 SERVINGS**

ACTIVE TIME: **15 MINUTES**

TOTAL TIME: **45 MINUTES**

INGREDIENTS

7 CUPS WATER

1 TABLESPOON KOSHER SALT

1⅔ CUPS COARSE-GRAINED CORNMEAL

4 TABLESPOONS UNSALTED BUTTER

½ CUP FRESHLY GRATED PARMESAN CHEESE

DIRECTIONS

1. Place the water in a saucepan and bring it to a boil. Add the salt, and then pour in the cornmeal in a slow stream while whisking to incorporate. Reduce the heat to low and stir constantly for 2 minutes. Cover the pan and gently simmer until the polenta is creamy, about 40 minutes. Remove the cover and stir for 1 minute every 10 minutes or so.

2. Stir in the butter and Parmesan. When they have melted and been incorporated, spoon the polenta into bowls and serve warm, or let it cool in the refrigerator overnight and then fry as a cake.

POLENTA FRIES

YIELD: **4 SERVINGS**

ACTIVE TIME: **30 MINUTES**

TOTAL TIME: **2 HOURS AND 30 MINUTES**

INGREDIENTS

2½ CUPS MILK

2½ CUPS VEGETABLE STOCK
(SEE PAGE 122)

2 CUPS COARSE-GRAIN CORNMEAL

2 TABLESPOONS UNSALTED BUTTER

1 TEASPOON KOSHER SALT, PLUS
MORE TO TASTE

½ TEASPOON BLACK PEPPER

½ TEASPOON DRIED OREGANO

½ TEASPOON DRIED THYME

½ TEASPOON DRIED ROSEMARY

CANOLA OIL, AS NEEDED

¼ CUP FRESHLY GRATED PARMESAN
CHEESE, FOR GARNISH

2 TABLESPOONS FINELY CHOPPED
FRESH ROSEMARY, FOR GARNISH

DIRECTIONS

1. Grease a large, rimmed baking sheet with nonstick cooking spray. Place the milk and stock in a saucepan and bring to a boil. Whisk in the cornmeal, reduce heat to low, and stir constantly for 2 minutes. Cover the pan and cook until the polenta is creamy, about 40 minutes. Remove the cover and stir for 1 minute every 10 minutes or so.

2. Stir in the butter, salt, pepper, oregano, thyme, and rosemary. When they have been incorporated, transfer the polenta to the greased baking sheet and even out the surface with a rubber spatula. Refrigerate for 2 hours.

3. Carefully invert the baking sheet over a cutting board so that the polenta falls onto it. Slice the polenta in half lengthwise and cut each piece into 4-inch-long and 1-inch-wide strips.

4. Add canola oil to a Dutch oven until it is 2 inches deep and warm it to 375°F over medium heat. Working in batches of two, place the strips in the oil and fry, turning as they cook, until golden brown, 2 to 4 minutes. Transfer the cooked fries to a paper towel–lined plate to drain. When all of the fries have been cooked, sprinkle the Parmesan and fresh rosemary over them and serve.

ARANCINI

YIELD: **8 SERVINGS**

ACTIVE TIME: **30 MINUTES**

TOTAL TIME: **1 HOUR AND 30 MINUTES**

INGREDIENTS

5 CUPS CHICKEN STOCK
(SEE PAGE 118)

1 STICK OF UNSALTED BUTTER

2 CUPS ARBORIO RICE

1 SMALL WHITE ONION, GRATED

1 CUP WHITE WINE

4 OZ. FONTINA CHEESE, GRATED

SALT AND PEPPER, TO TASTE

CANOLA OIL, AS NEEDED

6 LARGE EGGS, BEATEN

5 CUPS PANKO

DIRECTIONS

1. Bring the stock to a simmer in a large saucepan. In a skillet, melt the butter over high heat. Once the butter is foaming, add the rice and onion and cook until the rice has a toasty fragrance, about 4 minutes. Deglaze the skillet with the white wine and cook until the wine has almost completely been absorbed. Then, reduce the heat to medium-high and begin adding the stock ¼ cup at a time, stirring until it has been incorporated. Continue this process until the rice is al dente.

2. Turn off the heat, stir in the cheese, and season with salt and pepper. Pour the mixture onto a baking sheet and let it cool.

3. Add the oil to a Dutch oven until it is 2 inches deep and warm over medium heat until it reaches 350°F. When the rice mixture is cool, form it into golf ball–sized spheres. Dip them into in the eggs and then dip it into the panko until coated all over. Place the balls in the oil and fry until warmed through and golden brown. Transfer to a paper towel–lined plate until cool.

CAPRESE SALAD

YIELD: **4 SERVINGS**

ACTIVE TIME: **15 MINUTES**

TOTAL TIME: **15 MINUTES**

INGREDIENTS

1 LB. HEIRLOOM TOMATOES, SLICED
(IN SEASON IS A MUST)

SALT AND PEPPER, TO TASTE

1 LB. FRESH MOZZARELLA CHEESE,
SLICED

¼ CUP BASIL PESTO (SEE PAGE 78)

HIGHEST QUALITY EXTRA-VIRGIN
OLIVE OIL, TO TASTE

DIRECTIONS

1. Season the tomatoes with salt and pepper. While alternating, arrange them and the slices of mozzarella on a platter.

2. Drizzle the pesto and olive oil over the tomatoes and mozzarella and serve.

ROASTED GARLIC

YIELD: **6 SERVINGS**

ACTIVE TIME: **15 MINUTES**

TOTAL TIME: **45 MINUTES**

INGREDIENTS

6 HEADS OF GARLIC

EXTRA-VIRGIN OLIVE OIL,
AS NEEDED

SALT, TO TASTE

DIRECTIONS

1. Preheat the oven to 375°F. Cut the tops off each head of garlic and place them, cut side up, in a baking dish that is small enough for them to fit snugly. Add about ¼ inch of water to the dish, drizzle olive oil over the garlic, and season with salt.

2. Cover the dish with aluminum foil, place it in the oven, and roast for 20 minutes. Lift the foil and test to see if the garlic are soft. If not, re-cover the dish, add water if it has evaporated, and roast for another 10 minutes. Remove from the oven and, if desired, serve with Crostini (see page 40) and goat cheese.

SICILIAN MEATBALLS

YIELD: **4 SERVINGS**

ACTIVE TIME: **20 MINUTES**

TOTAL TIME: **45 MINUTES**

INGREDIENTS

2 TABLESPOONS EXTRA-VIRGIN OLIVE OIL

½ SMALL RED ONION, CHOPPED

2 GARLIC CLOVES, MINCED

1 LARGE EGG

2 TABLESPOONS WHOLE MILK

½ CUP ITALIAN BREAD CRUMBS

¼ CUP FRESHLY GRATED PARMESAN CHEESE

¼ CUP PINE NUTS, TOASTED

3 TABLESPOONS MINCED DRIED CURRANTS

2 TABLESPOONS FINELY CHOPPED FRESH MARJORAM

2 TABLESPOONS CHOPPED FRESH PARSLEY

¾ LB. GROUND PORK

½ LB. SWEET OR SPICY GROUND ITALIAN SAUSAGE

SALT AND PEPPER, TO TASTE

2 CUPS MARINARA SAUCE (SEE PAGE 77)

DIRECTIONS

1. Preheat the broiler to high, position a rack so that the tops of the meatballs will be approximately 6 inches below the broiler, and line a rimmed baking sheet with aluminum foil.

2. Place the oil in a large skillet and warm over medium-high heat. When it starts to shimmer, add the onion and garlic and sauté until the onion is translucent, about 3 minutes. Remove the pan from heat and set it aside.

3. Place the egg, milk, bread crumbs, Parmesan, pine nuts, currants, marjoram, and parsley in a mixing bowl and stir until combined. Add the pork, sausage, and onion mixture, season with salt and pepper, and stir until thoroughly combined. Working with wet hands, form the mixture into 1½-inch meatballs, arrange them on the baking sheet, and spray the tops with cooking spray.

4. Place the meatballs in the oven and broil until browned all over, turning them as they cook. Remove the meatballs from the oven and set them aside.

5. Place the sauce in the skillet and warm over medium heat. Add the meatballs to the sauce, reduce the heat to low, cover the pan, and simmer, turning the meatballs occasionally, until they are cooked through, about 15 minutes. Season with salt and pepper and serve.

SAUTÉED RADICCHIO WITH CHICKPEAS, PARMESAN & BALSAMIC

YIELD: **4 SERVINGS**

ACTIVE TIME: **1 HOUR**

TOTAL TIME: **24 HOURS**

INGREDIENTS

⅔ CUP DRIED CHICKPEAS, SOAKED OVERNIGHT

1 TABLESPOON EXTRA-VIRGIN OLIVE OIL

1 SMALL HEAD OF RADICCHIO, CORED AND SLICED THIN

1 SHALLOT, MINCED

1 GARLIC CLOVE, MINCED

¼ CUP WHITE WINE

¼ CUP VEGETABLE STOCK (SEE PAGE 122)

½ TEASPOON FINELY CHOPPED FRESH THYME

SALT AND PEPPER, TO TASTE

PARMESAN CHEESE, FRESHLY GRATED, FOR GARNISH

BALSAMIC VINEGAR, TO TASTE

DIRECTIONS

1. Drain the chickpeas. Place them in a large saucepan, cover them with water, and bring to a gentle simmer. Reduce the heat so that they simmer and cook, stirring occasionally, until tender, about 2 hours. Drain and let the chickpeas cool.

2. Place the oil in a skillet and warm over medium heat. When the oil starts to shimmer, add the radicchio and cook, stirring frequently, until it starts to wilt and brown, about 5 minutes. Stir in the shallot and garlic and sauté until the garlic starts to brown, about 1 minute. Deglaze the pan with the wine and stock.

3. Add the chickpeas to the radicchio mixture along with the thyme. Season the mixture with salt and pepper, cook until almost all of the liquid has evaporated, and then remove the pan from heat. Top with Parmesan and balsamic vinegar and serve.

   NOTE: If you have an infused balsamic vinegar, this dish is a perfect opportunity to break it out.

FRITTATA WITH PASTA

YIELD: **6 TO 8 SERVINGS**

ACTIVE TIME: **15 MINUTES**

TOTAL TIME: **2 HOURS AND 30 MINUTES**

INGREDIENTS

2 CUPS COOKED, LEFTOVER
SPAGHETTI

3 EGGS, BEATEN

2 TABLESPOONS FRESHLY GRATED
PARMESAN CHEESE

½ CUP CHOPPED FRESH HERBS

SALT AND PEPPER, TO TASTE

EXTRA-VIRGIN OLIVE OIL, AS
NEEDED

DIRECTIONS

1. Preheat the oven to 375°F. Place the pasta and eggs in a
    bowl, stir to combine, and then stir in the Parmesan and fresh
    herbs. Season with salt and pepper and set the mixture aside.

2. Add olive oil to a cast-iron skillet until it is about ½ inch deep
    and warm it over medium heat. Add the frittata mixture and
    cook until you can lift it up and look at the bottom of it. Place
    the frittata in the oven and bake until just firm to the touch.

3. Remove from the oven and let the frittata sit at room
    temperature for 2 hours before serving, or refrigerate, letting
    it return to room temperature before slicing and serving.

ASPARAGUS WITH PANCETTA AND GARLIC CREAM SAUCE

YIELD: **4 SERVINGS**

ACTIVE TIME: **20 MINUTES**

TOTAL TIME: **35 MINUTES**

INGREDIENTS

SALT AND PEPPER, TO TASTE

2 BUNCHES OF ASPARAGUS, TRIMMED

3 GARLIC CLOVES, MINCED

2 CUPS HEAVY CREAM

3 TABLESPOONS UNSALTED BUTTER

1 CUP DICED PANCETTA

DIRECTIONS

1. Bring a pot of salted water to boil. Add the asparagus and cook until tender, about 2 minutes. Drain and set aside.

2. Place the garlic, cream, and butter in a medium saucepan and bring to a simmer over medium heat.

3. Place the pancetta in a skillet and cook over medium-high heat until it turns a light golden brown. Add the pancetta to the garlic-and-cream mixture and stir to combine. Season to taste, pour over the asparagus, and serve.

ROASTED ASPARAGUS WITH FRIED EGGS & LEMON-PEPPER MAYONNAISE

YIELD: **4 TO 6 SERVINGS**

ACTIVE TIME: **20 MINUTES**

TOTAL TIME: **35 MINUTES**

INGREDIENTS

FOR THE ASPARAGUS & EGGS

SALT AND PEPPER, TO TASTE

2 BUNCHES OF ASPARAGUS, TRIMMED

2 TABLESPOONS EXTRA-VIRGIN OLIVE OIL

2 TABLESPOONS UNSALTED BUTTER

6 EGGS

PARMESAN CHEESE, FRESHLY GRATED, FOR GARNISH

FOR THE MAYONNAISE

1 CUP MAYONNAISE

3 TABLESPOONS FRESHLY GRATED PARMESAN CHEESE

1 TABLESPOON LEMON ZEST

3 TABLESPOONS FRESH LEMON JUICE

1½ TEASPOONS BLACK PEPPER

2 TEASPOONS KOSHER SALT

DIRECTIONS

1. Preheat the oven to 400°F. To begin preparations for the asparagus and eggs, bring a large pot of salted water to a boil and prepare an ice water bath in a large bowl.

2. Place the trimmed asparagus in the boiling water and cook for 30 seconds. Drain and transfer to the ice water bath until it is completely cool, about 3 minutes. Transfer to a kitchen towel to dry completely.

3. To prepare the mayonnaise, place all of the ingredients in a mixing bowl and whisk to combine. Set aside.

4. Pat the asparagus dry. Place the olive oil in a large skillet and warm over medium-high heat. Working in batches, add the asparagus just before the oil starts to smoke and cook until browned all over. Transfer cooked asparagus to a plate and tent with foil to keep warm.

5. Place the butter in a cast-iron skillet and melt over medium heat. Crack the eggs into the pan, taking care not to break the yolks. Season the eggs with salt and pepper and place the skillet in the oven. Cook until the whites are cooked through, 2 to 3 minutes. Remove from the oven.

6. To serve, spread some of the mayonnaise on a plate and lay some asparagus on top. Top with an egg and garnish with the grated Parmesan.

SAUTÉED SUNCHOKES

YIELD: **4 TO 6 SERVINGS**

ACTIVE TIME: **15 MINUTES**

TOTAL TIME: **45 MINUTES**

INGREDIENTS

SALT AND PEPPER, TO TASTE

1½ LBS. SUNCHOKES, PEELED

¼ CUP EXTRA-VIRGIN OLIVE OIL

1 GARLIC CLOVE, MINCED

1 TABLESPOON CHOPPED FRESH PARSLEY

DIRECTIONS

1. Bring water to a boil in a large saucepan. Add salt and the sunchokes and parboil for 30 seconds. Drain and let them cool. When the sunchokes are cool enough to handle, slice them thin and pat them dry with paper towels.

2. Place the olive oil in a large skillet and warm it over medium heat. When the oil starts to shimmer, add the garlic and cook, while stirring, for 1 minute. Add the sunchokes and parsley, season the mixture with salt and pepper, and cook, stirring occasionally, until the sunchokes are very tender, 10 to 15 minutes. Taste, adjust the seasoning as needed, and serve.

FAVA BEANS, ROMAN STYLE

YIELD: **4 SERVINGS**

ACTIVE TIME: **25 MINUTES**

TOTAL TIME: **50 MINUTES**

INGREDIENTS

2 TABLESPOONS EXTRA-VIRGIN OLIVE OIL

2 TABLESPOONS MINCED ONION

4 OZ. BACON, CHOPPED

¾ LB. SHELLED AND PEELED FAVA BEANS

SALT AND PEPPER, TO TASTE

DIRECTIONS

1. Place the olive oil in a large skillet and warm it over medium heat. When the oil starts to shimmer, add the onion and cook, stirring frequently, until it is translucent, about 3 minutes.

2. Add the bacon and cook, stirring occasionally, for 2 minutes. Add ⅓ cup of water and the beans, season the mixture with pepper, and bring to a gentle simmer. Cover the pan and cook until the fava beans are tender, 10 to 15 minutes.

3. Season the mixture with salt, raise the heat to high, and cook until the water has evaporated. Serve immediately.

CHAPTER 2

SAUCES

_____

*Yes, a classic Marinara Sauce (see page 77) is tough to beat. But
sticking strictly to just that is failing to get the most out of your
Italian meals. The sauces here are only a smattering of what's
available out there, but we're betting the variety is wide enough to
keep your most-beloved dishes from growing stale, and present you
with opportunities to try something new.*

MARINARA SAUCE

YIELD: **8 CUPS**

ACTIVE TIME: **30 MINUTES**

TOTAL TIME: **2 HOURS**

INGREDIENTS

4 LBS. RIPE ROMA TOMATOES, PEELED, SEEDED, AND CHOPPED

1 YELLOW ONION, SLICED

15 GARLIC CLOVES, CRUSHED

2 TEASPOONS FINELY CHOPPED FRESH THYME

2 TEASPOONS FINELY CHOPPED FRESH MARJORAM

2 TABLESPOONS EXTRA-VIRGIN OLIVE OIL

1½ TABLESPOONS KOSHER SALT, PLUS MORE TO TASTE

1 TEASPOON BLACK PEPPER, PLUS MORE TO TASTE

2 TABLESPOONS FINELY CHOPPED FRESH BASIL

1 TABLESPOON FINELY CHOPPED FRESH PARSLEY

DIRECTIONS

1. Place all of the ingredients, except for the basil and parsley, in a large saucepan and cook, stirring constantly, over medium heat until the tomatoes begin to collapse, about 10 minutes.

2. Reduce the heat to low and cook, stirring occasionally, for about 1½ hours, or until the flavor is to your liking.

3. Stir in the basil and parsley and season the sauce to taste. The sauce will be chunky. If you prefer a smoother texture, transfer the sauce to a food processor and blitz before serving with your pasta.

BASIL PESTO

YIELD: **1 CUP**

ACTIVE TIME: **10 MINUTES**

TOTAL TIME: **25 MINUTES**

INGREDIENTS

¼ CUP PINE NUTS

3 GARLIC CLOVES

SALT AND PEPPER, TO TASTE

2 CUPS FIRMLY PACKED FRESH BASIL LEAVES

½ CUP EXTRA-VIRGIN OLIVE OIL

¼ CUP FRESHLY GRATED PARMESAN CHEESE

1 TEASPOON FRESH LEMON JUICE

DIRECTIONS

1. Warm a small skillet over low heat for 1 minute. Add the pine nuts and cook, while shaking the pan, until they begin to give off a toasty fragrance, 2 to 3 minutes. Transfer to a plate and let cool completely.

2. Place the garlic, salt, and pine nuts in a food processor or blender and pulse until the mixture is a coarse meal. Add the basil and pulse it is until finely minced. Transfer the mixture to a medium bowl and, while whisking to incorporate, add the oil in a thin stream.

3. Add the cheese and stir until thoroughly incorporated. Stir in the lemon juice, taste, and adjust the seasoning as necessary. The pesto will keep in the refrigerator for up to 2 days.

    TIP: You can also make this pesto using a mortar and pestle, which will give it more texture.

LAMB RAGÙ

YIELD: **8 CUPS**

ACTIVE TIME: **40 MINUTES**

TOTAL TIME: **3 HOURS**

INGREDIENTS

2 TABLESPOONS EXTRA-VIRGIN OLIVE OIL

2 SMALL ONIONS, MINCED

2 CELERY STALKS, PEELED AND MINCED

SALT, TO TASTE

2 LBS. GROUND LAMB

1 CUP DRY RED WINE

2 TEASPOONS FRESH THYME

2 TEASPOONS FRESH MARJORAM

1 TEASPOON RED PEPPER FLAKES

2 (28 OZ.) CANS OF PEELED WHOLE SAN MARZANO TOMATOES, WITH THEIR LIQUID, CRUSHED BY HAND

DIRECTIONS

1. Place the olive oil in a Dutch oven and warm it over medium-high heat. When the oil starts to shimmer, add the onions, celery, and a couple of pinches of salt and stir to combine. When the mixture starts to sizzle, reduce the heat to low, cover, and cook, stirring occasionally, until the vegetables are very tender and a deep golden brown, about 30 minutes.

2. Add the ground lamb to the pot and cook, while breaking it apart with a fork, until it is no longer pink. Raise the heat to medium-high, add the wine, and cook until it has reduced by half, about 5 minutes.

3. Stir in the thyme, marjoram, and red pepper flakes and cook for 2 minutes. Add the tomatoes, season the sauce with salt and pepper, stir, and bring to a boil. Reduce the heat to medium-low and simmer, stirring occasionally, until the sauce has visibly thickened and the fat has separated and is bubbling on the surface, about 2 hours.

SALSA VERDE

YIELD: **1 CUP**

ACTIVE TIME: **10 MINUTES**

TOTAL TIME: **30 MINUTES**

INGREDIENTS

1 SHALLOT, MINCED

½ TEASPOON KOSHER SALT

RED WINE VINEGAR, TO TASTE

BUNCH OF FRESH PARSLEY, STEMMED AND CHOPPED

½ GARLIC CLOVE, GRATED

1 ANCHOVY FILLET, BONED AND MINCED

1 TEASPOON CAPERS, DRAINED, RINSED, AND MINCED

½ CUP EXTRA-VIRGIN OLIVE OIL

DIRECTIONS

1. Place the shallot and salt in a small bowl, stir to combine, and cover the mixture with the vinegar. Let sit for 15 minutes.

2. Drain the mixture, add the shallot to a clean bowl, and combine with the rest of the ingredients. Spoon over meats, vegetables, pasta, or anything you please.

ARRABBIATA SAUCE

YIELD: **3 CUPS**

ACTIVE TIME: **10 MINUTES**

TOTAL TIME: **25 MINUTES**

INGREDIENTS

2 TABLESPOONS EXTRA-VIRGIN OLIVE OIL

3 GARLIC CLOVES, CRUSHED

2 DRIED CHILI PEPPERS, SEEDED AND CHOPPED

1 (28 OZ.) CAN OF PEELED WHOLE SAN MARZANO TOMATOES, WITH THEIR LIQUID

1 HANDFUL OF FRESH PARSLEY, CHOPPED

SALT AND PEPPER, TO TASTE

DIRECTIONS

1. Warm a large, deep skillet over low heat for 1 to 2 minutes. Add the olive oil, garlic, and chilies, raise the heat to medium-low, and cook until the garlic begins to brown, about 1 minute. Remove the garlic and as much of the chili peppers as possible and add the tomatoes, breaking them up with your hands as you add them to the pan. Add the liquid from the can, raise the heat to medium-high, and bring to a boil. Reduce the heat to medium-low and cook, while stirring occasionally, until the sauce is thick and the oil has risen to the surface, about 20 minutes.

2. Stir in the parsley, season with salt and pepper, and serve with your favorite pasta.

PIZZA SAUCE

YIELD: **2 CUPS**

ACTIVE TIME: **5 MINUTES**

TOTAL TIME: **5 MINUTES**

INGREDIENTS

1 LB. CANNED, PEELED, AND WHOLE SAN MARZANO TOMATOES, WITH THEIR LIQUID, CRUSHED BY HAND

1½ TABLESPOONS EXTRA-VIRGIN OLIVE OIL

SALT, TO TASTE

DRIED OREGANO, TO TASTE

DIRECTIONS

1. Place the tomatoes and their juices in a bowl, add the olive oil, and stir until it has been thoroughly incorporated.

2. Season the sauce with salt and oregano and stir to incorporate. If using within 2 hours, leave the sauce at room temperature. If storing in the refrigerator, where the sauce will keep for up to 3 days, return to room temperature before using.

ROSE SAUCE

YIELD: **8 CUPS**

ACTIVE TIME: **15 MINUTES**

TOTAL TIME: **30 MINUTES**

INGREDIENTS

4 LBS. VERY RIPE ROMA TOMATOES, PEELED, SEEDED, AND CHOPPED

4 TABLESPOONS UNSALTED BUTTER

½ WHITE OR VIDALIA ONION, CUT INTO QUARTERS

SALT AND PEPPER, TO TASTE

2 CUPS HEAVY CREAM

DIRECTIONS

1. Place the tomatoes in a food processor and blitz until pureed.

2. Warm a medium saucepan over medium-low heat for 2 minutes. Add the butter and raise the heat to medium. Once the butter melts and stops foaming, add the onion and a pinch of salt and sauté until it begins to sizzle. Reduce the heat to low, cover the pan, and cook the onion, stirring occasionally, until the onion is soft, about 10 minutes.

3. Add the pureed tomatoes and a few pinches of salt. Bring to a boil, reduce the heat to low, and simmer until it has thickened and the flavor is to your liking, about 20 minutes. Remove as much of the onion as you can with a slotted spoon.

4. As the tomato sauce cooks, place the cream in a small saucepan and cook over low heat until it has reduced by about half. Remove the pan from heat and set the cream aside.

5. Stir the reduced cream into the tomato sauce, season it with salt and pepper, and serve.

FONTINA SAUCE

YIELD: **3 CUPS**

ACTIVE TIME: **40 MINUTES**

TOTAL TIME: **1 HOUR AND 15 MINUTES**

INGREDIENTS

FLORETS FROM 1 HEAD OF CAULIFLOWER

6½ TABLESPOONS EXTRA-VIRGIN OLIVE OIL

SALT AND PEPPER, TO TASTE

1 LB. CREMINI MUSHROOMS, STEMMED AND CHOPPED

3 TABLESPOONS FINELY CHOPPED FRESH THYME

6 OZ. BACON, CHOPPED

1 LARGE YELLOW ONION, GRATED

½ CUP CHICKEN STOCK (SEE PAGE 118)

1 CUP GRATED FONTINA CHEESE

¾ CUP HEAVY CREAM

1½ TEASPOONS WORCESTERSHIRE SAUCE

DIRECTIONS

1. Preheat the oven to 450°F. Place the cauliflower and 2 tablespoons of the olive oil in a large bowl and toss to coat. Transfer the cauliflower to a baking pan, season it with salt and pepper, cover the pan with foil, and then place in the oven. Cook for 15 minutes, remove from the oven, remove the foil, and turn the cauliflower over. Return the pan to the oven, uncovered, lower the oven's temperature to 400°F, and roast the cauliflower until it is tender and the edges are browned, about 40 minutes.

2. While the cauliflower is roasting, place the mushrooms in a large bowl with 2 tablespoons of the olive oil and toss to coat. Transfer to a parchment-lined baking sheet, season with salt and pepper, and sprinkle the thyme over the top. Place in the 400°F oven, roast for 15 minutes, and remove from oven. Carefully drain the liquid, return to the oven, and roast until the mushrooms are soft and lightly browned, about 25 minutes.

3. Warm a large skillet over medium-low heat for 2 minutes. Add 2 tablespoons of the olive oil and raise the heat to medium. When the oil starts to shimmer, add the bacon and sauté until it is browned and crisp, about 8 minutes. Transfer it to a small bowl and set aside.

4. Add the onion to the pan, season it with salt, and raise the heat to medium-high. Sauté until the onion starts to sizzle. Reduce the heat to low, cover the pan, and cook, while stirring occasionally, until the onion becomes very soft, about 15 minutes. Raise the heat to medium-high, stir in the stock, cheese, and cream, and cook until the mixture starts to bubble. Stir in the Worcestershire sauce, serve with pasta, and top with the bacon and roasted vegetables.

CALAMARI FRA DIAVOLO

YIELD: **6 CUPS**

ACTIVE TIME: **40 MINUTES**

TOTAL TIME: **1 HOUR**

INGREDIENTS

1 CUP DRY RED WINE

2 LBS. SQUID, BODIES CUT INTO RINGS, TENTACLES HALVED LENGTHWISE

3½ TABLESPOONS EXTRA-VIRGIN OLIVE OIL

4 GARLIC CLOVES, MINCED

1 TEASPOON RED PEPPER FLAKES

SALT, TO TASTE

3 ANCHOVY FILLETS, BONED AND CHOPPED

2 HANDFULS OF FRESH PARSLEY, CHOPPED

1 (28 OZ.) CAN OF PEELED WHOLE SAN MARZANO TOMATOES, WITH THEIR LIQUID, PUREED

½ CUP CLAM JUICE

DIRECTIONS

1. Place the wine in a small saucepan, bring it to a boil, and cook until it has reduced by half, about 5 minutes. Remove the pan from heat and set it aside.

2. Thoroughly rinse the squid thoroughly and transfer it to a paper towel–lined plate. Blot the squid with paper towels to remove as much surface moisture as possible.

3. Place the olive oil in a large, deep skillet and warm over medium heat for 2 to 3 minutes. When the oil starts to shimmer, add the garlic, half of the red pepper flakes, and a pinch of salt and sauté until the garlic starts to brown, about 1 minute. Raise the heat to medium-high and add the squid, anchovies, and half of the parsley. Cook, while occasionally, until the anchovies dissolve and the calamari is golden brown, about 5 minutes.

4. Add the reduced wine and continue to cook until the liquid in the mixture has reduced by one-third, about 5 minutes. Stir in the tomatoes, the clam juice, and remaining red pepper flakes, season with salt, bring to a boil, then reduce the heat to medium-low. Simmer until the sauce has thickened slightly, about 20 minutes, and serve with pasta.

AROMATIC WALNUT SAUCE

YIELD: **2 CUPS**

ACTIVE TIME: **20 MINUTES**

TOTAL TIME: **50 MINUTES**

INGREDIENTS

1 CUP DAY-OLD BREAD PIECES

1 CUP WALNUTS

1 GARLIC CLOVE, SLICED THIN

¼ CUP BREAD CRUMBS

HANDFUL OF FRESH PARSLEY, CHOPPED

2 TABLESPOONS FINELY CHOPPED FRESH MARJORAM

3 TABLESPOONS WALNUT OIL

3 TABLESPOONS HEAVY CREAM

5 TABLESPOONS UNSALTED BUTTER, AT ROOM TEMPERATURE

SALT, TO TASTE

DIRECTIONS

1. Place the bread in a small bowl, cover it with warm water, and let it soak for 30 minutes. Drain, squeeze the bread to remove as much water from it as possible, and set it aside.

2. Bring a small saucepan of water to a boil, add the walnuts, cook for 2 minutes, drain, and let them cool. When cool enough to handle, rub off their skins and place on paper towels to dry. When dry, chop the walnuts and transfer them to a small bowl.

3. Place the bread, walnuts, garlic, bread crumbs, parsley, and half of the marjoram in a food processor and pulse until the mixture is a smooth paste. Transfer to a bowl, stir in the walnut oil until it has been thoroughly incorporated, and then stir in the cream and the butter. Season with salt and serve over pasta.

PUTTANESCA SAUCE

YIELD: **3 CUPS**

ACTIVE TIME: **15 MINUTES**

TOTAL TIME: **30 MINUTES**

INGREDIENTS

½ CUP EXTRA-VIRGIN OLIVE OIL

3 GARLIC CLOVES, MINCED

1 (28 OZ.) CAN OF PEELED WHOLE SAN MARZANO TOMATOES, WITH THEIR LIQUID, CRUSHED BY HAND

½ LB. BLACK OLIVES, PITTED

¼ CUP CAPERS, DRAINED AND RINSED

5 ANCHOVY FILLETS PACKED IN OLIVE OIL, BONED

1 TEASPOON RED PEPPER FLAKES

SALT AND PEPPER, TO TASTE

DIRECTIONS

1. Place the olive oil in a large, deep skillet and warm over medium heat. When the oil begins to shimmer, add the garlic and sauté until fragrant, about 1 minute.

2. Add the tomatoes and their liquid, olives, capers, and anchovies and stir, pressing down on the anchovies to break them up. Cook until the anchovies have dissolved. Stir in the red pepper flakes, season with salt and pepper, stir to combine, and raise the heat to medium. Simmer, stirring occasionally, until the sauce thickens slightly, about 10 minutes. Taste and adjust seasoning if necessary before serving.

RABBIT RAGÙ

YIELD: **4 CUPS**

ACTIVE TIME: **45 MINUTES**

TOTAL TIME: **2 HOURS AND 30 MINUTES**

INGREDIENTS

¼ CUP EXTRA-VIRGIN OLIVE OIL

2½- TO 3½-LB. RABBIT, CUT INTO 8 BONE-IN PIECES

SALT AND PEPPER, TO TASTE

1 CUP ALL-PURPOSE FLOUR

1 YELLOW ONION, CHOPPED

2 CELERY STALKS, PEELED AND CHOPPED

2 CARROTS, PEELED AND CHOPPED

1 GARLIC CLOVE, MINCED

2 TABLESPOONS TOMATO PASTE

½ CUP DRY RED WINE

1 (28 OZ.) CAN OF CRUSHED TOMATOES, WITH THEIR LIQUID

1 CUP CHICKEN STOCK (SEE PAGE 118)

2 BAY LEAVES

2 SPRIGS OF FRESH ROSEMARY

4 SPRIGS OF FRESH THYME

DIRECTIONS

1. Place the olive oil in a Dutch oven and warm it over medium heat. Season the rabbit with salt and pepper, dredge it in the flour, and shake to remove any excess. When the oil starts to shimmer, add the rabbit and cook until it is browned on both sides, about 4 minutes per side.

2. Use a slotted spoon to remove the rabbit and set it aside. Add the onion, celery, carrots, and garlic and sauté until the onion starts to brown, about 8 minutes. Stir in the tomato paste and cook for another 4 minutes.

3. Add the wine and let the mixture come to a rolling boil. Reduce the heat so that the sauce simmers and cook until the wine has reduced by half, about 10 minutes.

4. Stir in the tomatoes, stock, bay leaves, rosemary, and thyme and simmer for 2 minutes. Return the rabbit to the pot and simmer until it is extremely tender, about 1½ hours.

5. Use a slotted spoon to remove the rabbit and set it aside. Remove the bay leaves, rosemary, and thyme. When the rabbit is cool enough to handle, remove the meat from the bones and shred it. Discard the bones and return the meat to the sauce before serving over pasta.

BOLOGNESE SAUCE

YIELD: **8 CUPS**

ACTIVE TIME: **45 MINUTES**

TOTAL TIME: **2 HOURS**

INGREDIENTS

2 TABLESPOONS EXTRA-VIRGIN OLIVE OIL

½ LB. BACON

1½ LBS. GROUND BEEF

SALT AND PEPPER, TO TASTE

1 ONION, CHOPPED

1 CARROT, PEELED AND MINCED

3 CELERY STALKS, PEELED AND CHOPPED

2 GARLIC CLOVES, MINCED

1 TEASPOON FRESH THYME

2 CUPS SHERRY

8 CUPS MARINARA SAUCE (SEE PAGE 77)

1 CUP WATER

1 CUP HEAVY CREAM

2 TABLESPOONS CHOPPED FRESH SAGE

1 CUP FRESHLY GRATED PARMESAN CHEESE

DIRECTIONS

1. Place the olive oil in a Dutch oven and warm over medium heat. When the oil starts to shimmer, add the bacon and cook until it is crispy, about 6 minutes. Add the ground beef, season it with salt and pepper, and cook, breaking up the meat with a fork as it browns, until it is cooked through, about 8 minutes. Remove the bacon and the ground beef from the pot and set them aside.

2. Add the onion, carrot, celery, and garlic to the Dutch oven, season with salt, and sauté until the carrot is tender, about 8 minutes. Return the bacon and ground beef to the pot, add the thyme and sherry, and cook until the sherry has nearly evaporated. Stir in the Marinara Sauce and water, reduce the heat to low, and cook for approximately 45 minutes, stirring often, until the sauce has thickened noticeably.

3. Stir the cream and sage into the sauce and cook for an additional 15 minutes.

4. Add the Parmesan and stir until melted. Taste and adjust the seasoning if necessary before serving.

ROASTED TOMATO & GARLIC SAUCE

YIELD: **6 CUPS**

ACTIVE TIME: **15 MINUTES**

TOTAL TIME: **2 HOURS**

INGREDIENTS

3 LBS. TOMATOES, HALVED

¼ CUP EXTRA-VIRGIN OLIVE OIL

5 LARGE GARLIC CLOVES, UNPEELED

SALT AND PEPPER, TO TASTE

1 HANDFUL OF FRESH BASIL LEAVES

DIRECTIONS

1. Preheat the oven to 350°F. Place the tomatoes on a parchment-lined baking sheet and drizzle the olive oil over them. Stir to ensure the tomatoes are coated evenly, place them in the oven, and lower the oven's temperature to 325°F. Roast the tomatoes for 1 hour.

2. Remove the baking sheet from the oven, place the garlic cloves on the baking sheet, return it to the oven, and roast for another 30 minutes.

3. Remove the sheet from the oven and let the tomatoes and garlic cool slightly.

4. When the garlic is cool enough to handle, peel them and place them in a bowl. Add the tomatoes, season the mixture with salt and pepper, and let cool completely.

5. Place the roasted tomatoes, garlic, and basil leaves in a food processor and blitz until pureed. Place the puree in a medium saucepan and bring to a simmer over medium heat, stirring occasionally. Taste and adjust the seasoning if necessary before serving.

TOMATO & EGGPLANT SAUCE ALLA NORMA

YIELD: **6 CUPS**

ACTIVE TIME: **40 MINUTES**

TOTAL TIME: **1 HOUR AND 30 MINUTES**

INGREDIENTS

2 MEDIUM EGGPLANTS, CHOPPED

2 TABLESPOONS SALT, PLUS MORE TO TASTE

3 TABLESPOONS EXTRA-VIRGIN OLIVE OIL

5 CUPS MARINARA SAUCE (SEE PAGE 77)

1 CUP RICOTTA CHEESE

BLACK PEPPER, TO TASTE

DIRECTIONS

1. Place the eggplants in a colander and sprinkle the salt over them. Let rest for 30 minutes, rinse the eggplants, and pat them dry with paper towels.

2. Preheat the oven to 400°F. Place the eggplants in a large mixing bowl, drizzle the olive oil over the top, and stir to make sure the pieces are evenly coated. Place the eggplants on a parchment-lined baking sheet, place it in the oven, and roast, stirring occasionally, until the eggplants are tender and golden brown, about 25 minutes. Remove from the oven and let the eggplants cool.

3. Place the eggplants, sauce, and ricotta in a large saucepan, stir to combine, and bring to a simmer over medium heat. Taste and season with salt and pepper if necessary before serving.

SOFIA'S SPICED PORK SAUCE

YIELD: **4 CUPS**

ACTIVE TIME: **20 MINUTES**

TOTAL TIME: **1 HOUR AND 30 MINUTES**

INGREDIENTS

6 TABLESPOONS UNSALTED BUTTER

1 YELLOW ONION, GRATED

2 CELERY STALKS, PEELED AND GRATED

SALT, TO TASTE

1½ LBS. GROUND PORK

1 CUP MILK

½ TEASPOON GROUND CLOVES

1 CUP CHICKEN STOCK
(SEE PAGE 118)

2 TABLESPOONS TOMATO PASTE

2 BAY LEAVES

6 FRESH SAGE LEAVES

DIRECTIONS

1. Place half of the butter in a large saucepan and melt it over medium-high heat. Add the onion, celery, and a few pinches of salt and sauté until the onion is translucent, about 3 minutes. Reduce the heat to low, cover the pan, and cook, stirring occasionally, until the vegetables are very tender, about 30 minutes.

2. Add the ground pork to the pot and raise the heat to medium-high. Season the pork with salt and cook, using a fork to break it up as it browns. When the pork is browned all over, stir in the milk and cook until the milk has completely evaporated, about 10 minutes.

3. Stir in the cloves, cook for 2 minutes, and then add the stock, tomato paste, and bay leaves. Bring the sauce to a boil, reduce the heat to low, and let the sauce simmer, stirring occasionally, until the flavor has developed to your liking, about 45 minutes.

4. Place the remaining butter in a small skillet and melt it over medium-low heat. Add the sage leaves and cook until the leaves are slightly crispy. Remove the sage leaves and discard them. Stir the seasoned butter into the sauce, taste, and adjust the seasoning if necessary before serving.

SHRIMP & PISTOU SAUCE

YIELD: **5 CUPS**

ACTIVE TIME: **35 MINUTES**

TOTAL TIME: **1 HOUR**

INGREDIENTS

1½ LBS. SHRIMP, PEELED AND
DEVEINED

4 GARLIC CLOVES

5 TABLESPOONS TOMATO PASTE

SALT AND PEPPER, TO TASTE

½ CUP FRESHLY GRATED PARMESAN
CHEESE

2 HANDFULS OF FRESH BASIL LEAVES,
TORN

6½ TABLESPOONS EXTRA-VIRGIN
OLIVE OIL

3 CUPS MARINARA SAUCE
(SEE PAGE 77)

½ CUP WATER

DIRECTIONS

1. Place the shrimp on a paper towel–lined plate and let them
    come to room temperature. Place the garlic, tomato paste,
    and a generous pinch of salt in a food processor and pulse
    until thoroughly combined. Add the Parmesan and pulse
    to incorporate. Add the basil and pulse once. Transfer the
    mixture to a small bowl and whisk in ¼ cup of the olive oil.
    Set the pistou aside.

2. Place the remaining olive oil in a large, deep skillet and warm
    it over medium heat. Pat the shrimp dry with paper towels.
    When the oil starts to shimmer, add the shrimp to the pan,
    working in batches to ensure there is plenty of room between
    them. Cook for 2 minutes on each side, transfer the cooked
    shrimp to a plate, and tent it with aluminum foil.

3. Place the sauce and water in the skillet and bring to a simmer
    over medium-high heat. Stir in the pistou, taste, and season
    with salt and pepper. Serve the sauce over pasta and top with
    the cooked shrimp.

CHAPTER 3

SOUPS
& STEWS

---

*While pizza and pasta have granted Italy the comfort crown, soup is
still the most comforting dish in every cuisine. From the agricultural
celebration that is Minestrone to the Ribollita and Pasta e Fagioli that
rely on odds and ends and allow you to make the most of everything
you bring into your kitchen, these preparations are key to developing
the patience and palate necessary to improving as a cook.*

MINESTRONE

YIELD: **4 SERVINGS**

ACTIVE TIME: **30 MINUTES**

TOTAL TIME: **1 HOUR AND 15 MINUTES**

INGREDIENTS

2 TABLESPOONS EXTRA-VIRGIN OLIVE OIL

1 GARLIC CLOVE, MINCED

2 ONIONS, MINCED

2 CARROTS, PEELED AND MINCED

1 LEEK, WHITE PART ONLY, RINSED WELL AND MINCED

2 YELLOW BELL PEPPERS, STEMMED, SEEDED, AND MINCED

2 RED BELL PEPPERS, STEMMED, SEEDED, AND MINCED

2 ZUCCHINI, MINCED

8 CHERRY TOMATOES, CHOPPED

2 (28 OZ.) CANS OF PEELED WHOLE SAN MARZANO TOMATOES, WITH THEIR LIQUID, PUREED

½ TEASPOON CHOPPED FRESH THYME

½ TEASPOON CHOPPED FRESH ROSEMARY

SALT AND PEPPER, TO TASTE

PARMESAN CHEESE, SHAVED, FOR GARNISH

DIRECTIONS

1. Place the oil in a large saucepan and warm it over medium heat. When the oil starts to shimmer, add the garlic, onions, carrots, and leek and cook, stirring frequently, until the vegetables start to soften, about 5 minutes.

2. Add the peppers, cook for 5 minutes, and then stir in the zucchini and cherry tomatoes. Cook for 3 minutes, add the pureed tomatoes, thyme, and rosemary, and bring to a boil.

3. Reduce the heat so that the soup simmers and cook until the vegetables are tender, about 20 minutes. Season with salt and pepper, ladle into warmed bowls, and garnish with the Parmesan.

SPICY ITALIAN SAUSAGE SOUP

YIELD: **4 SERVINGS**

ACTIVE TIME: **20 MINUTES**

TOTAL TIME: **1 HOUR**

INGREDIENTS

2 TABLESPOONS EXTRA-VIRGIN OLIVE OIL

1 LB. HOT ITALIAN SAUSAGE

1 ONION, CHOPPED

2 CARROTS, PEELED AND CHOPPED

1 CELERY STALK, PEELED AND CHOPPED

2 GARLIC CLOVES, MINCED

6 CUPS BEEF STOCK (SEE SIDEBAR)

1 ZUCCHINI, QUARTERED AND CHOPPED

1 (14 OZ.) CAN OF WHOLE TOMATOES, DRAINED AND CHOPPED

1 (14 OZ.) CAN OF CANNELLINI BEANS, DRAINED AND RINSED

2 CUPS BABY SPINACH

SALT AND PEPPER, TO TASTE

DIRECTIONS

1. Place the olive oil in a medium saucepan and warm it over medium heat. When the oil starts to shimmer, add the sausage and cook, turning it occasionally, until it is evenly browned, about 5 minutes. Use a slotted spoon to remove the sausage and set it aside.

2. Add the onion, carrots, celery, and garlic to the pan and cook, stirring frequently, until the onion starts to soften, about 5 minutes.

3. Add the stock and bring the soup to a boil. Reduce the heat so that it simmers and cook for 10 minutes.

4. Add the zucchini, tomatoes, and beans and cook until the zucchini is tender, about for 15 minutes.

5. Slice the sausage, add it to the soup along with the spinach, and simmer until the sausage is cooked through, about 10 minutes. Season the soup with salt and pepper and ladle it into warmed bowls.

BEEF STOCK

Place 3 lbs. beef bones in a stockpot and cover with cold water. Bring to a simmer over medium-high heat, skimming to remove any impurities that rise to the surface. Reduce the heat to low, add 2 chopped yellow onions, 3 chopped carrots, 4 chopped celery stalks, 3 crushed garlic cloves, 3 sprigs of fresh thyme, 1 teaspoon whole black peppercorns, 1 bay leaf, and salt to taste, and simmer for 5 hours, skimming to remove any impurities that rise to the surface. Strain, let cool slightly, and transfer to the refrigerator. Leave uncovered and let cool completely. Remove the layer of fat and cover. The stock will keep in the refrigerator for 3 to 5 days, and in the freezer for up to 3 months.

CHICKEN STOCK

Place 3 lbs. rinsed chicken bones in a large stockpot, cover them with water, and bring to a boil. Add 1 chopped onion, 2 chopped carrots, 3 chopped celery stalks, 3 unpeeled, smashed garlic cloves, 3 sprigs of fresh thyme, 1 teaspoon black peppercorns, 1 bay leaf, and salt to taste and reduce the heat so that the stock simmers. Cook for 2 hours, skimming to remove any impurities that rise to the surface. Strain the stock through a fine sieve, let the stock cool slightly, and place it in the refrigerator, uncovered, to chill. Remove the fat layer and cover. The stock will keep in the refrigerator for 3 to 5 days, and in the freezer for up to 3 months.

CHICKEN SOUP WITH MEATBALLS, FARFALLE & SPINACH

YIELD: **8 SERVINGS**

ACTIVE TIME: **35 MINUTES**

TOTAL TIME: **1 HOUR**

INGREDIENTS

FOR THE MEATBALLS

1 CUP FRESH BREAD CRUMBS

1 LB. GROUND CHICKEN

1 CUP FRESHLY GRATED PARMESAN
CHEESE

3 TABLESPOONS TOMATO PASTE

1 HANDFUL OF FRESH PARSLEY,
CHOPPED

3 LARGE EGGS

SALT AND PEPPER, TO TASTE

2 TABLESPOONS EXTRA-VIRGIN
OLIVE OIL

FOR THE SOUP

2 TABLESPOONS EXTRA-VIRGIN
OLIVE OIL

2 LEEKS, TRIMMED, RINSED WELL,
AND CHOPPED

SALT AND PEPPER, TO TASTE

5 GARLIC CLOVES, SLICED THIN

8 CUPS CHICKEN STOCK (SEE
SIDEBAR)

5 CARROTS, PEELED AND SLICED

½ LB. FARFALLE (SEE PAGE 166)

2 HANDFULS OF BABY SPINACH
LEAVES

¼ CUP FRESHLY GRATED PARMESAN
CHEESE, PLUS MORE FOR GARNISH

DIRECTIONS

1. To begin preparations for the meatballs, place the bread crumbs, chicken, Parmesan, tomato paste, parsley, and eggs in a mixing bowl, season with salt and pepper, and work the mixture with your hands until thoroughly combined. Working with wet hands, form the mixture into ½-inch balls.

2. Place the olive oil in a large skillet and warm it over medium heat. When the oil starts to shimmer, add the meatballs in batches and cook, turning them occasionally, until browned all over, about 8 minutes per batch. Transfer the browned meatballs to a paper towel–lined plate to drain.

3. To begin preparations for the soup, place the olive oil in a Dutch oven and warm it over medium heat. When the oil starts to shimmer, add the leeks, season them with salt and pepper, and cook, stirring frequently, until they are translucent, about 3 minutes. Reduce the heat to low, cover the pot, and cook, stirring occasionally, until the leeks are very soft, about 15 minutes.

4. Add the garlic, cook for 1 minute, and then stir in the stock, carrots, and meatballs. Raise the heat to medium-high and bring the soup to a gentle boil. Reduce the heat to medium-low and simmer the soup until the meatballs are cooked through and the carrots are tender, about 15 minutes.

5. Add the farfalle and cook until tender, about 8 minutes. Remove the Dutch oven from heat and stir in the spinach and Parmesan. Cover the pot and let it rest until the spinach has wilted, about 5 minutes. Ladle the soup into warmed bowls and garnish each portion with additional Parmesan.

TOMATO SOUP WITH CHICKPEAS & DITALINI

YIELD: **4 SERVINGS**

ACTIVE TIME: **20 MINUTES**

TOTAL TIME: **35 MINUTES**

INGREDIENTS

2 TABLESPOONS EXTRA-VIRGIN OLIVE OIL

1 ONION, CHOPPED

2 GARLIC CLOVES, MINCED

2 (28 OZ.) CANS OF PEELED WHOLE SAN MARZANO TOMATOES, WITH THEIR LIQUID, PUREED

2 TABLESPOONS FINELY CHOPPED FRESH THYME

4 CUPS CHICKEN STOCK
(SEE PAGE 118)

½ CUP DITALINI

1 (14 OZ.) CAN OF CHICKPEAS, DRAINED AND RINSED

¼ CUP CHOPPED FRESH PARSLEY

¼ CUP FRESHLY GRATED PARMESAN CHEESE, PLUS MORE FOR GARNISH

SALT AND PEPPER, TO TASTE

FRESH BASIL, CHOPPED, FOR GARNISH

DIRECTIONS

1. Place the olive oil in a large saucepan and warm over medium heat. When the oil starts to shimmer, add the onion and sauté until it starts to soften, about 5 minutes. Add the garlic, cook for 1 minute, and then stir in the pureed tomatoes, thyme, and stock.

2. Bring the soup to a boil, reduce the heat so that the soup simmers, and add the pasta. Cook until it is tender, about 8 minutes.

3. Stir in the chickpeas, parsley, and Parmesan and cook for 3 minutes. Season with salt and pepper, ladle into warmed bowls, and garnish with additional Parmesan and the basil.

VEGETABLE STOCK

Place 2 tablespoons extra-virgin olive oil, 2 trimmed and well rinsed leeks, 2 peeled and sliced carrots, 2 celery stalks, 2 sliced onions, and 3 unpeeled, smashed garlic cloves in a large stockpot and cook over low heat until the liquid the vegetables release has evaporated. Add 2 sprigs of fresh parsley and thyme, 1 bay leaf, 8 cups water, ½ teaspoon black peppercorns, and salt to taste. Raise the heat to high and bring the stock to a boil. Reduce heat so that the stock simmers and cook for 2 hours, skimming to remove any impurities that float to the surface. Strain the stock through a fine sieve, let the stock cool slightly, and place it in the refrigerator, uncovered, to chill. Remove the fat layer and cover. The stock will keep in the refrigerator for 3 to 5 days, and in the freezer for up to 3 months.

BROCCOLI & ANCHOVY SOUP

YIELD: **4 SERVINGS**

ACTIVE TIME: **20 MINUTES**

TOTAL TIME: **45 MINUTES**

INGREDIENTS

1 TABLESPOON EXTRA-VIRGIN OLIVE OIL

1 TABLESPOON UNSALTED BUTTER

1 ONION, CHOPPED

1 GARLIC CLOVE, MINCED

1½ CUPS CHOPPED PORTOBELLO MUSHROOMS

1 CHILI PEPPER, STEMMED, SEEDED, AND CHOPPED

2 ANCHOVY FILLETS, BONED AND MINCED

2 TOMATOES, PEELED, SEEDED, AND CHOPPED

¼ CUP WHITE WINE

4 CUPS VEGETABLE STOCK (SEE SIDEBAR)

2 CUPS BROCCOLI FLORETS

½ LB. ORECCHIETTE (SEE PAGE 169)

SALT AND PEPPER, TO TASTE

PARMESAN CHEESE, FRESHLY GRATED, FOR GARNISH

DIRECTIONS

1. Place the olive oil and butter in a saucepan and warm over low heat. When the butter has melted, add the onion, garlic, mushrooms, chili pepper, and anchovies and cook, stirring frequently, until the onion starts to soften, about 5 minutes.

2. Stir in the tomatoes and the white wine and simmer, stirring occasionally, for 10 minutes.

3. Add the stock, raise the heat to medium-high, and bring the soup to a boil. Reduce the heat so that the soup simmers. Add the broccoli florets and pasta cook until they are tender, about 10 minutes.

4. Season with salt and pepper, ladle the soup into warmed bowls, and garnish with Parmesan cheese.

CHICKEN PARM SOUP

YIELD: **4 SERVINGS**

ACTIVE TIME: **20 MINUTES**

TOTAL TIME: **1 HOUR**

INGREDIENTS

2 TABLESPOONS EXTRA-VIRGIN OLIVE OIL

2 BONELESS, SKINLESS CHICKEN BREASTS, CUT INTO ½-INCH PIECES

1 ONION, CHOPPED

2 GARLIC CLOVES, MINCED

1 TEASPOON RED PEPPER FLAKES

¼ CUP TOMATO PASTE

1 (14 OZ.) CAN OF DICED TOMATOES, WITH THEIR LIQUID

6 CUPS CHICKEN STOCK (SEE PAGE 118)

½ LB. PENNE

2 CUPS SHREDDED MOZZARELLA CHEESE

1 CUP FRESHLY GRATED PARMESAN CHEESE, PLUS MORE FOR GARNISH

SALT AND PEPPER, TO TASTE

FRESH BASIL, CHOPPED, FOR GARNISH

DIRECTIONS

1. Place the olive oil in a medium saucepan and warm it over medium-high heat. When the oil starts to shimmer, add the chicken and cook, stirring occasionally, until it is browned all over, about 6 minutes.

2. Add the onion and cook, stirring frequently, until it starts to soften, about 5 minutes. Stir in the garlic, red pepper flakes, tomato paste, tomatoes, and stock and bring the soup to a boil. Reduce heat so that the soup simmers and cook for 10 minutes.

3. Add the penne and cook until it is tender, about 10 minutes. Stir in the mozzarella and Parmesan and cook until they have melted. Season the soup with salt and pepper, ladle it into bowls, and garnish each portion with the basil and additional Parmesan.

GREAT NORTHERN BEAN SOUP

YIELD: **4 SERVINGS**

ACTIVE TIME: **20 MINUTES**

TOTAL TIME: **35 MINUTES**

INGREDIENTS

2 TABLESPOONS EXTRA-VIRGIN OLIVE OIL

1 SMALL YELLOW ONION, DICED

2 GARLIC CLOVES, MINCED

1 (14 OZ.) CAN OF GREAT NORTHERN BEANS, DRAINED AND RINSED

4 CUPS CHICKEN STOCK (SEE PAGE 118)

4 SLICES OF PROSCIUTTO, TORN

SALT AND PEPPER, TO TASTE

2 TABLESPOONS CHOPPED FRESH PARSLEY

2 TEASPOONS FRESH LEMON JUICE

1 TEASPOON LEMON ZEST

DIRECTIONS

1. Place the olive oil in a large saucepan and warm it over medium heat. When the oil starts to shimmer, add the onion to the pan and cook, stirring frequently, until it just starts to soften, about 5 minutes. Add the garlic and sauté until it begins to brown, about 1 minute.

2. Add the beans and stock to the pot and simmer for about 10 minutes.

3. Transfer the soup to a blender or food processor and puree until smooth. Set the soup aside.

4. Place the prosciutto in a small skillet and cook, stirring occasionally, over medium heat until it is just starting to brown, about 5 minutes. Transfer to a plate and set aside.

5. Warm the white bean puree over medium heat and season with salt and pepper. Ladle into warmed bowls and top each portion with the prosciutto, parsley, lemon juice, and lemon zest.

BROKEN PASTA SOUP

YIELD: **4 SERVINGS**

ACTIVE TIME: **20 MINUTES**

TOTAL TIME: **45 MINUTES**

INGREDIENTS

1 TABLESPOON EXTRA-VIRGIN OLIVE OIL

1 ONION, CHOPPED

2 GARLIC CLOVES, MINCED

2 CARROTS, PEELED AND CHOPPED

1 ZUCCHINI, CHOPPED

4 CELERY STALKS, PEELED AND CHOPPED

1 (28 OZ.) CAN OF DICED TOMATOES, WITH THEIR LIQUID

4 CUPS VEGETABLE STOCK (SEE PAGE 122)

1 CUP BROKEN SPAGHETTI

2 TABLESPOONS CHOPPED FRESH PARSLEY

SALT AND PEPPER, TO TASTE

DIRECTIONS

1. Place the oil in a large saucepan and warm over medium heat. When the oil starts to shimmer, add the onion and cook, stirring frequently, until it starts to soften, about 5 minutes.

2. Add the garlic, carrots, zucchini, and celery and cook for 5 minutes. Add the tomatoes and stock and bring the soup to a boil. Reduce heat so that the soup simmers and cook for 15 minutes.

3. Add the spaghetti and cook until the pasta is tender, 6 to 8 minutes.

4. Stir in the parsley and season the soup with salt and pepper. Ladle into warmed bowls and serve.

SAUSAGE, SPINACH & BEAN SOUP

YIELD: **4 SERVINGS**

ACTIVE TIME: **20 MINUTES**

TOTAL TIME: **40 MINUTES**

INGREDIENTS

2 TABLESPOONS EXTRA-VIRGIN
OLIVE OIL

1 LB. HOT ITALIAN SAUSAGE, SLICED

2 POTATOES, CHOPPED

2 GARLIC CLOVES, MINCED

½ TEASPOON RED PEPPER FLAKES

1 LB. BABY SPINACH

1 (14 OZ.) CAN OF CANNELLINI
BEANS, DRAINED AND RINSED

6 CUPS CHICKEN STOCK
(SEE PAGE 118)

1 BAY LEAF

SALT AND PEPPER, TO TASTE

1 CUP PARMESAN CHEESE, FRESHLY
GRATED, FOR GARNISH

DIRECTIONS

1. Place the olive oil in a large saucepan and warm it over medium heat. When the oil starts to shimmer, add the sausage and cook, stirring frequently, until it is nicely browned, about 5 minutes.

2. Add the potatoes, garlic, red pepper flakes, and baby spinach and cook, stirring frequently, until the spinach has wilted, about 3 minutes.

3. Add the beans, stock, and bay leaf, raise the heat to high, and bring the soup to a boil. Reduce the heat so that the soup simmers and cook until the potatoes are fork-tender, about 15 minutes.

4. Remove the bay leaf, season the soup with salt and pepper, ladle into warmed bowls, and garnish each one generously with Parmesan.

SEAFOOD MINESTRONE WITH BASIL PESTO

YIELD: **6 SERVINGS**

ACTIVE TIME: **45 MINUTES**

TOTAL TIME: **1 HOUR AND 30 MINUTES**

INGREDIENTS

½ CUP WHITE WINE

30 MUSSELS, RINSED AND DEBEARDED

1 TABLESPOON EXTRA-VIRGIN OLIVE OIL

4 STRIPS OF THICK-CUT BACON, CHOPPED

1 GARLIC CLOVE, MINCED

1 ONION, CHOPPED

2 CELERY STALKS, PEELED AND CHOPPED

1 TABLESPOON TOMATO PASTE

1 TEASPOON FRESH ROSEMARY, CHOPPED

1 TEASPOON FRESH THYME, CHOPPED

1 BAY LEAF

1 TEASPOON FRESH LEMON JUICE

½ CUP CANNED KIDNEY BEANS, DRAINED AND RINSED

6 TABLESPOONS RICE

1 TOMATO, CHOPPED

6 CUPS FISH STOCK (SEE SIDEBAR)

6 OZ. SHRIMP, SHELLED AND DEVEINED

MEAT OF 12 OYSTERS, JUICES RESERVED

SALT AND PEPPER, TO TASTE

PARMESAN CHEESE, SHAVED, FOR GARNISH

BASIL PESTO (SEE PAGE 78), FOR SERVING

DIRECTIONS

1. Place the wine and mussels in a large saucepan, cover the pan, and cook over medium heat until the majority of the mussels have opened. Discard any that do not open.

2. Strain the soup through a fine sieve, reserving the mussels and the cooking liquid. Remove the mussels from their shells and set them aside.

3. Place the olive oil in a large saucepan and warm it over medium heat. When the oil starts to shimmer, add the bacon and cook until it starts to brown, about 4 minutes. Add the garlic, onion, and celery and cook, stirring frequently, until the onion and celery start to soften, about 5 minutes.

4. Stir in the tomato paste, rosemary, thyme, bay leaf, lemon juice, kidney beans, rice, and tomato and cook for 2 minutes.

5. Add the stock and bring the soup to a boil. Reduce the heat so that the soup simmers and cook until the rice is tender, about 12 minutes.

6. Add the mussels, shrimp, and oysters. Season to taste and simmer until the shrimp and oysters are cooked through, about 3 minutes.

7. Ladle the soup into warmed bowls, garnish with Parmesan, and serve with the Basil Pesto.

FISH STOCK

Place ¼ cup olive oil in a stockpot and warm over low heat. Add 1 trimmed, rinsed, and chopped leek, 1 unpeeled, chopped onion, 2 chopped carrots, 1 chopped celery stalk and cook until the liquid they release has evaporated. Add ¾ lb. of whitefish bodies, 4 sprigs of fresh parsley, 3 sprigs of fresh thyme, 2 bay leaves, 1 teaspoon of black peppercorns and salt, and 8 cups water, raise the heat to high, and bring to a boil. Reduce heat so that the stock simmers and cook for 3 hours, while skimming to remove any impurities that rise to the surface. Strain the stock through a fine sieve, let it cool slightly, and place in the refrigerator, uncovered, to chill. When the stock is completely cool, remove the fat layer from the top and cover. The stock will keep in the refrigerator for 3 to 5 days, and in the freezer for up to 3 months.

PASTA E FAGIOLI

YIELD: **8 SERVINGS**

ACTIVE TIME: **30 MINUTES**

TOTAL TIME: **1 HOUR AND 15 MINUTES**

INGREDIENTS

2 TABLESPOONS EXTRA-VIRGIN OLIVE OIL

4 OZ. PANCETTA OR BACON, CHOPPED

1 ONION, MINCED

1 CELERY STALK, PEELED AND MINCED

3 CARROTS, PEELED AND CHOPPED

SALT AND PEPPER, TO TASTE

3 GARLIC CLOVES, SLICED THIN

3 ANCHOVY FILLETS, BONED

1 (28 OZ.) CAN OF PEELED WHOLE SAN MARZANO TOMATOES, WITH THEIR JUICES, CRUSHED BY HAND

1 PARMESAN CHEESE RIND

3 (14 OZ.) CANS OF CANNELLINI BEANS, DRAINED AND RINSED

6½ CUPS CHICKEN STOCK (SEE PAGE 118)

½ LB. PASTA

¼ CUP CHOPPED FRESH PARSLEY

1 CUP FRESHLY GRATED PARMESAN CHEESE

DIRECTIONS

1. Place the olive oil in a Dutch oven and warm it over medium heat. When the oil starts to shimmer, place the pancetta or bacon in the pot and cook, stirring occasionally, until crispy, about 8 minutes.

2. Add the onion, celery, carrots, and a couple pinches of salt and sauté until the onion turns translucent, about 3 minutes. Reduce the heat to low, cover the pot, and cook, stirring occasionally, until the vegetables are very soft, about 20 minutes.

3. Stir in the garlic and anchovies and cook, stirring frequently, until the anchovies dissolve, about 1 minute. Add the tomatoes and scrape up any browned bits from the bottom of the pot. Raise the heat to medium-high, add the Parmesan rind, beans, and stock, and bring the soup to a boil. Reduce the heat to low and simmer, stirring occasionally, until the flavors have developed to your liking, about 45 minutes.

4. Remove the Parmesan rind and discard it. Stir in the pasta and cook until it is al dente, about 10 minutes. Remove the pot from heat, season the soup with salt and pepper, and top with the parsley and Parmesan.

ITALIAN WEDDING SOUP

YIELD: **4 SERVINGS**

ACTIVE TIME: **30 MINUTES**

TOTAL TIME: **1 HOUR AND 15 MINUTES**

INGREDIENTS

FOR THE MEATBALLS

¾ LB. GROUND CHICKEN

⅓ CUP PANKO

1 GARLIC CLOVE, MINCED

2 TABLESPOONS CHOPPED FRESH PARSLEY

¼ CUP FRESHLY GRATED PARMESAN CHEESE

1 TABLESPOON MILK

1 EGG, BEATEN

⅛ TEASPOON FENNEL SEEDS

⅛ TEASPOON RED PEPPER FLAKES

½ TEASPOON PAPRIKA

SALT AND PEPPER, TO TASTE

FOR THE SOUP

2 TABLESPOONS EXTRA-VIRGIN OLIVE OIL

1 ONION, CHOPPED

2 CARROTS, PEELED AND MINCED

1 CELERY STALK, PEELED AND MINCED

6 CUPS CHICKEN STOCK
(SEE PAGE 118)

¼ CUP WHITE WINE

½ CUP SMALL PASTA

2 TABLESPOONS CHOPPED FRESH DILL

6 OZ. BABY SPINACH

SALT AND PEPPER, TO TASTE

PARMESAN CHEESE, FRESHLY GRATED, FOR GARNISH

DIRECTIONS

1. Preheat the oven to 350°F. To prepare the meatballs, place all of the ingredients in a mixing bowl and work the mixture with your hands until combined. Working with wet hands, form the mixture into 1-inch balls and place them on a parchment-lined baking sheet. Place the meatballs in the oven and bake for 12 to 15 minutes, until browned and cooked through. Remove from the oven and set the meatballs aside.

2. To begin preparations for the soup, place the olive oil in a saucepan and warm it over medium heat. When the oil starts to shimmer, add the onion, carrots, and celery and cook, stirring frequently, until they start to soften, about 5 minutes.

3. Stir in the stock and the wine and bring the soup to a boil. Reduce the heat so that the soup simmers, add the pasta, and cook until it is tender, about 8 minutes.

4. Add the cooked meatballs and simmer for 5 minutes. Stir in the dill and the spinach and cook until the spinach has wilted, about 2 minutes. Season the soup with salt and pepper, ladle it into warmed bowls, and garnish with the Parmesan.

RIBOLLITA

YIELD: **4 SERVINGS**

ACTIVE TIME: **30 MINUTES**

TOTAL TIME: **1 HOUR AND 30 MINUTES**

INGREDIENTS

5 TABLESPOONS EXTRA-VIRGIN
OLIVE OIL

1 SMALL YELLOW ONION, CHOPPED

1 CARROT, PEELED AND CHOPPED

1 CELERY STALK, PEELED AND
CHOPPED

2 GARLIC CLOVES, MINCED

SALT AND PEPPER, TO TASTE

2 CUPS CANNED CANNELLINI BEANS,
RINSED WELL

1 LB. CANNED, PEELED, AND WHOLE
SAN MARZANO TOMATOES, WITH
THEIR JUICES, CRUSHED BY HAND

4 CUPS VEGETABLE STOCK
(SEE PAGE 122)

1 SPRIG OF FRESH ROSEMARY

1 SPRIG OF FRESH THYME

1 LB. KALE OR ESCAROLE, CHOPPED

4 LARGE, THICK SLICES OF DAY-OLD
BREAD, TOASTED

1 SMALL RED ONION, SLICED THIN

½ CUP FRESHLY GRATED PARMESAN
CHEESE

DIRECTIONS

1. Place 2 tablespoons of the oil in a large saucepan and warm it over medium heat. When the oil starts to shimmer, add the yellow onion, carrot, celery, and garlic, season the mixture with salt and pepper, and cook, stirring occasionally, until the vegetables are soft, about 10 minutes.

2. Preheat the oven to 500°F. Add the beans to the pot along with the tomatoes and their juices, the stock, rosemary, and thyme. Bring to a boil, reduce the heat so the soup simmers, and cover the pan. Cook, stirring occasionally, until the flavors have developed, 15 to 20 minutes.

3. Remove the rosemary and thyme and discard. Stir in the kale or escarole, taste the soup, and adjust the seasoning if necessary. Lay the bread slices on top of the stew so they cover as much of the surface as possible. Sprinkle the red onion and Parmesan on top and drizzle the remaining olive oil over everything.

4. Place the pot in the oven and bake until the bread, onions, and cheese are browned and crisp, 10 to 15 minutes. Ladle the soup and bread into warmed bowls and serve.

ARTICHOKE SOUP

YIELD: **4 SERVINGS**

ACTIVE TIME: **20 MINUTES**

TOTAL TIME: **45 MINUTES**

INGREDIENTS

6 ARTICHOKES

1 TABLESPOON EXTRA-VIRGIN OLIVE
OIL

1 TABLESPOON UNSALTED BUTTER

1 YELLOW ONION, CHOPPED

1 GARLIC CLOVE, MINCED

1 CUP RIESLING

1 TEASPOON FRESH THYME

4 CUPS HEAVY CREAM

1 CUP VEGETABLE STOCK
(SEE PAGE 122)

1 CUP PLAIN GREEK YOGURT

1 TEASPOON GROUND FENNEL

SALT AND PEPPER, TO TASTE

FRESH DILL, CHOPPED, FOR GARNISH

DIRECTIONS

1. Peel the artichokes, remove the hearts, and slice them thin.
    Place the oil and butter in a medium saucepan and warm
    over medium heat. When the butter has melted, add the
    artichoke hearts and onion and cook, stirring frequently, until
    they are starting to brown, about 10 minutes.

2. Add the garlic, Riesling, and thyme and cook until the wine
    has reduced by half. Add the heavy cream and the stock and
    simmer for 10 minutes.

3. While the soup is simmering, place the yogurt and fennel in a
    bowl and stir to combine. Set the mixture aside.

4. Transfer the soup to a food processor or blender, puree until
    smooth, and strain through a fine sieve. Season with salt and
    pepper, ladle into warmed bowls, top each portion with a
    dollop of the fennel yogurt, and garnish with dill.

CHICKEN LIVER & FARFALLE SOUP

YIELD: **4 SERVINGS**

ACTIVE TIME: **25 MINUTES**

TOTAL TIME: **1 HOUR**

INGREDIENTS

1 TABLESPOON EXTRA-VIRGIN OLIVE OIL

1 TABLESPOON UNSALTED BUTTER

½ CUP CHOPPED CHICKEN LIVERS

4 GARLIC CLOVES, MINCED

2 TABLESPOONS WHITE WINE

2 TABLESPOONS CHOPPED FRESH PARSLEY

2 TABLESPOONS CHOPPED FRESH MARJORAM

2 TABLESPOONS CHOPPED FRESH SAGE

1 TEASPOON FRESH THYME, CHOPPED

6 FRESH BASIL LEAVES, FINELY CHOPPED

6 CUPS CHICKEN STOCK (SEE PAGE 118)

2 CUPS PEAS

1 CUP FARFALLE (SEE PAGE 166)

3 SCALLION WHITES, SLICED

SALT AND PEPPER, TO TASTE

DIRECTIONS

1. Place the oil and butter in a medium saucepan and warm over medium-high heat. When the butter has melted, add the chicken livers and garlic and sauté until the chicken livers are browned all over, about 5 minutes. Add the wine and cook until it evaporates. Stir in the herbs and cook for 2 minutes. Remove pan from heat and set aside.

2. Place the stock in a large saucepan and bring it to a boil. Reduce the heat so that the stock simmers, add the peas, and cook for 5 minutes.

3. Return the broth to a boil and add the Farfalle. Reduce the heat so that the broth simmers and cook until the pasta is al dente, about 4 minutes.

4. Add the chicken livers and scallions and simmer for 3 minutes. Season the soup with salt and pepper and ladle it into warmed bowls.

CHAPTER 4

PASTA: FRESH DOUGHS & NOODLES

The dream of making fresh pasta is a common one. It is a fantasy that is also frequently drowned out by the ease of opening a box and dumping its contents into a pot of boiling water. Too often, in our opinion. Because there's nothing out of reach about whipping up a simple dough, letting it rest, and running it through a pasta maker before cutting it into your desired shape.

Making your own pasta's not miraculous, it only tastes like it. This chapter intends to introduce you to a few basic doughs that will help you turn out classic noodles like spaghetti, linguine, and fettuccine, as well as a few off–the–beaten path options that will soon become as cherished as those standards. So start fresh, and shift pasta from a last-resort dish to an immersive experience that everyone looks forward to.

MAKING YOUR OWN PASTA

Making your own pasta is not rocket science. At the end of the day, it can be as simple as combining two ingredients, eggs and flour, or flour and water. Should you decide to use the all-purpose flour in your pantry and high-quality eggs, you'll make pasta more delicious than anything you could purchase from the market, even those from high-end grocers.

If, on the other hand, you would like to delve deeper into understanding the subtleties of the ingredients that go into pasta making, read on. Once you begin experimenting with different types of flour and ingredients you will quickly be able to discern the slightest of differences, which is a profoundly satisfying development.

FLOUR: THE FOUNDATION OF PASTA

A passion for making great pasta translates into a knowledge of flour. There's no way around it. Otherwise, it's akin to trying to master the piano without understanding anything about chord structure.

To understand how flour will aid in your pasta-making exploits, it is important to recognize the role protein plays in flour and how it affects the dough. Once water is added to flour and the kneading process begins, proteins come into contact and form a bond that creates a network of fine strands in the dough known as gluten. This network is what gives dough its structure and strength.

In the seminal book *On Food and Cooking*, author and food scientist Harold McGee relates that the Chinese call gluten "the muscle of flour." It is an apt description, as gluten gives dough its elasticity and plasticity, which is the ability to take on a shape and keep it. The right amount of gluten results in a pasta dough that is easier to knead, put through the pasta maker, and stretch without tearing when handled. This explains why bread flour contains higher amounts of protein and why pasta noodles, which need to be more malleable, require less.

Before we begin exploring the different flours used in pasta making, it is worth noting that flour is not a static product. If "a rose is a rose is a rose" in Gertrude Stein's world, then "flour is not flour is not flour" in ours. In other words, the bag of flour in your pantry is probably very different from your next-door neighbor's. In fact, flour varies greatly depending on whether it comes from a nearby mill, a regional manufacturer, or a nationally recognized one. That's because when flour is milled, its composition, and thus performance, depends on the wheat grain variety, growing season, the soil in which it is grown, protein content, milling technique, temperature of the grain at the time of milling, and storage. National brands are the exception. Blended specifically for consistency, they combine different hard and soft wheat varieties to guarantee certain protein-level compositions. Because of this, they are often the flour of choice among professional bakers, who value predictability and consistency above all else.

Ultimately, the decision on what flour to use is yours. As I mentioned earlier, fresh pasta made with a national brand of flour and good quality eggs will be delicious. Its only shortcoming will be its neutral flavor, which will contain none of the aromatic notes of nuts, tobacco, and even grass that you would find in a freshly milled flour.

UNBLEACHED ALL-PURPOSE FLOUR: Typically produced from a blend of hard, high-protein bread flours and soft, low-protein pastry flours, all-purpose flour contains a moderate level of protein that ranges from 9 percent to 12 percent in national flour brands, though it can go as low as 7.5 percent in small regional brands. Blended and milled to be versatile, it is strong enough to make bread and soft enough to create tender, delicate scones, cakes, and biscuits. It also makes perfectly tender pasta, though combining it with other flours such as semolina results in tastier and slightly firmer noodles. Avoid bleached flour whenever possible, as it is treated with chemicals like benzoyl peroxide and chlorine gas to speed up the flour's aging process. The unbleached version is aged naturally, through oxidation.

"00" FLOUR: Produced from soft wheat, and ground so fine it is almost talcum-like, "00" flour is fairly low in protein content. It is the flour of choice in most Italian homes because it produces soft dough that is easy to roll and yields pastas and noodles that are smooth and silky. Tender egg pastas such tagliatelle, garganelli, and corzetti have most likely been prepared with a dough made from "00" flour and eggs. Occasionally the categorization of "00" flour causes some confusion because despite always being finely milled into powdery form, it can be made from soft or hard varieties of wheat and consequently contains different percentages of protein by weight. Soft wheat is lower in protein and creates soft and tender pasta that readily absorbs and takes on the flavor of a tasty sauce. Hard wheat is higher in protein content and creates a sturdy dough that is ideal for trapping air bubbles, like bread dough, but that quality makes it almost impossible to roll into sheets for pasta. When purchasing it, you will find "00" flour designated for bread and pizza or for pasta, with protein contents ranging from 5 percent to 12 percent. Be sure to select a "00" flour toward the lower end of this range (or one specifically designated for making pasta). If this flour is not readily available in your area, it is only a click away on the internet.

SEMOLINA FLOUR AND DURUM FLOUR: Both of these come from milling durum wheat berries, which have the highest protein content. Semolina comes from milling the innermost layer, called the endosperm, of the berry. It is characteristically coarse and golden in color as a result of its high concentration of carotenoids (the same compounds responsible for the carrot's bright orange color). It creates a strong pasta dough that holds any shape and strengthens when heated. Experienced pasta makers often add small amounts of semolina flour to pasta dough made predominantly with "00" flour to add a pleasant chewiness and subtle nutty flavor, as well as increase the dough's elasticity during rolling. Semolina flour also makes an excellent alternative to cornmeal, and can be used to dust formed pasta and work surfaces intended for pasta making. As the word *semolina* is also used to describe the innermost layer of any grain, such as corn and rice, some confusion can arise when people encounter this term.

Durum flour has a very fine texture that makes it look like golden all-purpose flour. A byproduct of milling semolina flour, it creates a malleable pasta dough that is easily fed through pasta makers and will curl or bend during cooking. Again, if either of these flours is not readily available in your area, look for it online.

WHOLE WHEAT FLOUR: This flour is ground from the entire wheat berry of either hard red spring or winter wheat: the endosperm, germ, and bran. Brown in color and lightly speckled, whole wheat adds a full-bodied wheaty flavor that, due to the tannins in the outer bran, can at times verge on bitterness. Chock-full of naturally occurring vitamins, minerals, and fiber, it is a viable option for health-oriented individuals who don't mind its assertive flavor. For best results, it is advisable to add some all-purpose flour to your dough to make it more pliable and the pasta more tender. Whole wheat flour also tends to absorb more moisture than white flour, so you'll need to adjust for that if you're substituting it in a recipe. There is also white whole wheat flour, which is ground from hard white spring or winter wheat berries; it possesses the same nutritional profile as whole wheat flour but is milder in flavor and lighter in color.

EGGS: TENDER PASTA'S NOT-SO-SECRET INGREDIENT

For the purposes of making pasta, and eating the most wholesome food possible, it is best to secure the highest quality eggs available to you.

Eggs play a vital role in many fresh pasta recipes. Not only do they enrich the noodles from a nutritional standpoint, they also add an appealing pale yellow color and a subtle flavor to the dough. Eggs also contribute two additional elements that may be more important to a pasta maker. First, they provide more protein, which, when combined with the gluten in the dough, enhances its structure, making the dough elastic, soft, and easier to roll out thin without tearing. Secondly, the egg whites provide additional heft and firmness to the dough while preventing the loss of starch as the pasta cooks.

It is important to use eggs that have a vibrantly orange yolk, as it is a sign of a healthy, happy, and well-fed chicken. Egg yolks get their color from carotenoids, which are also responsible for strengthening the chicken's immune system. Because chickens only hatch eggs if they have sufficient levels of carotenoids, the yolks possess deep hues of dark gold and orange. Paler yolks are often a result of chickens feeding on barley or white cornmeal, foods that don't nourish them as thoroughly as a diet based on yellow corn and marigold petals.

Using brown or white eggs is up to the discretion of the individual, since they both share the same nutritional profiles and taste the same. Aliza Green, author of the wonderful book *Making Artisan Pasta,* makes a good argument for buying brown eggs. First, brown eggs come from larger breeds that eat more, take longer to produce their eggs, and produce eggs with thicker protective shells, which prevents internal moisture loss over time and helps maintain freshness. Also, because brown eggs are considered a specialty product, she adds, their quality tends to be higher.

Eggs in the US are graded according to the thickness of their shell and the firmness of their egg whites. Agricultural advances have made it possible for large egg producers to assess the quality of each individual egg and to efficiently sort them by size, weight, and quality. With almost scientific precision, eggs are graded AA (top quality), A (good quality found in most supermarkets), and B (substandard eggs with thin shells and watery whites that don't reach consumers, but are used commercially and industrially). They are also further categorized by size: medium, large (the most common size), and extra large.

The past decade or so has also seen a rise in popularity of free-range and organic eggs. The product of smaller-scale enterprises, these chickens are given organic feed and are caged with slightly more space at their disposal than what is available on industrial-scale chicken farms. While the jury is still out on whether this last category tastes betters, it nonetheless constitutes an additional, and perhaps politically oriented, option for pasta makers.

For the purposes of making pasta, it is best to secure the freshest eggs available, so check the expiration dates before buying them and buy them when they are well within that window.

When making pasta it is important to avoid cold at all costs, so make sure to use room-temperature eggs. Also, do not work on a naturally cold surface such as marble or stainless steel. Wood is best; otherwise Corian or linoleum will work.

WATER

The water you use, its mineral content, and its temperature can impact the quality of your pasta dough.

Mineral-rich water from your tap is best for making pasta. The only exception is if your water is particularly hard, or excessively high in minerals like magnesium and calcium. In that case, you may be better off using spring water, as too much magnesium or calcium can produce a tighter gluten network in the dough and result in a firmer, and sometimes too firm, dough. Always use warm water, around 105°F (or two parts cold water to one part boiling water), as it makes it easier for the flour to absorb the liquid.

SALT

Use fine-grain iodized salt (table salt) or slightly coarser kosher salt, as both work nicely and contribute a hint of salty flavor to your pasta. Try to avoid using sea salt in either fine or coarse-grained forms, as its high mineral content can cause dough to develop a tighter gluten network, resulting in a firmer, and sometimes too firm, noodle.

USING YOUR PASTA MAKER

First, since you're enough of a pasta-phile to purchase a book about a cuisine that is largely built around it, we're assuming that you already have a pasta maker. But if not, better-than-satisfactory versions are available for around $40.

Once you have cut and rolled your dough, set the pasta maker for the flat roller (no teeth) on the widest setting (typically notch 1). Now feed the dough into the rollers. As a rather rough, thick sheet comes out the other end, make sure to support it with one of your hands. Fold the sheet of dough over itself twice, as you would a letter, and then turn the folded dough 90 degrees and feed it back through the pasta maker. Repeat this folding and feeding it back into the pasta maker three more times. This process is called "laminating" and it makes the dough more sturdy and manageable to handle.

Set the pasta maker to the second-widest setting (typically notch 2) and feed the dough into the rollers. Again, support the pasta as it comes out the other side. Fold it as you would a letter and feed it into the rollers. Repeat three additional times.

Set the pasta maker to the third-widest setting (typically notch 3) and feed the dough into the rollers. Again, support the pasta as it comes out the other side. Fold it as you would a letter and feed it into the rollers. Repeat three additional times.

Set the pasta maker to the second-smallest setting (typically notch 4). Feed the pasta into the rollers. Again, support the pasta as it comes out the other side. At this point, there is no need to laminate the pasta.

Stop rolling at this point if making sheets of pasta that are ⅛ inch thick for pansoti, agnolotti, maltagliati, farfalle, and cappellacci dei briganti. If you like your fettuccine, pappardelle, and tagliatelle a little thicker, then this is the setting for you.

If thinner sheets of pasta are desired, set the pasta maker to the smallest setting (typically notch 5). Cut the pasta sheet in half and feed it into the rollers. Again, support the pasta as it comes out the other side.

This last setting makes pasta sheets that are about 1/16 inch thick—that's so thin you can see light through them. It is ideal for filled pastas like ravioli, ravioloni, tortellini, anolini, cappellacci di zucca, and caramelle, whose fillings can easily be overshadowed by too much surrounding dough, as well as fazzoletti and quadretti. If you like your fettuccine, pappardelle, and tagliatelle very thin, then this is the setting for you.

The just-rolled pasta will be very delicate, so be gentle handling it. If the pasta sheet is too long to easily handle, carefully cut it in half. Lightly dust each sheet with flour and lay it on a surface lined with wax or parchment paper. Repeat all the above steps with the remaining pieces of dough.

The dough needs to dry for approximately 15 minutes after it has been rolled out and before it is cut into strands or other shapes. This drying time makes the dough less sticky and easier to handle. Keep in mind that when the pasta is very thick or wide it will need to be turned over to ensure thorough and even drying (not necessary for thinner noodles). The notable exception to this rule is if you are making stuffed pasta. In this case, not letting the dough dry is best because the slight stickiness helps the pasta adhere better and create a better seal.

Once fresh pasta has been cut, toss it with some semolina flour, place it on a semolina flour–dusted surface, and allow it to dry for at least 15 minutes before cooking. This drying period is important because it allows the pasta to become firmer and less sticky, which prevents the pasta from sticking together as it cooks (noodles also hold their shape better when allowed to dry slightly before cooking). More specific drying times are indicated in individual recipes. Just note that the drying process can be fickle. Depending on temperature, humidity levels, and the size of the noodles or pasta, the process may take a longer or shorter period of time than stated in the recipes. Also, it is probably best to avoid making pasta on very humid days. If you can't avoid it, turn on the air conditioner or even an oscillating fan to help the air circulate more effectively.

YIELD: ¾ **LB.**

ACTIVE TIME: **20 MINUTES**

TOTAL TIME: **2 HOURS AND 30 MINUTES**

INGREDIENTS

2¾ CUPS ALL-PURPOSE FLOUR, PLUS MORE AS NEEDED

3 LARGE EGGS

1 EGG YOLK

2 TABLESPOONS WARM WATER (105°F), PLUS MORE AS NEEDED

BASIC PASTA DOUGH

DIRECTIONS

1. Place the flour in a mixing bowl. Create a well in the center and place the eggs, egg yolk, and the water in the well. Using a fork or your fingers, gradually start incorporating the flour into the well until the dough starts holding together in a single mass. Incorporate more water, 1 tablespoon at a time, if the mixture is too dry to hold together. Once the dough feels firm and dry and can be formed into a ball, it's time to start kneading.

2. Place the dough on a flour-dusted work surface. Using the heel of your hand, push the ball of dough away from you. Turn the dough 45 degrees each time you repeat this motion, as doing so incorporates the flour more evenly. As you continue to knead, you'll notice the dough getting less and less floury. Eventually it will have a smooth, elastic texture. If the dough still feels wet or tacky, dust it with flour and continue kneading. If it feels too dry and is not completely sticking together, wet your hands with water and continue kneading. Wet your hands as many times as you need to until the dough is smooth and springy, about 8 to 10 minutes. The dough has been sufficiently kneaded when it gently pulls back when stretched.

3. Wrap the ball of dough tightly in plastic wrap and let it rest for 2 hours at room temperature. The dough will keep for up to 3 days in the refrigerator, but may experience some discoloration.

4. Cut the dough into four even pieces. Set one piece on a smooth work surface and wrap up the rest in plastic wrap to prevent them from drying out. Shape the piece of dough into a ball, place it on the surface, and, with the palm of your hand, push down on it so that it looks like a thick pita. Using a rolling pin, roll the dough to ½ inch thick. Try as much as possible to keep the thickness and width of the dough even, as it will make it easier to fit the through the pasta maker.

TIP: This dough is suitable for popular noodles such as fettuccine (¼ to ½ inch wide), pappardelle (1- to 1½-inch-wide), tagliatelle (¾ inch wide), and tortellini (see page 165).

ALL-YOLK PASTA DOUGH

YIELD: ¾ LB.

ACTIVE TIME: 20 MINUTES

TOTAL TIME: 2 HOURS AND 30 MINUTES

INGREDIENTS

1½ CUPS ALL-PURPOSE FLOUR

⅓ CUP "00" FLOUR, PLUS MORE AS NEEDED

8 LARGE EGG YOLKS

2 TABLESPOONS WARM WATER (105°F), PLUS MORE AS NEEDED

DIRECTIONS

1. Place the flours in a mixing bowl. Create a well in the center and place the egg yolks and the water in the well. Using a fork or your fingers, gradually start incorporating the flour into the well until the dough starts holding together in a single mass. Incorporate more water, 1 tablespoon at a time, if the mixture is too dry to hold together. Once the dough feels firm and dry and can be formed into a ball, it's time to start kneading.

2. Place the dough on a flour-dusted work surface. Using the heel of your hand, push the ball of dough away from you. Turn the dough 45 degrees each time you repeat this motion, as doing so incorporates the flour more evenly. As you continue to knead, you'll notice the dough getting less and less floury. Eventually it will have a smooth, elastic texture. If the dough still feels wet or tacky, dust it with flour and continue kneading. If it feels too dry and is not completely sticking together, wet your hands with water and continue kneading. Wet your hands as many times as you need to until the dough is smooth and springy, about 8 to 10 minutes. The dough has been sufficiently kneaded when it gently pulls back when stretched.

3. Wrap the ball of dough tightly in plastic wrap and let it rest for 2 hours at room temperature. The dough will keep for up to 3 days in the refrigerator, but may experience some discoloration.

Continued...

4. Cut the dough into four even pieces. Set one piece on a smooth work surface and wrap up the rest in plastic wrap to prevent them from drying out. Shape the piece of dough into a ball, place it on the surface, and, with the palm of your hand, push down on it so that it looks like a thick pita. Using a rolling pin, roll the dough to ½ inch thick. Try as much as possible to keep the thickness and width of the dough even, as it will make it easier to fit the through the pasta maker.

TIP: This dough is suitable for noodles such as lasagna, cannelloni, and tajarin, and should be used right away.

YIELD: ¾ **LB.**

ACTIVE TIME: **20 MINUTES**

TOTAL TIME: **2 HOURS AND 30 MINUTES**

INGREDIENTS

4 CUPS FINE WHOLE WHEAT FLOUR,
PLUS MORE AS NEEDED

1½ TEASPOONS SALT

4 LARGE EGG YOLKS

1 TABLESPOON EXTRA-VIRGIN OLIVE
OIL

2 TABLESPOONS WATER, PLUS MORE
AS NEEDED

WHOLE WHEAT PASTA DOUGH

DIRECTIONS

1. Place the flour and salt in a mixing bowl and form the mixture into a mound. Create a well in the center and place the egg yolks, olive oil, and the water in the well. Using a fork or your fingers, gradually start incorporating the flour into the well until the dough starts holding together in a single mass. Incorporate more water, 1 tablespoon at a time, if the mixture is too dry to hold together. Once the dough feels firm and dry and can be formed into a ball, it's time to start kneading.

2. Place the dough on a flour-dusted work surface. Using the heel of your hand, push the ball of dough away from you. Turn the dough 45 degrees each time you repeat this motion, as doing so incorporates the flour more evenly. As you continue to knead, you'll notice the dough getting less and less floury. Eventually it will have a smooth, elastic texture. If the dough still feels wet or tacky, dust it with flour and continue kneading. If it feels too dry and is not completely sticking together, wet your hands with water and continue kneading. Wet your hands as many times as you need to until the dough is smooth and springy, about 8 to 10 minutes. The dough has been sufficiently kneaded when it gently pulls back when stretched.

3. Wrap the ball of dough tightly in plastic wrap and let it rest for 2 hours at room temperature. The dough will keep for up to 3 days in the refrigerator, but may experience some discoloration.

4. Cut the dough into four even pieces. Set one piece on a smooth work surface and wrap up the rest in plastic wrap to prevent them from drying out. Shape the piece of dough into a ball, place it on the surface, and, with the palm of your hand, push down on it so that it looks like a thick pita. Using a rolling pin, roll the dough to ½ inch thick. Try as much as possible to keep the thickness and width of the dough even, as it will make it easier to run the dough through the pasta maker.

TIP: This dough is perfect for those who are looking for a slightly chewier pappardelle or linguine. Whole wheat pasta is also great with thick, creamy sauces.

RAVIOLI

YIELD: ¾ LB.

ACTIVE TIME: 30 MINUTES

TOTAL TIME: 1 HOUR

INGREDIENTS

2 CUPS "00" FLOUR, PLUS MORE AS NEEDED

PINCH OF KOSHER SALT, PLUS MORE TO TASTE

9 EGG YOLKS, BEATEN

2 TEASPOONS EXTRA-VIRGIN OLIVE OIL

1 EGG

1 TABLESPOON WATER

DIRECTIONS

1. Place the flour and salt in a mixing bowl, stir to combine, and make a well in the center. Place the egg yolks and olive oil in the well and slowly incorporate the flour until the dough holds together. Knead the dough until smooth, about 5 minutes. Cover the bowl with plastic wrap and let stand at room temperature for 30 minutes.

2. To form the ravioli, divide the dough into two pieces. Use a pasta maker to roll each piece into a long, thin rectangle. Place one of the rectangles over a flour-dusted ravioli tray and place a teaspoon of your desired filling into each of the depressions. Place the egg and water in a small bowl and beat until combined. Dip a pastry brush or a finger into the egg wash and lightly coat the edge of each ravioli with it. Gently lay the other rectangle over the piece in the ravioli tray. Use a rolling pin to gently cut out the ravioli. Remove the cut ravioli and place them on a flour-dusted baking sheet.

3. To cook the ravioli, bring a large saucepan of water to a boil. When the water is boiling, add salt and the ravioli, stir to make sure they do not stick to the bottom, and cook until tender but still chewy, about 2 minutes.

TORTELLINI

YIELD: **1 LB.**

ACTIVE TIME: **1 HOUR**

TOTAL TIME: **5 HOURS**

INGREDIENTS

BASIC PASTA DOUGH
(SEE PAGES 156–157)

SEMOLINA FLOUR, AS NEEDED

SALT, TO TASTE

DIRECTIONS

1. Prepare the dough as directed, rolling it to the thinnest setting (generally notch 5) for pasta sheets that are about $\frac{1}{16}$ inch thick. Dust the sheets with flour, place them on flour-dusted, parchment-lined baking sheets, and cover with plastic wrap.

2. Working with one pasta sheet at a time, place it on a flour-dusted work surface and, using a round stamp or pastry cutter, cut as many 1¼-inch rounds or squares out of it as possible. Transfer the rounds or squares to flour-dusted, parchment-lined baking sheets and cover with plastic wrap. Repeat with all the pasta sheets. Gather the scraps together into a ball, put it through the pasta maker to create additional pasta sheets, and cut those as well.

3. Place ½ teaspoon of your desired filling in the center of each round or square. Lightly moisten the edge of the pasta with a fingertip dipped in water. Fold the dough over to form a half-moon or a triangle. Now draw the two corners together; if using a pasta round, this will form a nurse's cap; for a square, it will have a kerchief shape. Press down around the joined sides to create a tight seal. As you do this, try to push out any air from around the filling, which prevents the tortellini from coming apart in the water when boiling due to vapor pressure. Press one more time to ensure you have a tight seal. Dust with flour, place the sealed tortellini on baking sheets, and let them dry for 2 hours.

4. To cook the tortellini, place them in a large saucepan of boiling, salted water and cook until they are tender but still chewy, 2 to 3 minutes.

FARFALLE

YIELD: ¾ **LB.**

ACTIVE TIME: **1 HOUR**

TOTAL TIME: **3 HOURS AND 30 MINUTES**

INGREDIENTS

ALL-YOLK PASTA DOUGH
(SEE PAGES 158–159)

SEMOLINA FLOUR, AS NEEDED

SALT, TO TASTE

DIRECTIONS

1. Prepare the dough as directed, rolling the dough to the second thinnest setting (generally notch 4) for pasta sheets that are about ⅛ inch thick. Lay the pasta sheets on flour-dusted, parchment-lined baking sheets and cover loosely with plastic wrap. Work quickly to keep the pasta sheets from drying out, which makes it harder for the pasta to stick together.

2. Working with one pasta sheet at a time, place it on a flour-dusted work surface and trim both ends to create a rectangle. Using a pastry cutter, cut the pasta sheet lengthwise into 1- to 1¼-inch-wide ribbons. Carefully separate the ribbons from each other, then, using a ridged pastry cutter, cut the ribbons into 2-inch pieces. To form the butterfly shape, place the index finger of your weak hand on the center of the piece of pasta. Then place the thumb and index finger of your dominant hand on the sides of the rectangle, right in the middle, and pinch the dough together to create a butterfly shape. Firmly pinch the center again to help it hold its shape. Leave the ruffled ends of the farfalle untouched. Repeat with all the pasta sheets.

3. Set the farfalle on lightly floured, parchment-lined baking sheets so they are not touching. Allow them to air-dry for at least 30 minutes and up to 3 hours, and then cook. Alternatively, you can place them, once air-dried, in a bowl, cover with a kitchen towel, and refrigerate for up to 3 days. Or freeze on the baking sheets, transfer to freezer bags, and store in the freezer for up to 2 months. Do not thaw them prior to cooking (they will become mushy) and add an extra minute or so to their cooking time.

4. To cook the farfalle, bring a large pot of salted water to a boil. Add the farfalle and cook until the pasta is tender but still chewy, 2 to 3 minutes.

YIELD: **1 LB.**

ACTIVE TIME: **45 MINUTES**

TOTAL TIME: **4 HOURS**

INGREDIENTS

2 CUPS SEMOLINA FLOUR, PLUS
MORE AS NEEDED

1 TEASPOON SALT, PLUS MORE TO
TASTE

¾ CUP WATER, PLUS MORE AS
NEEDED

ORECCHIETTE

DIRECTIONS

1. Combine the flour and salt in a large bowl. Add the water a little at a time and work the mixture with a fork until it starts holding together. If it is too dry to stick together, incorporate more water, 1 teaspoon at a time, until it does. Work the dough with your hands until it feels firm and dry and can be formed into a ball.

2. Transfer the dough to a flour-dusted work surface and knead it. Because it is made with semolina flour, the dough can be quite stiff and hard. You can also knead this in a stand mixer; don't try it with a handheld mixer—the dough will be too stiff and could burn the motor out. Using the heel of your hand, push the ball of dough away from you in a downward motion. Turn the dough 45 degrees each time you repeat this motion, as doing so incorporates the flour more evenly. Wet your hands as needed if the dough is too sticky. After 10 minutes of kneading, the dough will only be slightly softer (most of the softening is going to occur when the dough rests, which is when the gluten network within the dough will relax). Shape the dough into a ball, cover it tightly with plastic wrap, and let rest in the refrigerator for 2 hours.

3. Cut the dough into four equal pieces. Take one piece and shape it into an oval. Cover the remaining pieces with plastic wrap to prevent them from drying out. Place the dough on a flour-dusted work surface and roll it into a long, ½-inch-thick rope. Using a sharp paring knife, cut the rope into ¼-inch discs, dusting them with semolina flour so they don't stick together.

4. To form the orecchiette, place a disc on the work surface. Dip your thumb in semolina flour, place it on top of the disc, and, applying a little pressure, drag your thumb across the dough to create an earlike shape. For best results, dip your thumb in semolina flour your thumb before making each orecchiette. Dust the formed orecchiette with flour and set them on flour-dusted, parchment-lined baking sheets, making sure they are not touching. Let them dry for 1 hour, turning them over once halfway through.

5. To cook the orecchiette, place in a large pot of boiling, salted water until they are tender but still chewy, 3 to 4 minutes.

PIZZOCCHERI

YIELD: **1 LB.**

ACTIVE TIME: **30 MINUTES**

TOTAL TIME: **2 HOURS AND 15 MINUTES**

INGREDIENTS

1 CUP BUCKWHEAT FLOUR

1 CUP ALL-PURPOSE FLOUR, PLUS
MORE AS NEEDED

½ TEASPOON SALT, PLUS MORE TO
TASTE

¼ CUP VERY WARM WATER (160°F),
PLUS MORE AS NEEDED

2 LARGE EGGS

SEMOLINA FLOUR, AS NEEDED

DIRECTIONS

1. Place the flours and salt in a mixing bowl and form the mixture into a mound. Create a well in the center and place the water and eggs in the well. Using a fork or your fingers, gradually start incorporating the flour into the well until the dough starts holding together in a single mass. Incorporate more water, 1 tablespoon at a time, if the mixture is too dry to hold together. Once the dough feels firm and dry and can be formed into a ball, it's time to start kneading.

2. Place the dough on a flour-dusted work surface. Using the heel of your hand, push the ball of dough away from you. Turn the dough 45 degrees each time you repeat this motion, as doing so incorporates the flour more evenly. As you continue to knead, you'll notice the dough getting less and less floury. Eventually it will have a smooth, elastic texture. If the dough still feels wet or tacky, dust it with flour and continue kneading. If it feels too dry and is not completely sticking together, wet your hands with water and continue kneading. Wet your hands as many times as you need to until the dough is smooth and springy, about 8 to 10 minutes. The dough has been sufficiently kneaded when it gently pulls back when stretched.

3. Wrap the ball of dough tightly in plastic wrap and let it rest for 40 minutes hours at room temperature. The dough will keep for up to 3 days in the refrigerator, but may experience some discoloration.

Continued...

4. Cut the dough into four even pieces. Set one piece on a smooth work surface and wrap up the rest in plastic wrap to prevent them from drying out. Shape the piece of dough into a ball, place it on the surface, and, with the palm of your hand, push down on it so that it looks like a thick pita. Using a rolling pin, roll the dough to ½ inch thick. Try as much as possible to keep the thickness and width of the dough even, as it will help the dough fit through the pasta machine more easily.

5. Lightly dust the piece of dough with semolina flour and, using a rolling pin, roll it until it is approximately 4 inches wide and 8 inches long. Run the dough three times through the widest setting of the pasta machine. The dough will now be 12 to 15 inches long and 4 to 5 inches wide. Repeat this process with the remaining pieces of dough. Hang the pieces of dough across a wooden drying rack and let them dry for 30 minutes, turning the sheets over twice during that time.

6. Lightly dust one sheet of dough with semolina flour and gently roll it up. Gently slice the roll across into ⅓-inch wide ribbons, taking care not to compress the roll too much as you slice through it. Repeat with the remaining pieces of dough. Lightly dust the pasta coils with semolina flour, then unroll them and place them on parchment-lined baking sheets. Let them rest for 30 minutes before cooking.

FAZZOLETTI

YIELD: **1 LB.**

ACTIVE TIME: **45 MINUTES**

TOTAL TIME: **4 HOURS**

INGREDIENTS

BASIC PASTA DOUGH
(SEE PAGES 156–157)

SEMOLINA FLOUR, AS NEEDED

SALT, TO TASTE

DIRECTIONS

1. Prepare the dough as directed, rolling the dough to the thinnest setting (generally notch 5) for pasta sheets that are about $\frac{1}{16}$ inch thick. Lay the pasta sheets on flour-dusted, parchment-lined baking sheets and let them dry for 15 minutes.

2. Cut each pasta sheet into as many 2½-inch squares as possible. Set them on flour-dusted, parchment-lined baking sheets so they are not touching. Gather any scraps into a ball, put it through the pasta maker to create additional pasta sheets, and cut those as well. Allow them to dry for 1 hour, turning them over once halfway through, and then cook. Alternatively, you can place them, once dried, in a bowl, cover with a kitchen towel, and refrigerate for up to 3 days.

3. To cook the fazzoletti, cook for about 1 minute in a pot of boiling, salted water, until they are tender but still chewy.

GARGANELLI

YIELD: **1½ LBS.**

ACTIVE TIME: **1 HOUR**

TOTAL TIME: **4 HOURS**

INGREDIENTS

2¼ CUPS SEMOLINA FLOUR, PLUS MORE AS NEEDED

1½ TEASPOONS SALT, PLUS MORE TO TASTE

3 LARGE EGGS

2 TABLESPOONS EXTRA-VIRGIN OLIVE OIL

2 TABLESPOONS WATER

DIRECTIONS

1. Place the flour and salt in a mixing bowl and form it into a mound. Create a well in the center and place the eggs, olive oil, and the water in the well. Using a fork or your fingers, gradually start incorporating the flour into the well until the dough starts holding together in a single mass. Incorporate more water, 1 tablespoon at a time, if the mixture is too dry to hold together. Once the dough feels firm and dry and can be formed into a ball, it's time to start kneading.

2. Place the dough on a flour-dusted work surface. Using the heel of your hand, push the ball of dough away from you. Turn the dough 45 degrees each time you repeat this motion, as doing so incorporates the flour more evenly. As you continue to knead, you'll notice the dough getting less and less floury. Eventually it will have a smooth, elastic texture. If the dough still feels wet or tacky, dust it with flour and continue kneading. If it feels too dry and is not completely sticking together, wet your hands with water and continue kneading. Wet your hands as many times as you need to until the dough is smooth and springy, about 8 to 10 minutes. The dough has been sufficiently kneaded when it gently pulls back when stretched.

3. Wrap the ball of dough tightly in plastic wrap and let it rest for 2 hours at room temperature. The dough will keep for up to 3 days in the refrigerator, but may experience some discoloration.

Continued...

4. Cut the dough into four even pieces. Set one piece on a smooth work surface and wrap up the rest in plastic wrap to prevent them from drying out. Shape the piece of dough into a ball, place it on the surface, and, with the palm of your hand, push down on it so that it looks like a thick pita. Using a rolling pin, roll the dough to ½ inch thick. Try as much as possible to keep the thickness and width of the dough even, as it will make it easier to run the dough through the pasta maker.

5. Run the dough through the pasta maker, rolling the dough to the second-thinnest setting (generally notch 4) for pasta sheets that are about 1/8 inch thick. Lay the pasta sheets on flour-dusted, parchment-lined baking sheets and cover them loosely with plastic wrap.

6. Working with one sheet at a time, lightly dust it with flour. Cut it into 1½-inch-wide strips and then cut the strips into 1½-inch squares. Repeat with the remaining pasta sheets. Cover the squares loosely with plastic wrap. Gather any scraps together into a ball, put it through the pasta maker to create additional pasta sheets, and cut those in the same fashion.

7. To make each garganello, place one square of pasta dough on a flour-dusted work surface with one of the corners pointing toward you. Using a chopstick, gently roll the square of pasta around the chopstick, starting from the corner closest to you, until a tube forms. Once completely rolled, press down slightly as you seal the ends together, then carefully slide the tube of pasta off the chopstick and lightly dust it with flour. Set them on flour-dusted, parchment-lined baking sheets and allow them to dry for 1 hour, turning them over halfway through.

8. To cook the garganelli, cook for 2 to 3 minutes in a pot of boiling, salted water, until they are tender but still chewy.

YIELD: **1 LB.**

ACTIVE TIME: **45 MINUTES**

TOTAL TIME: **5 HOURS**

INGREDIENTS

1¾ CUPS SEMOLINA FLOUR, PLUS
MORE AS NEEDED

1 TEASPOON SALT, PLUS MORE TO
TASTE

½ TEASPOON FENNEL SEEDS,
GROUND FINE

⅔ CUP WARM WATER (105°F)

NODI

DIRECTIONS

1. Place the flour, salt, and fennel seeds in a large bowl and add the water. Work the mixture with a fork until it starts to stick together and look coarse. Transfer it to a flour-dusted work surface.

2. Using the heel of your hand, push the ball of dough away from you. Turn the dough 45 degrees each time you repeat this motion, as doing so incorporates the flour more evenly. As you continue to knead, you'll notice the dough getting less and less floury. Eventually it will have a smooth, elastic texture. If the dough still feels wet or tacky, dust it with flour and continue kneading. If it feels too dry and is not completely sticking together, wet your hands with water and continue kneading. Wet your hands as many times as you need to until the dough is smooth and springy, about 8 to 10 minutes. The dough has been sufficiently kneaded when it gently pulls back when stretched.

3. Wrap the ball of dough tightly in plastic wrap and let it rest for 2 hours at room temperature. The dough will keep for up to 3 days in the refrigerator, but may experience some discoloration.

4. Place the dough on a flour-dusted work surface, roll it into a 2-inch-thick log and cut it into 18 rounds. Cover all the pieces but the one you are working on with plastic wrap to keep them from drying out.

5. Roll each piece of dough into a long rope that is ⅛ inch thick. Starting at one end of the rope, tie a simple knot, gently pull on both ends to tighten the knot slightly, then cut the knot off the rope, leaving a tail on each side of about ⅜ inch long. Keep making and cutting off knots in this manner until you use up all of the rope. Repeat with the remaining pieces of dough. Set the finished knots on flour-dusted, parchment-lined baking sheets, making sure they are not touching. Allow them to dry for 2 hours, turning them over once halfway through.

6. To cook the nodi, place in a large pot of boiling, salted water for 2 to 3 minutes, until they are tender but still firm.

TAJARIN

YIELD: ½ **LB.**

ACTIVE TIME: **45 MINUTES**

TOTAL TIME: **3 HOURS AND 30 MINUTES**

INGREDIENTS

ALL-YOLK PASTA DOUGH
(SEE PAGES 158–159)

SEMOLINA FLOUR, AS NEEDED

SALT, TO TASTE

DIRECTIONS

1. Prepare the dough as directed, rolling the dough to the thinnest setting (generally notch 5) for pasta sheets that are about ¹⁄₁₆ inch thick. Cut the pieces into 8-inch-long sheets, lay them on flour-dusted, parchment-lined baking sheets, and let them dry for 15 minutes.

2. Working with one sheet at a time, dust it with semolina flour and gently roll it up. Using a very sharp knife, gently slice the roll into ¹⁄₁₂-inch-wide strips. Dust the strips with flour, then gently unfold the strips, one at a time, shaking off any excess flour. Arrange them on flour-dusted, parchment-lined baking sheets, either straight and spread out or curled into a coil. Repeat with all the pasta sheets. Allow the tajarin to dry for 30 minutes before cooking.

3. To cook the tajarin, place in a large pot of boiling, salted water until they are tender but still chewy, typically no more than 2 minutes.

TROFIE

YIELD: **1 LB.**

ACTIVE TIME: **45 MINUTES**

TOTAL TIME: **5 HOURS**

INGREDIENTS

2¾ CUPS ALL-PURPOSE FLOUR

1 TEASPOON SALT, PLUS MORE TO TASTE

1 CUP WATER

SEMOLINA FLOUR, AS NEEDED

DIRECTIONS

1. Place the flour and salt in a large bowl, stir to combine, and add the water. Work the mixture with a fork until all the water has been incorporated. Work the mixture with your hands until a coarse dough forms.

2. Transfer the dough, along with any bits that stuck to the bowl, to a flour-dusted work surface and knead the dough. Using the heel of your hand, push the ball of dough away from you in a downward motion. Turn the dough 45 degrees each time you repeat this motion, as doing so incorporates the flour more evenly. Knead the dough until it is smooth and elastic, about 10 minutes. Cover the dough with plastic wrap and let it rest at room temperature for 2 hours.

3. Place the dough on a flour-dusted work surface and roll it into a 2-inch-thick log. Cut it into eight pieces, leave one out, and cover the rest with plastic wrap. Shape each piece of dough into a ball, roll it out until it is a long, ½-inch-thick rope. Cut it into ½-inch pieces and dust them with flour. Working with one piece at a time, press down on the dough with your fingertips and roll it down the palm of your other hand. This will cause the piece of dough to turn into a narrow spiral with tapered ends. Repeat with the remaining pieces of dough. Dust the spirals with flour, place them on flour-dusted, parchment-lined baking sheets, and allow them to dry for 2 hours, turning them over halfway through.

4. To cook the trofie, place in a large pot of boiling, salted water until they are tender but still chewy, 3 to 4 minutes.

GNOCCHI

YIELD: 1½ LBS.

ACTIVE TIME: 1 HOUR

TOTAL TIME: 2 HOURS AND 30 MINUTES

INGREDIENTS

3 LBS. YUKON GOLD POTATOES

2 LARGE EGGS

2½ CUPS ALL-PURPOSE FLOUR, PLUS MORE AS NEEDED

1 TABLESPOON SALT, PLUS MORE TO TASTE

DIRECTIONS

1. Preheat the oven to 400°F. Place the potatoes on a baking sheet, prick them several times with a fork, and bake until they are soft all the way through, about 1 hour. Remove from oven, slice them open, and let cool completely.

2. When the potatoes are cool enough to handle, scoop the flesh into a mixing bowl and mash until smooth. Make a well in the center of the potatoes and add the eggs, 1½ cups of the flour, and the salt. Work the mixture with your hands to combine, and then add the remaining flour in small increments. Knead the dough to incorporate and stop adding flour as soon as the dough holds together and is no longer tacky.

3. Place a handful of dough on a flour-dusted work surface and roll it into a ¾-inch-thick rope. Repeat with the remaining dough. Cut the ropes into ½-inch-wide pieces and roll the gnocchi over the tines of a fork, or a gnocchi board, while gently pressing down to create ridges. If the gnocchi start sticking to the fork, dip it into flour before pressing the gnocchi against it. Place the shaped gnocchi on a parchment-lined baking sheet and dust them with flour.

4. To cook the gnocchi, bring a large pot of water to a boil. Working in small batches, add salt and the gnocchi and stir to keep the gnocchi from sticking to the bottom. The gnocchi will eventually float to the surface. Cook for 1 more minute, remove, and transfer to a parchment-lined baking sheet to cool.

   TIP: Sautéing gnocchi in butter or olive oil after boiling them adds a nice bit of flavor.

SWEET POTATO GNOCCHI

YIELD: **1 LB.**

ACTIVE TIME: **1 HOUR**

TOTAL TIME: **2 HOURS AND 30 MINUTES**

INGREDIENTS

2½ LBS. SWEET POTATOES

½ CUP RICOTTA CHEESE

1 EGG

2 EGG YOLKS

1 TABLESPOON KOSHER SALT, PLUS MORE TO TASTE

1 TEASPOON BLACK PEPPER

3 TABLESPOONS LIGHT BROWN SUGAR

2 TABLESPOONS REAL MAPLE SYRUP

2 CUPS ALL-PURPOSE FLOUR, PLUS MORE AS NEEDED

1 CUP SEMOLINA FLOUR

2 TABLESPOONS EXTRA-VIRGIN OLIVE OIL

DIRECTIONS

1. Preheat the oven to 350°F. Wash the sweet potatoes, place them on a parchment-lined baking sheet, and use a knife to poke several holes in the tops of the potatoes. Place in the oven and cook until they are soft all the way through, 45 minutes to 1 hour. Remove from the oven, slice them open, and let cool completely.

2. Scrape the cooled sweet potato flesh into a mixing bowl and mash until smooth. Add the ricotta, egg, egg yolks, salt, pepper, brown sugar, and maple syrup and stir until thoroughly combined. Add the flours 1 cup at a time and work the mixture with your hands until incorporated. The dough should not feel tacky when touched. If it is tacky, incorporate more all-purpose flour, 1 teaspoon at a time, until it has the right texture. Coat a mixing bowl with the olive oil and set it aside.

3. Transfer the dough to a lightly floured work surface and cut it into 10 even pieces. Roll each piece into a long rope and cut the ropes into ¾-inch-wide pieces. Roll the gnocchi over a fork, or a gnocchi board, pressing down gently to form them into the desired shapes. Place the formed gnocchi on a parchment-lined, flour-dusted baking sheet.

4. To cook the gnocchi, bring a large pot of water to a boil. Add salt once the water is boiling. Working in small batches, add the gnocchi and stir to keep them from sticking to the bottom. The gnocchi will eventually float to the surface. Cook for 1 more minute, remove, and transfer to the bowl containing the olive oil. Toss to coat and place on a parchment-lined baking sheet to cool.

CHICKPEA GNOCCHETTI

YIELD: ¾ **LB.**

ACTIVE TIME: **1 HOUR**

TOTAL TIME: **1 HOUR**

INGREDIENTS

1 (14 OZ.) CAN OF CHICKPEAS, DRAINED AND RINSED

4 LARGE EGG YOLKS

1 TABLESPOON WATER

1½ CUPS ALL-PURPOSE FLOUR, PLUS MORE AS NEEDED

1½ TEASPOONS SALT, PLUS MORE TO TASTE

DIRECTIONS

1. Remove the outer skin from each chickpea. Place the chickpeas, egg yolks, and water in a food processor and puree until smooth. Transfer the puree to a mixing bowl and add the flour and salt. Knead until a soft, tacky dough forms, about 8 minutes. The dough should have no elasticity whatsoever. If you poke it with a finger, the indentation should remain.

2. Dust a work surface with flour. Tear off a handful of the dough and cover the remainder with plastic wrap to keep it from drying out. Roll the dough into a long rope that is about ½ inch thick and cut the ropes into ½-inch-wide pieces. Roll the gnocchetti over the tines of a fork, or a gnocchi board, while gently pressing down to create ridges. If the gnocchetti start sticking to the fork, dip it into flour before pressing the gnocchetti against it. Place the shaped dumplings on a parchment-lined baking sheet and dust them with flour.

3. To cook the gnocchetti, bring a large pot of water to a boil. Working in small batches, add salt and the gnocchetti and stir to keep them from sticking to the bottom. The gnocchetti will eventually float to the surface. Cook for 1 more minute, remove, and transfer to a parchment-lined baking sheet to cool.

PASSATELLI

YIELD: **1 LB.**

ACTIVE TIME: **20 MINUTES**

TOTAL TIME: **2 HOURS AND 30 MINUTES**

INGREDIENTS

1¼ CUPS VERY FINE BREAD CRUMBS

1¼ CUPS FRESHLY GRATED PARMESAN CHEESE

2 TABLESPOONS UNSALTED BUTTER, MELTED

1 HANDFUL OF FRESH PARSLEY LEAVES, FINELY CHOPPED

3 LARGE EGGS, PLUS MORE AS NEEDED

1 TEASPOON FRESHLY GRATED NUTMEG OR LEMON ZEST

1 TEASPOON SALT, PLUS MORE TO TASTE

½ TEASPOON WHITE PEPPER

DIRECTIONS

1. Place the bread crumbs, Parmesan, butter, parsley, eggs, nutmeg or lemon zest, salt, and pepper in a large mixing bowl. Work the mixture with your hands until a firm, slightly tacky dough forms. If the mixture feels too wet, incorporate more bread crumbs, 1 tablespoon at a time. Cover the dough with plastic wrap and let it rest at room temperature for 15 minutes.

2. Bring water to a boil in a small saucepan. Form a pinch of dough into a ball and drop it in the water. If it falls apart, add another egg to the dough and stir to incorporate. Working in batches, place handfuls of dough into the cup of a spätzle maker that has been oiled with nonstick cooking spray. Press down to squeeze long ropes of dough out the other side. Cut the ropes into 1½-inch-long pieces and transfer them to a parchment-lined baking sheet. Let dry for 1½ hours.

3. To cook the passatelli, bring a large pot of water to a boil. Reduce the heat so that the water comes to a gentle boil and add salt and the passatelli. After they float to the surface, about 4 minutes, let them cook for a minute longer.

   NOTE: Spätzle makers are very reasonably priced, about $7 for a serviceable one. If you do not have one, you can use a box grater to form the long ropes.

PIZZICOTTI

YIELD: **1 LB.**

ACTIVE TIME: **30 MINUTES**

TOTAL TIME: **2 HOURS AND 45 MINUTES**

INGREDIENTS

4 CUPS ALL-PURPOSE FLOUR

2½ TEASPOONS ACTIVE DRY YEAST

2 TEASPOONS SALT, PLUS MORE TO
TASTE

1¼ CUPS WARM WATER (105°F)

SEMOLINA FLOUR, AS NEEDED

DIRECTIONS

1. Place the all-purpose flour, yeast, and salt in a large bowl and stir to combine. Gradually incorporate the water and work the mixture with a fork until it starts holding together. Work the dough with your hands until it feels firm and dry. Transfer the dough to a flour-dusted work surface and knead it until it is very smooth and gently pulls back into place when stretched, 8 to 10 minutes. Place the dough in a large bowl, cover it with plastic wrap, and let it rise in a naturally warm place until it doubles in size, about 1 hour.

2. Remove the dough from the bowl and knead it just enough to remove any air trapped inside. Place the dough on a parchment-lined baking sheet, cover it with a kitchen towel, and let it rise for another hour in a naturally warm place.

3. Bring a large pot of water to a boil. Add salt to the water once it is boiling. Knead the dough to remove any air, pinch off peanut-sized pieces of the dough, and drop them in the boiling water, working in batches if necessary. Cook until they float to the surface, 2 to 3 minutes, and drain.

   TIP: Pizzicotti are wonderful with rich, thick sauces, such as the Lamb Ragù on page 81.

PICI

YIELD: ¾ **LB.**

ACTIVE TIME: **45 MINUTES**

TOTAL TIME: **2 HOURS**

INGREDIENTS

2½ CUPS ALL-PURPOSE FLOUR, PLUS
MORE AS NEEDED

1¾ CUPS SEMOLINA FLOUR, PLUS
MORE AS NEEDED

1¼ CUPS WATER, PLUS MORE AS
NEEDED

DIRECTIONS

1. Combine the flours and water in the work bowl of a stand mixer fitted with the paddle attachment. Mix on low until the dough starts holding together. Replace the paddle attachment with the dough hook and work the dough on medium speed until it forms a ball, about 5 minutes. Dust a work surface with all-purpose flour and place the dough on it. Gently knead it until smooth and elastic. Cover the dough in plastic wrap and refrigerate for at least 45 minutes.

2. Cut the dough into four pieces and roll the dough out to the third thinnest setting (generally notch 3). Dust a baking sheet with semolina flour and dust a work surface with all-purpose flour. Place one sheet of pasta on the work surface, cut it into 5-inch squares, stack the squares, and cut them into ⅛-inch-wide strips. Using your fingers, roll one strip into a 10-inch-long strand, place it on the baking sheet, and dust it with semolina flour. Repeat with the remaining strips and sheets of pasta.

3. To cook the pici, bring a large pot of salted water to a boil. Add the pici and cook until the pasta is tender but still chewy, 2 to 3 minutes.

CHAPTER 5

PIZZA & FOCACCIA

Some may be surprised to see focaccia standing shoulder-to-shoulder with pizza—conqueror of hearts the world over—but those who have been to Italy will understand. Focaccia is not only the proto-pizza, it is also representative of the diverse cultures that call Italy home, as it seems every little dale and village has its own version of this flatbread.

We've collected the best of those here, and, for those whose thinking is strictly circular when it comes to Italian flatbreads, there's a host of traditional and modern-leaning pizzas to provide plenty of inspiration and enjoyment.

MAKING PIZZA & FOCACCIA AT HOME

Different pizza and focaccia doughs will require different ingredients. But there are basic ingredients that most pizzas and focaccias share, such as flour, water, salt, fat, and yeast.

FLOUR

Not all flours are the same—not even all wheat flour is the same—and this must be kept in mind when setting out to make pizza or focaccia. One important aspect to consider is how extensible and elastic the dough needs to be for a particular style of pizza. A weaker flour may provide plenty of stretch, but it is generally not elastic, meaning that the resulting dough will not spring back when spread out. Another factor that is important is the amount of time the dough is supposed to ferment. Stronger flours will withstand long fermentation times, while doughs made with weaker flours will lose their structure in an extended fermenting process. Based on these considerations—stretchiness vs. elasticity and fermentation time—we can choose the strength we want in our flour for each type of pizza. An easy way to have an approximate idea of the flour strength is to think of it like this: anything with less than 10 percent protein content is weak. Anything over 12.5 percent is strong. Most flours are somewhere in the middle.

As focaccia is extremely varied, it is difficult to generalize about "ideals." As a rule of thumb, however, most focaccia require a moderately strong flour, one that can produce a dough that has the strength to bear the weight of the toppings without releasing the carbon dioxide created by fermentation, while also being extensible enough to not spring back too energetically once it has been stretched. In other words, we need a flour with a protein content between 10.5 and 11 percent. A good all-purpose flour could do the job, but if the protein content is too low, it is recommended that you blend it with a stronger flour, such as a standard bread flour. Several focaccia require the use of durum wheat flour, alone or in combination with soft wheat flour. In these instances, the optimal durum wheat flour is semolina.

For Neapolitan pizza, there is a consensus that a very fine soft wheat flour, such as the Italian "00" flour, is ideal. However, the term "00" says nothing about the strength of the flour, which can be anything from 7 to 14 percent. If looking into popular Italian "00" flours, the protein content tends to be higher than an all-purpose flour, between 11.5 and 12.5 percent—the same level commonly found in bread flour. Such proportions of gluten proteins should enable the dough to be extensible but also elastic, since a Neapolitan pizza dough does need to spring back quite energetically after it is spread out.

You can buy the specialty pizza flours, but be aware that you can achieve acceptable results with even a common bread flour.

SALT

In baking, salt is not only used for taste; it serves several functions that influence the chemistry and development of a dough. For pizza, salt is generally used in higher percentages as compared to other baking preparations. This is done to increase the tenacity of the dough, which, especially in Neapolitan pizza, needs enough elasticity to spring back once spread out. It is important to avoid adding the salt at the same time as the yeast, because salt can inhibit the activity of the yeast. The proper time to add salt depends on how tenacious and elastic we want the dough to be. For a round pizza, like a Neapolitan-style one, the salt is added quite close to the beginning of making the dough.

For focaccia, it is better to add the salt toward the end of the kneading process, because this type of dough needs to be more extensible than elastic. Regarding the type of salt, any type works, as the differences in results between table, kosher, and the other varieties are truly minimal.

YEAST

There are several types of yeasts available, and they will all do the job. But instant yeast is by far the easiest to manage. Unlike fresh yeast, instant yeast can be stored for a long amount of time (up to two months when opened and refrigerated), but, like fresh yeast and unlike active dry yeast, it does not need to be activated.

That said, pizza dough can be made with any of the three main types of yeast.

There will be some discrepancy in how much is required of each. For 1 teaspoon of instant yeast, 1¼ teaspoons of active dry yeast, and 1 tablespoon of fresh yeast will be required.

OLD DOUGH & PRE-FERMENTS

A pre-ferment is a mixture of flour and water that a leavening agent has been added to and left to ferment, from a few hours to a few days, which is then added to new dough. In pizza making, it is common to use pre-ferments both with yeast and on their own.

The easiest pre-ferment you can use is a piece of dough from a previous bake. Old dough, *pasta di riporto* in Italian, can keep in the fridge for up to five days, and it simply needs to be taken out and added to your fresh dough, adding complexity to the flavor of your crust. For the occasional home baker, it will be difficult to have old dough on hand, so a pre-ferment will have to be created for the occasion. This is achieved by combining a small amount of yeast with water and flour and letting the mixture rest at room temperature for several hours.

You may be wondering: What about sourdough?

In Italy, sourdough is rarely used for pizza or focaccia. In rural contexts, sourdough was surely used for focaccia, but over the last two centuries yeast has become by far the most common leavening agent for pizza and focaccia. That said, many home bakers, and a limited number of professional bakers, have embraced sourdough for pizza. And good results can be obtained when utilizing a wild yeast.

FATS

The fat of election for most focaccia and for almost every pizza is extra-virgin olive oil. One exception to olive oil's supremacy is the focaccia tradition of northern Italy—excepting Liguria—where butter, whole milk, and lard are the go-to options; some deep-dish pizza recipes will also call for butter.

SAUCES

Tomatoes are not native to Europe and only became popular in Italy in the 1800s. One can therefore find a large number of focaccia and pizza recipes that do not include tomato sauce.

For all the recipes that do include tomato sauce, like the famed Neapolitan, it is important to know that the best sauce for pizza is uncooked. When putting an already-cooked tomato sauce on pizza dough, the result will be a sauce that is overdone, if not burned, and does no justice to the tomato.

The best tomatoes for sauce are peeled, whole, canned tomatoes, ideally the San Marzano variety. There is truly no need to use dedicated pizza sauces. The practice of using precooked tomato sauce over pizza is likely a result of the low quality of the canned tomatoes available in the past in the US. This led to people correcting the taste with vinegar, sugar, and seasonings. When using high-quality canned tomatoes, however, little adulteration is required. The sauce should leave the tomato as untouched as possible in an effort to preserve the original flavor. To make a perfect sauce, simply crush the peeled tomatoes, add salt and olive oil, and, *voilà*, the sauce is ready.

The sauce will be cooked to perfection in the oven. If using fresh tomatoes, peeling will be required, and a brief sautéing. In any case, make sure you do not use hot tomato sauce over the uncooked pizza dough. A cold tomato sauce will also be detrimental to the optimal rise in the oven. The best option is to always have your tomato sauce at room temperature before applying it to pizza dough.

BASIC MIXING METHODS

The creation of both focaccia and pizza doughs have some basic methods in common. The following is a brief introduction to these fundamental techniques, which will be expanded upon further in specific recipes.

There are two main methods to making a pizza or focaccia dough: by hand and with a stand mixer. You may feel more comfortable with a specific one or alternate between them based on your mood, the amount of time and energy available, or a specific outcome you have in mind.

When mixing by hand, it is important to start by combining the flour and water, followed by any other ingredients; depending on the recipe, the additional ingredients can be incorporated later in a large mixing bowl. The use of a mixing bowl will minimize the mess that is inevitably created when mixing by hand. Once the flour is combined with the water to form a dough, it can be transferred to a flour-dusted work surface and kneaded.

There are several kneading techniques, but a method that is quite easy to follow is to work the dough for only a few minutes at a time before covering it with a damp kitchen towel and letting it rest for a bit before kneading for another few minutes, repeating the process until the dough feels smooth and springs back when pulled from one corner.

SIMPLE KNEADING: After combining the flour, water, and yeast in a bowl, turn the dough out onto a flour-dusted work surface and work it with the palms of your hands until the mass comes together. Add the salt and any other ingredients and keep working the dough with your palms until they are thoroughly incorporated. At this point, you can start stretching the dough—pulling it toward you with one hand, pushing it away with the other, and then folding it over itself. Continue to stretch and fold the dough until the dough is well developed, smooth, and extensible (you are able to extend it without tearing it).

STRETCHING AND FOLDING IN THE BOWL: When the water-to-flour ratio is high (see the 24-hour doughs on page 215 and page 261), it is possible to knead the dough directly in the bowl you used to combine the flour, water, and yeast in. After combining them, let the dough rest for a minimum of 15 minutes and a maximum of 30 minutes (the optimal amount of time will depend on the amount of yeast included in the recipe). The salt is then worked into the dough until thoroughly incorporated. Over the next hour, stretch and fold the dough, pulling up one side with both hands, folding it back on itself, and letting it rest for 15 to 20 minutes before repeating the stretch-and-fold two more times. When the dough is well developed, it is then left to rest to complete bulk fermentation.

SLAP AND FOLD: This is a modern technique developed by Richard Bertinet, the renowned French baker, and it works best with highly hydrated doughs. This method involves turning your mixed dough out on your countertop, picking it up with one hand on each side, slapping the dough down on the work surface, and folding the upper part of the dough over the bottom. The dough is then turned 90 degrees and the movement is repeated until the dough appears smooth and well developed.

Keep in mind that kneading by hand is a rather intuitive process. It is best to let your hands inform your brain as to when the dough is ready, a feel that can be developed only with practice.

To check whether a dough has been worked enough, it is common to perform the "windowpane" test. This simply means taking a piece of dough and stretching it between your fingers: if it can be stretched to where you can almost see through it and it does not tear, the dough is ready.

When using a stand mixer, always start by setting the machine at one of the slowest settings. If mixing very small batches of dough, it is best to add the water first, then the flour and yeast. If mixing larger batches of dough, proceed as usual, adding the flour first, then the water and yeast.

It is generally best to add the salt and any fats at a later stage, allowing the water to hydrate the flour and start changing its structure without any interference.

Overall, machine mixing should not last more than 15 active minutes, combined with a minimum of 15 minutes of rest in between intervals of active mixing.

The first interval of active mixing is done at low speed, with the aim of incorporating the water into the flour. This stage should not last more than 5 minutes. The dough is then left to rest, covered, for about 10 to 15 minutes. After this rest, salt and fats can be added and the dough is worked at low speed for another 5 minutes. If additional water is required, this stage is a good time to incorporate it. Let the dough rest for another 15 minutes before commencing the final stage, which should be done at a higher speed to achieve ideal gluten development. When the dough is well developed, it should adhere to the dough hook attachment and should not break when pulled away from one side.

Ultimately, there is not one way to produce a dough, but many. The best method is whichever gives you the best feel for the dough and the confidence to work it energetically. But, for a moment, think about the original bakers: as bread was the main staple, it needed to be good, meaning that everyone needed to learn quickly. The best way to do this is to mix the dough by hand. Don't be nervous, just imagine your ancestors and follow your "dough instinct"—we bet you'll be surprised.

If all of this sounds like too much to comprehend, there's a technique known as "no-knead mixing," which involves mixing ingredients by hand or machine just enough to combine them—which generally takes only a few minutes—and then letting the dough rest in a covered bowl for an extended amount of time. This technique is particularly effective with doughs featuring high hydration. These types of doughs can be helped by simply stretching the mass and folding it on itself a few times during the first hours of fermentation. The dough is developed mostly through autolysis, where time allows the dough to catalyze its own transformation.

FERMENTATION

Pizza and focaccia are living doughs, meaning doughs that ferment through the interaction of the myriad microorganisms living in them. It is therefore useful to understand fermentation techniques, which will help considerably in your attempt to master the recipes in this book.

To start, we need to talk about the distinction between doughs fermented directly, by simply adding yeast to the mix, and doughs that are instead fermented indirectly with a starter, the so-called pre-ferment. The direct method is pretty straightforward. Sourdough is an example of a pre-ferment, but it is far from the only one. Below are several types of pre-ferments that can be added to the mix when creating a dough.

BIGA: Originally from Italy, this is a stiff pre-ferment based on yeast and made with half as much water as flour.

POOLISH: Originally from Poland, this is a pre-ferment based on yeast and made with equal amounts of water and flour.

SOURDOUGH: This pre-ferment relies on wild yeasts and lactic acid rather than commercial yeast; sourdough cultures can thrive with various water-to-flour ratios.

OLD DOUGH: The simplest pre-ferment is a piece of old dough from a previous batch. This helps leaven the dough while at the same time enhancing the flavor by adding complexity.

The fermentation process begins the moment the leavening agent, either yeast or a pre-ferment, is added to the dough. Every dough requires a period of rest after mixing, which allows the the carbon dioxide generated by the yeast—and lactic acid in sourdough—to foment, a process that makes the dough grow visibly. This period of development before shaping is called bulk fermentation. It is helpful to have a few large bowls (or containers) with lids for this specific part of pizza and focaccia making.

After the first fermentation, when the dough has expanded to 1½ to 2 times its original size, it needs to be shaped according to the specific recipe. The period of rest generally given to a dough after the shaping stage is called the second fermentation, or proofing. During this stage, the dough continues to expand while the microorganisms in it keep "eating" the sugars present in the flour.

It is important to end the second fermentation before all of the sugars have been consumed, so that there is room for a final expansion. This final expansion happens at high temperature during the first stages of baking, and is commonly referred to as "oven spring."

When a proofing stage has exceeded optimal fermentation and all of the sugars have been exhausted, the dough is defined as "overproofed." This will generally result in harder and flatter crusts, owing to the loss of the gluten network that traps the carbon dioxide inside the dough, allowing it to become soft and voluminous.

To prevent overproofing, you need to keep a close eye on the dough and observe when it is losing its elasticity. A common way to monitor the fermentation process is by simply poking the dough with a finger. Simply press the dough with your index finger and then observe how fast or slow the dough springs back to its original shape. If the dough does not spring back at all, it is overproofed. The refrigerator is a great ally in controlling fermentation, as is altering the amount of leavening agent used initially.

SHORT VS. LONG FERMENTATION

Although it is important to avoid overproofing, pizza and focaccia do benefit from extended fermentation times. While there are "cheat" recipes with short leavening times, in most cases it's better not to expedite the process by overloading the dough with excessive amounts of yeast.

Besides producing clearly inferior taste and structure, a fermentation of less than four hours will result in products that are less digestible.

This is particularly true for Neapolitan pizza, which requires a very short baking time of just a few minutes. During the fermentation process, wheat starches and proteins are pre-digested by the microorganisms present in yeasts, and by wild yeasts and lactic acid in sourdough. These microorganisms transform the complex carbohydrates and proteins present in cereal flours, which are otherwise indigestible, into a proper food for our bodies. A further transformation of the starches occurs during baking, particularly during prolonged baking. A quick fermentation paired with a short time in the oven makes for a pizza with mediocre flavor and texture, and adverse effects on your digestive system.

Conversely, pizza and focaccia fermented for an extended amount of time, sometimes even days, results in an extremely light crust that will melt in your mouth and also agrees with your stomach. The good news about long fermentation is that it does not require much effort, just a bit of planning ahead. At the end of the day, time is the most important ingredient in a tasty and digestible crust.

SHAPING FOCACCIA & PIZZA

After the initial rise, the leavened focaccia dough generally needs to complete its second rise directly on the baking sheet or pan that it will be cooked upon.

First, the baking sheet or pan should always be greased before the dough is placed upon it. Place the focaccia dough in the center of the pan and drizzle olive oil over it. The spreading of the focaccia should happen in a very deliberate fashion, rather than all at once. This will allow the dough to slowly relax and become more extensible. Spreading the dough too quickly will result in deflating it excessively, producing a tough focaccia, rather than the soft and light version that is ideal.

To stretch the focaccia, shape the dough into an oval by spreading it with the palms of your hands, pushing each hand in opposite directions.

Let the dough rest for 15 to 20 minutes, and then proceed to a new round of stretching. It will be very useful to keep the surface of the dough moist by adding olive oil, or an emulsion of olive oil and water, after each interval.

After three to four stages of stretching, the focaccia should have extended to cover the entire pan without having lost its volume. A final period of rest, lasting at least 30 minutes, will be required before putting the toppings on the focaccia and baking it.

Depending on the toppings and of the amount of yeast used, the focaccia can benefit from an extra period of rest after the toppings are applied before going in the oven.

There are numerous ways to shape a pizza and, with time, you will develop your own style.

As a rule of thumb, pizza does not require the use of a rolling pin. Exceptions are specific regional varieties that require a crust that departs from the classical Neapolitan style.

One method relies on gravity. The trick is to slightly flatten the ball of pizza dough, then ball your hands into fists, turn them so that your fingers are facing toward you, and slide them beneath the dough. Lift the dough and pass it along the tops of your fists, allowing the dough to slowly stretch on all sides. If done properly, this technique will provide a perfectly shaped disk of dough that will be thinner in the center and thicker on the edge.

An alternative method involves placing the dough on a work surface that has been dusted with semolina or cornmeal and gently stretching the dough by pressing in opposite directions with each hand. The dough is rotated on the surface while being stretched until the desired shape is achieved.

Whatever approach is used, the most important thing when shaping pizza dough is making sure the dough is thicker around the edge.

Lastly, when getting acquainted with pizza making it is essential to learn how to master the loading of the pizza onto the peel and into the oven without altering the pizza's shape or losing the toppings. One way is to heavily dust a peel (or a flat baking sheet) with semolina or cornmeal and place the dough on the peel before distributing the toppings. Another method consists of stretching the dough directly on a piece of semolina-dusted parchment paper. This final method will ensure that the transfer to the heated baking implement in the oven is uneventful.

EQUIPMENT

A standard, 18 x 13–inch baking sheet with a rim will do the job for most focaccia. For pizza, some specialized equipment is needed. A baking stone or a baking steel is highly recommended. In a pinch, or if you would like to get some experience making pizza before making a bit of an investment, an upside-down baking sheet will do the trick. A peel is also crucial to quality pizzas that maintain their shape. If one is not available, a flat, rimless baking sheet is worth a shot.

The trickiest part of baking pizza at home, especially Neapolitan-style pizza, is the conventional oven. Some will tell you is impossible to reproduce Neapolitan pizza at a temperature below 700°F. This is true, to a certain extent.

With a regular oven, the crust will never be exactly the same as what a good pizzeria can produce. But it can still be very good, especially if you employ a few tricks. You want to place your baking stone or steel on the floor of the oven and preheat the oven to the highest temperature it can achieve for 1 hour. Do that, and you'll be ready to produce a quality pizza.

An outdoor grill can be a surprisingly great ally in making a perfect pizza crust. With the right accessories, you can even achieve that wood-fired touch that is so in demand today. What you'll need are a grill lid and a baking stone or steel. The lid will retain the steam from the cooking pizza and will also help to keep the temperature high.

The stone/steel will allow the temperature of the grill to be maximized and not dispersed. If you are thinking of using the grill to make pizza, be sure to buy a stone/steel that will fit on your grill.

A scale will make life a whole lot easier, no matter what kind of focaccia or pizza you are making. There are plenty of inexpensive scales on the market, and learning to measure ingredients when making a dough is the only way to really master the craft. By weighing ingredients, it is also easier to calculate percentages and scale ingredients for batches of different sizes. As most of the ingredients in this chapter are listed by weight, a scale will come in very handy.

A stand mixer makes the preparation of pizza and focaccia dough a much less messy concern, as ingredients are just mixed in a bowl rather than flying all over the kitchen while you knead them by hand. Mixing with a machine not only saves you energy and time, it also ensures more consistent results when it comes to dough development and strength.

One final note: all ovens are different. How long you allow your oven to preheat, how it holds heat, and whether or not a pizza stone or steel is being used will make a difference in cooking times. You'll want to watch what you're making and judge for yourself, using the recipe's timing as a guideline. There is also personal preference to take into account here, too, as some people like their crust crispier or their cheese more browned than others.

QUICK FOCACCIA DOUGH

YIELD: **DOUGH FOR 1 LARGE FOCACCIA**

ACTIVE TIME: **15 MINUTES**

TOTAL TIME: **1 HOUR AND 15 MINUTES**

INGREDIENTS

2½ TEASPOONS INSTANT YEAST OR 3½ TEASPOONS ACTIVE DRY YEAST

2 CUPS WARM WATER (105°F)

17.6 OZ. BREAD FLOUR

7 OZ. ALL-PURPOSE FLOUR, PLUS MORE AS NEEDED

2 TEASPOONS SUGAR

5 TABLESPOONS EXTRA-VIRGIN OLIVE OIL, PLUS MORE AS NEEDED

2½ TEASPOONS TABLE SALT

DIRECTIONS

1. If using active dry yeast, dissolve the yeast in the water and let the mixture rest for a few minutes, until it starts to foam.

2. In a large bowl, combine the flours, sugar, yeast, and water and work the mixture until it just holds together. Transfer it to a flour-dusted work surface and knead the dough until it is compact, smooth, and elastic.

3. Add the olive oil and salt and knead until the dough is developed, elastic, and extensible, about 5 minutes. Form the dough into a ball and place it in an airtight container that has been greased with olive oil. Let rest in a naturally warm spot (in the oven with the light on is a good option) until it has doubled in size, about 1 hour.

4. After 1 hour, the dough can be spread and flavored as desired. It will need another 30 minutes to 1 hour for the second rise before baking.

BASIC FOCACCIA DOUGH

YIELD: **DOUGH FOR 1 LARGE FOCACCIA**

ACTIVE TIME: **30 MINUTES**

TOTAL TIME: **3 HOURS AND 30 MINUTES**

INGREDIENTS

½ TEASPOON INSTANT YEAST OR ¾ TEASPOON ACTIVE DRY YEAST

17.3 OZ. WATER

21.1 OZ. BREAD FLOUR

3.5 OZ. ALL-PURPOSE FLOUR, PLUS MORE AS NEEDED

2 TABLESPOONS EXTRA-VIRGIN OLIVE OIL, PLUS MORE AS NEEDED

2 TEASPOONS TABLE SALT

DIRECTIONS

1. If using active dry yeast, warm 3½ tablespoons of the water until it is about 105°F. Add the water and the yeast to a bowl and gently stir. Let sit until it starts to foam.

2. In a large bowl, combine the flours, yeast, and water. Work the mixture until it just holds together. Transfer it to a flour-dusted work surface and knead the dough until it is compact, smooth, and elastic.

3. Add the olive oil and salt and knead until the dough is developed, elastic, and extensible, about 5 minutes. Form the dough into a ball, cover it with a damp kitchen towel or greased plastic wrap, and let it rest at room temperature until it has doubled in size, 3 to 4 hours. The time for this first fermentation can be reduced if you place the dough in a naturally warm spot. In the oven with the light on is a good option if you're going to go this route.

4. Stretch and flavor the dough as desired. It will need another 1½ to 2 hours for the second rise before baking. The extra rising time can only benefit the dough, as the relatively low amount of yeast means the risk of overproofing is small.

24-HOUR FOCACCIA DOUGH

YIELD: **DOUGH FOR 1 LARGE FOCACCIA**

ACTIVE TIME: **30 MINUTES**

TOTAL TIME: **24 HOURS**

INGREDIENTS

¾ TEASPOON (SCANT) INSTANT YEAST OR 1 TEASPOON (SCANT) ACTIVE DRY YEAST

13 OZ. WATER

21.1 OZ. BREAD FLOUR OR "00" FLOUR

2½ TEASPOONS TABLE SALT

2 TABLESPOONS EXTRA-VIRGIN OLIVE OIL

DIRECTIONS

1. If using active dry yeast, warm 3½ tablespoons of the water until it is about 105°F. Add the water and the yeast to a bowl and gently stir. Let sit until it starts to foam.

2. In a large bowl, combine the flour, yeast, and water. Work the mixture until it just holds together. Transfer it to a flour-dusted work surface and knead the dough until it is compact, smooth, and elastic.

3. Add the salt and knead until the dough is developed, elastic, and extensible, about 5 minutes. Add the olive oil and knead the dough until the oil has been incorporated. Form the dough into a ball, place it in an airtight container that is at least three times bigger, cover, and refrigerate for 24 hours.

4. Remove the dough from the refrigerator and let it warm to room temperature before making focaccia.

NO-KNEAD FOCACCIA DOUGH

YIELD: **DOUGH FOR 1 LARGE FOCACCIA**

ACTIVE TIME: **30 MINUTES**

TOTAL TIME: **17 TO 21 HOURS**

INGREDIENTS

¼ TEASPOON INSTANT YEAST OR ¼ TEASPOON PLUS 1 PINCH ACTIVE DRY YEAST

18.7 OZ. WATER

1½ LBS. BREAD FLOUR

1 TABLESPOON (SCANT) TABLE SALT

2 TABLESPOONS EXTRA-VIRGIN OLIVE OIL, PLUS MORE AS NEEDED

DIRECTIONS

1. If using active dry yeast, warm 3½ tablespoons of the water until it is about 105°F. Add the water and the yeast to a bowl and gently stir. Let sit until it starts to foam.

2. In a large bowl, combine the flour, yeast, and water. Work the mixture until it just holds together. Add the salt and olive oil and work them into the dough. Cover the bowl with plastic wrap and let the dough rest at room temperature for 12 to 16 hours.

3. Grease an 18 x 13-inch baking sheet generously with olive oil and place the dough on it. Let the dough spread to the edges of the pan, helping it along by gently stretching on occasion, being careful not to deflate the dough. Let the dough rest in the pan for 1 hour and then flavor as desired.

BIGA

Combine 3.5 oz. of bread flour, 1.75 oz. water, and ⅛ teaspoon instant yeast (if using active dry yeast, make it ⅛ teaspoon plus a pinch) in a mixing bowl and work the mixture until it is a sticky dough. Place the biga in a greased bowl, cover with plastic wrap, place it in a naturally cool spot, and let it sit until it has tripled in size, about 18 hours. Use immediately or store in the refrigerator for up to 5 days.

FOCACCIA DOUGH WITH BIGA

YIELD: **DOUGH FOR 1 LARGE FOCACCIA**

ACTIVE TIME: **30 MINUTES**

TOTAL TIME: **27 HOURS**

INGREDIENTS

¼ TEASPOON INSTANT YEAST OR ¼
TEASPOON PLUS 1 PINCH ACTIVE
DRY YEAST

2 CUPS WATER

BIGA (SEE SIDEBAR)

14 OZ. BREAD FLOUR

8.8 OZ. ALL-PURPOSE FLOUR

2 TABLESPOONS EXTRA-VIRGIN
OLIVE OIL

1 TABLESPOON TABLE SALT

DIRECTIONS

1. If using active dry yeast, warm 3½ tablespoons of the water until it is about 105°F. Add the water and the yeast to a bowl and gently stir. Let sit for 5 to 10 minutes.

2. In a large bowl, combine the Biga, flours, yeast, and water. Work the mixture until it just holds together.

3. If kneading by hand, transfer the dough to a flour-dusted surface. Work it until it is smooth and elastic. The stretch-and-fold as well as the slap-and-fold techniques are particularly effective for wet doughs such as this.

4. Add the olive oil and salt and work the dough until it is developed, elastic, and extensible, about 5 minutes. Form the dough into a ball and place it in an airtight container that is at least three times bigger.

5. Let the dough rest 1 hour at room temperature. After the 1-hour interval, refrigerate the dough in its container for a minimum of 20 hours.

6. Remove the dough from the refrigerator and let it warm to room temperature. Stretch and flavor the dough as desired. It will need another 2 to 3 hours for the second rise before baking.

PEAR & RICOTTA FOCACCIA

YIELD: **1 LARGE FOCACCIA**

ACTIVE TIME: **45 MINUTES**

TOTAL TIME: **3 HOURS**

INGREDIENTS

1 BATCH OF FOCACCIA DOUGH

ALL-PURPOSE FLOUR, AS NEEDED

EXTRA-VIRGIN OLIVE OIL, AS NEEDED

5.3 OZ. LOW-MOISTURE MOZZARELLA CHEESE, CUBED

SALT, TO TASTE

8.8 OZ. RICOTTA CHEESE

½ CUP WALNUTS, CHOPPED

1 LB. PEARS, CORED AND SLICED

¼ CUP ARUGULA

HONEY, WARMED, TO TASTE

DIRECTIONS

1. Once the dough has finished its initial rise, place it on a flour-dusted work surface and form it into a loose ball, making sure not to compress the core of the dough. Grease an 18 × 13–inch baking pan with olive oil, place the dough in the center, and gently stretch it into an oval. Brush the dough with olive oil, cover it with plastic wrap, and let rest at room temperature for 1 hour. Preheat the oven to 445°F.

2. Use your hands to flatten the dough and stretch it toward the edges of the pan. When the dough is covering the pan, let it rest for 30 minutes.

3. Top the dough with the mozzarella, pressing the cheese partially into the dough. Season with salt and drizzle olive oil over the focaccia.

4. Place the focaccia in the oven and bake for 15 to 20 minutes, until the focaccia starts to brown. Remove from the oven, top with dollops of the ricotta, the walnuts, and the pears, drizzle olive oil over the focaccia, and return it to the oven. Bake for another 5 to 10 minutes, until the edges are crispy. Remove from the oven, top with the greens, drizzle honey over the top, and let the focaccia cool slightly before slicing and serving.

FOCACCIA WITH PUMPKIN CREAM

YIELD: **1 LARGE FOCACCIA**

ACTIVE TIME: **45 MINUTES**

TOTAL TIME: **3 HOURS**

INGREDIENTS

1 BATCH OF FOCACCIA DOUGH

ALL-PURPOSE FLOUR, AS NEEDED

EXTRA-VIRGIN OLIVE OIL, AS NEEDED

1 PUMPKIN, HALVED AND SEEDED

SALT AND PEPPER, TO TASTE

FRESH THYME, TO TASTE

4 ANCHOVY FILLETS, BONED AND CHOPPED

¾ LB. BURRATA CHEESE, TORN

DIRECTIONS

1. Once the dough has finished its initial rise, place it on a flour-dusted work surface and form it into a loose ball, making sure not to compress the core of the dough. Grease an 18 × 13–inch baking pan with olive oil, place the dough in the center, and gently stretch it into an oval. Brush the dough with olive oil, cover it with plastic wrap, and let rest at room temperature for 1 hour. Preheat the oven to 445°F.

2. Place the pumpkin halves cut side up on a baking sheet, season with salt, and drizzle olive oil over them. Place in the oven and roast until the flesh is tender, about 30 minutes. Remove, let the pumpkin cool slightly, and then scrape 1 pound of the flesh into a food processor. Add olive oil, salt, and thyme to taste and blitz until the mixture is smooth and creamy. Set the pumpkin cream aside. Reserve any remaining pumpkin for another preparation.

3. Use your hands to flatten the dough and stretch it toward the edges of the pan. When the dough is covering the pan, let it rest for 30 minutes.

4. Drizzle olive oil over the focaccia and season it with salt. Place it in the oven and bake for 15 to 20 minutes, until the focaccia starts to brown. Remove from the oven, top with the pumpkin cream and anchovies, drizzle olive oil over the top, and return the focaccia to the oven. Bake for another 5 to 10 minutes, until the edges are crispy. Remove from the oven, top the focaccia with the burrata, season it with pepper, and drizzle olive oil over the top. Let the focaccia cool slightly before slicing and serving.

SPINACH & FETA FOCACCIA

YIELD: **1 LARGE FOCACCIA**

ACTIVE TIME: **45 MINUTES**

TOTAL TIME: **3 HOURS**

INGREDIENTS

1 BATCH OF FOCACCIA DOUGH

ALL-PURPOSE FLOUR, AS NEEDED

EXTRA-VIRGIN OLIVE OIL, AS NEEDED

SALT AND PEPPER, TO TASTE

½ LB. FRESH SPINACH

¾ LB. FETA CHEESE, CUBED

DIRECTIONS

1. Once the dough has finished its initial rise, place it on a flour-dusted work surface and form it into a loose ball, making sure not to compress the core of the dough. Grease an 18 × 13-inch baking pan with olive oil, place the dough in the center, and gently stretch it into an oval. Brush the dough with olive oil, cover it with plastic wrap, and let rest at room temperature for 1 hour. Preheat the oven to 445°F.

2. Use your hands to flatten the dough and stretch it toward the edges of the pan. When the dough is covering the pan, let it rest for 30 minutes.

3. Drizzle olive oil over the focaccia and season it with salt. Place the focaccia in the oven and bake for 15 to 20 minutes, until the focaccia starts to brown. Remove from the oven, top with the spinach and feta, season with salt and pepper, and drizzle olive oil over the focaccia.

4. Return to the oven and bake for another 5 to 10 minutes, until the edges are crispy. Remove from the oven and let the focaccia cool slightly before slicing and serving.

FOCACCIA WITH OLIVES & LEMON

YIELD: **1 LARGE FOCACCIA**

ACTIVE TIME: **45 MINUTES**

TOTAL TIME: **3 HOURS**

INGREDIENTS

1 BATCH OF FOCACCIA DOUGH

ALL-PURPOSE FLOUR, AS NEEDED

EXTRA-VIRGIN OLIVE OIL, AS NEEDED

COARSE SEA SALT, TO TASTE

½ LB. PITTED KALAMATA OLIVES, SLICED

1½ LEMONS, SLICED THIN

LEAVES FROM 6 SPRIGS OF FRESH ROSEMARY

BLACK PEPPER, TO TASTE

DIRECTIONS

1. Once the dough has finished its initial rise, place it on a flour-dusted work surface and form it into a loose ball, making sure not to compress the core of the dough. Grease an 18 × 13–inch baking pan with olive oil, place the dough in the center, and gently stretch it into an oval. Brush the dough with olive oil, cover it with plastic wrap, and let rest at room temperature for 1 hour. Preheat the oven to 445°F.

2. Use your hands to flatten the dough and stretch it toward the edges of the pan. When the dough is covering the pan, let it rest for 30 minutes.

3. Drizzle olive oil over the focaccia and season with the coarse-grained salt. Press the olives into the dough and then top it with the lemon slices and rosemary.

4. Drizzle olive oil over the focaccia, place it in the oven, and bake for 20 to 25 minutes, until the focaccia is golden brown. Remove, season with salt and pepper, and let cool slightly before slicing and serving.

SMACAFAM

YIELD: **1 MEDIUM FOCACCIA**

ACTIVE TIME: **10 MINUTES**

TOTAL TIME: **1 HOUR**

INGREDIENTS

BUTTER, AS NEEDED

14 OZ. ALL-PURPOSE FLOUR, PLUS
MORE AS NEEDED

2½ CUPS WHOLE MILK

2 EGGS

½ LB. SWEET ITALIAN SAUSAGE,
CHOPPED

2 TEASPOONS TABLE SALT

2 PINCHES OF BLACK PEPPER

DIRECTIONS

1. Preheat the oven to 360°F and grease a 9 x 13–inch baking sheet with butter. Add all of the ingredients, except for about 3 oz. of the sausage, to a mixing bowl and stir until the batter looks smooth. Pour the batter into the pan and sprinkle the remaining sausage over the top.

2. Place the focaccia in the oven and bake for 30 to 40 minutes, until the edges are golden brown. Remove and let cool briefly before serving.

FOCACCIA DI GIAVENO

YIELD: **1 LARGE FOCACCIA**

ACTIVE TIME: **30 MINUTES**

TOTAL TIME: **4 HOURS**

INGREDIENTS

2 TEASPOONS INSTANT YEAST OR 2½ TEASPOONS ACTIVE DRY YEAST

WATER, AS NEEDED

7 OZ. ALL-PURPOSE FLOUR, PLUS MORE AS NEEDED

17.6 OZ. BREAD FLOUR

15.5 OZ. WHOLE MILK

2.6 OZ. SUGAR, PLUS MORE TO TASTE

3 EGG YOLKS

ZEST OF ½ LEMON

ZEST OF ½ ORANGE

1 TEASPOON TABLE SALT

½ TEASPOON PURE VANILLA EXTRACT

3.5 OZ. UNSALTED BUTTER, CHOPPED, PLUS MORE AS NEEDED

DIRECTIONS

1. If using active dry yeast, add the yeast and 3½ tablespoons of 90°F water to a bowl and gently stir. Let the mixture sit until it starts to foam.

2. In a large bowl, combine the two flours. Add the milk and yeast and work the mixture until it just holds together. Transfer it to a flour-dusted work surface and knead the dough until it is compact, smooth, and elastic.

3. Incorporate all of the remaining ingredients, except for the butter, into the dough one at a time. When incorporated, knead until the dough is developed, elastic, and extensible, about 5 minutes. Gradually incorporate the butter and work the dough until it does not feel sticky. Let the dough rest in a warm spot until it has doubled in size, about 2 hours. A good option is your oven with the light on and the door cracked open slightly. You can also place a pot of simmering water on the bottom of the oven.

4. Grease an 18 x 13–inch baking sheet with butter. Place the dough on the sheet and gently flatten it into an approximately ¾-inch-thick disk. There is no need to cover the whole pan with the dough. Cover with a kitchen towel and let the focaccia rest at room temperature for 1 hour. Preheat the oven to 430°F.

5. Dip your fingers in butter and press down on the dough to make deep indentations in it. Sprinkle sugar generously over the top, place in the oven, and bake for 15 to 20 minutes, until the focaccia is a light golden brown. Remove from the oven, sprinkle more sugar over the focaccia, and let cool briefly before serving.

PIZZA AL PADELLINO

YIELD: **1 SMALL FOCACCIA**

ACTIVE TIME: **15 MINUTES**

TOTAL TIME: **3 HOURS**

INGREDIENTS

1 BALL OF 24-HOUR PIZZA DOUGH
(SEE PAGE 261)

1 TABLESPOON EXTRA-VIRGIN OLIVE
OIL, PLUS MORE TO TASTE

1 CUP CRUSHED TOMATOES

½ TEASPOON (SCANT) TABLE SALT,
PLUS MORE TO TASTE

2 PINCHES OF DRIED OREGANO

7 OZ. FRESH MOZZARELLA CHESSE,
SLICED

DIRECTIONS

1. Place the ball of dough on a piece of parchment paper, cover with a kitchen towel, and let rest at room temperature until it looks soft and fully risen, 2 to 3 hours.

2. Place the dough in a 10-inch cast-iron skillet and gently spread it to the edge of the pan, being careful not to deflate the dough. Brush the dough with olive oil, cover the skillet with plastic wrap, and let it rest at room temperature for 30 minutes.

3. Preheat the oven to 480°F. Place the tomatoes, salt, dried oregano, and olive oil in a mixing bowl and stir to combine. Spread the sauce over the focaccia, season with salt, and generously drizzle olive oil over the top.

4. Place the focaccia in the oven and bake for about 10 minutes, until it is a light golden brown. Remove the focaccia, top with the mozzarella, and return it to the oven. Bake until the mozzarella has melted and the edges of the focaccia are golden brown, about 10 minutes. Remove and let cool briefly before serving.

FOCACCIA GENOVESE

YIELD: **1 LARGE FOCACCIA**

ACTIVE TIME: **2 HOURS**

TOTAL TIME: **27 HOURS**

INGREDIENTS

FOCACCIA DOUGH WITH BIGA
(SEE PAGES 218–219)

ALL-PURPOSE FLOUR, AS NEEDED

2 TABLESPOONS EXTRA-VIRGIN
OLIVE OIL, PLUS MORE AS NEEDED

⅔ CUP WATER

1 TEASPOON TABLE SALT

COARSE SEA SALT, TO TASTE

DIRECTIONS

1. Place the dough on a flour-dusted work surface and form it into a loose ball, making sure not to compress the core of the dough and deflate it. Grease an 18 ×13–inch baking pan with olive oil, place the dough on the pan, and gently flatten the dough into an oval. Cover with a kitchen towel and let rest at room temperature for 30 minutes to 1 hour.

2. Stretch the dough toward the edges of the baking pan. If the dough does not want to extend to the edges of the pan right away, let it rest for 15 to 20 minutes before trying again. Cover with the kitchen towel and let rest for another 30 minutes to 1 hour.

3. Place the olive oil, water, and table salt in a mixing bowl and stir to combine. Set the mixture aside. Lightly dust the focaccia with flour and press down on the dough with two fingers to make deep indentations. Cover the focaccia with half of the olive oil mixture and let it rest for another 30 minutes.

4. Preheat the oven to 445°F. Cover the focaccia with the remaining olive oil mixture and sprinkle the coarse sea salt over the top. Place in the oven and bake for 15 to 20 minutes, until the focaccia is a light golden brown. As this focaccia is supposed to be soft, it's far better to remove it too early as opposed to too late. Remove and let cool briefly before serving.

FUGASSA CO A CIÒULA

YIELD: **1 LARGE FOCACCIA**

ACTIVE TIME: **20 MINUTES**

TOTAL TIME: **4 HOURS AND 45 MINUTES**

INGREDIENTS

24-HOUR FOCACCIA DOUGH
(SEE PAGE 215)

ALL-PURPOSE FLOUR, AS NEEDED

3 TABLESPOONS EXTRA-VIRGIN
OLIVE OIL, PLUS MORE AS NEEDED

½ CUP WATER

1 TEASPOON TABLE SALT

2 LARGE WHITE ONIONS, SLICED
THIN

DIRECTIONS

1. Remove the dough from the refrigerator and let the dough rest at room temperature for 30 minutes.

2. Place the dough on a flour-dusted work surface and form it into a loose ball, making sure not to compress the core of the dough. Grease an 18 x 13–inch baking sheet with olive oil, place the dough on the pan, and gently flatten the dough into an oval. Cover with plastic wrap and let rest at room temperature for 1 hour.

3. Stretch the dough toward the edges of the baking sheet. If the dough does not want to extend to the edges of the pan right away, let it rest for 15 to 20 minutes before trying again.

4. Add the olive oil, water, and salt to a mixing bowl and stir to combine. Cover the focaccia with half of the mixture, cover with plastic wrap, and let it rest for another hour.

5. Preheat the oven to 445°F. Distribute the onions over focaccia and drizzle the rest of the olive oil mixture over the onions. Place in the oven and bake for 20 to 25 minutes, until the onions look slightly charred and the focaccia is a deep golden brown. Remove from the oven and let cool slightly before serving.

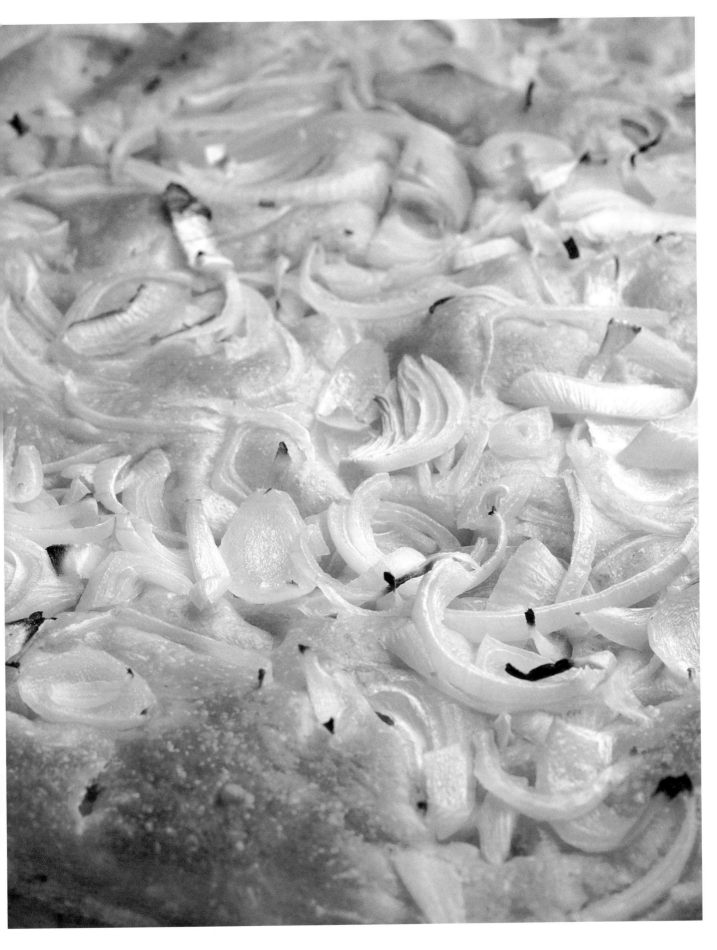

FARINATA

YIELD: **1 LARGE FOCACCIA**

ACTIVE TIME: **20 MINUTES**

TOTAL TIME: **3 TO 24 HOURS**

INGREDIENTS

14 OZ. CHICKPEA FLOUR

2 TEASPOONS TABLE SALT

5 CUPS WATER

3.5 OZ. EXTRA-VIRGIN OLIVE OIL,
PLUS MORE AS NEEDED

LEAVES FROM 3 SPRIGS OF FRESH
ROSEMARY (OPTIONAL)

BLACK PEPPER, TO TASTE

DIRECTIONS

1. In a large bowl, combine the chickpea flour and the salt. While whisking constantly, gradually add the water. If possible, use a handheld mixer, as you do not want lumps to form in the dough. When all of the water has been incorporated, cover the batter with a kitchen towel and let rest at room temperature for 2 to 3 hours. If time allows, let the batter rest overnight.

2. Preheat the oven to 480°F. Remove the foam that has gathered on the surface of the batter and discard. Stir the olive oil and, if desired, the rosemary into the batter.

3. Grease an 18 x 13–inch baking sheet with olive oil, pour the batter into the pan, and use a rubber spatula to even the surface. Drizzle olive oil generously over the top.

4. Place the focaccia on the upper rack in the oven and bake for 10 to 15 minutes, until it is set and lightly brown. Remove and let cool briefly before seasoning with pepper and cutting into squares.

PIADINA

YIELD: **4 PIADINA**

ACTIVE TIME: **30 MINUTES**

TOTAL TIME: **1 HOUR**

INGREDIENTS

4.8 OZ. LUKEWARM WATER (90°F)

2 TEASPOONS TABLE SALT

18 OZ. ALL-PURPOSE FLOUR, PLUS
MORE AS NEEDED

1½ TEASPOONS BAKING SODA

3.5 OZ. LARD OR EXTRA-VIRGIN
OLIVE OIL, PLUS MORE AS NEEDED

DIRECTIONS

1. Combine the water and salt and stir until the salt has
    dissolved. In a large mixing bowl, combine the flour and the
    baking soda. Add the lard or olive oil and the salted water
    and work the mixture until it just holds together. Transfer it
    to a flour-dusted work surface and knead the dough until it
    is compact, smooth, and elastic. Grease an airtight container
    with lard or olive oil, form the dough into a ball, place it in the
    container, and let it rest at room temperature for 30 minutes.

2. Place the dough on a flour-dusted work surface and divide it
    into four pieces. Form the pieces into balls and roll each one
    until it is an approximately ⅛-inch-thick disk.

3. Warm a dry skillet over medium-high heat. When the skillet is
    hot, cook one piadina at a time. Cook until dark brown spots
    appear on both sides, about 5 minutes per side. Pop any big
    bubbles with a fork as the piadina cooks.

YIELD: **1 LARGE FOCACCIA**

ACTIVE TIME: **45 MINUTES**

TOTAL TIME: **5 HOURS**

INGREDIENTS

½ TEASPOON INSTANT YEAST OR ⅔ TEASPOON ACTIVE DRY YEAST

11 OZ. WATER

½ LB. PROSCIUTTO

½ LB. PANCETTA

24.75 OZ. BREAD FLOUR, PLUS MORE AS NEEDED

2.5 OZ. LARD OR EXTRA-VIRGIN OLIVE OIL, PLUS MORE AS NEEDED

½ LB. BIGA (SEE PAGE 218)

1 TABLESPOON SUGAR

2⅔ TEASPOONS TABLE SALT

CRESCENTA BOLOGNESE

DIRECTIONS

1. If using active dry yeast, warm 3½ tablespoons of the water until it is about 90°F. Add the water and the yeast to a bowl and gently stir. Let the mixture sit until it starts to foam.

2. Place the prosciutto and pancetta in a food processor and blitz until very fine. Set the mixture aside.

3. In a large bowl, combine the flour, lard or olive oil, Biga, sugar, yeast, and water and work the mixture until it just holds together. Transfer it to a flour-dusted work surface and knead the dough until it is compact, smooth, and elastic.

4. Add the salt and the cured meat mixture and knead the dough until it is developed, elastic, and extensible, about 5 minutes. Cover the dough with a kitchen towel and let it rest in a warm spot until it has doubled in size, about 2 hours. A good option is your oven with the light on and the door cracked open slightly. You can also place a pot of simmering water on the bottom of the oven.

5. Place the dough on a flour-dusted work surface and form it into a ball. Grease an 18 x 13–inch baking sheet with lard or olive oil and place the dough in the center. Brush the surface of the dough with lard or olive oil and gently press it into an oval. Cover and let rest for 1 hour.

6. Stretch the dough toward the edges of the baking sheet. If the dough does not want to extend to the edges of the pan right away, let rest for 15 to 20 minutes before trying again. Once it has been stretched to the edges of the pan, cover with a kitchen towel and let rest until fully risen, about 1 hour. You may need to stretch the dough again halfway through this final rise to get the desired rise.

7. Preheat the oven to 430°F and place a rack in the center position. Brush the focaccia with lard or olive oil, place it in the oven, and bake for 25 to 30 minutes, until golden brown. Remove from the oven and let cool slightly before serving.

PIZZA ASSETTATA

YIELD: **1 LARGE FOCACCIA**

ACTIVE TIME: **25 MINUTES**

TOTAL TIME: **1 HOUR AND 15 MINUTES**

INGREDIENTS

12.3 OZ. BREAD FLOUR, PLUS MORE
AS NEEDED

12.3 OZ. SEMOLINA FLOUR

2 TEASPOONS TABLE SALT

16.6 OZ. WARM WATER (110°F)

1.75 OZ. EXTRA-VIRGIN OLIVE OIL,
PLUS MORE AS NEEDED

1 TABLESPOON FENNEL SEEDS

1 TEASPOON RED PEPPER FLAKES

COARSE-GRAINED SEA SALT, AS
NEEDED

DIRECTIONS

1. Preheat the oven to 430°F. In a large bowl, combine the flours and table salt. Gradually incorporate the water and work the mixture with your hands until it just holds together. Add the oil, fennel seeds, and red pepper flakes and knead the dough until they have been incorporated.

2. Transfer the dough to a flour-dusted work surface and knead until it is smooth, compact, and elastic, about 10 minutes. Form the dough into a ball, envelop it in plastic wrap, and let rest at room temperature for 30 minutes. Preheat the oven to 430°F.

3. Grease an 18 x 13–inch baking sheet with olive oil, roll the dough out into a rectangle that will fit within the pan, and place the dough in the pan. Drizzle olive oil over the dough and sprinkle the coarse-grained sea salt on top. Place in the oven and bake for 20 to 25 minutes, until it is a light golden brown. Remove and let cool slightly before serving.

PARIGINA

YIELD: **1 LARGE FOCACCIA**

ACTIVE TIME: **20 MINUTES**

TOTAL TIME: **3 HOURS**

INGREDIENTS

EXTRA-VIRGIN OLIVE OIL,
AS NEEDED

24-HOUR FOCACCIA DOUGH
(SEE PAGE 215)

22.9 OZ. CANNED TOMATOES,
DRAINED

SALT, TO TASTE

½ LB. HAM, SLICED

14 OZ. CACIOCAVALLO CHEESE
OR LOW-MOISTURE MOZZARELLA
CHEESE, SLICED THIN

1 SHEET OF FROZEN PUFF PASTRY,
THAWED

¼ CUP HEAVY CREAM

2 EGG YOLKS

DIRECTIONS

1. Grease an 18 x 13–inch baking sheet with olive oil, place the
   dough on it, and stretch it toward the edges of the pan,
   taking care not to tear it. Cover the dough with a kitchen
   towel and let rest at room temperature for 2 hours. As the
   dough rests, stretch it toward the edges of the pan every 20
   minutes until it covers the entire pan.

2. Preheat the oven to 390°F. Place the tomatoes in a bowl,
   season with salt, and mash the tomatoes. Spread the
   tomatoes over the dough, making sure to leave a 1-inch
   border of dough at the edges. Cover with a layer of ham
   and top this with a layer of cheese. Cover the focaccia with
   the puff pastry, beat the cream and egg yolks together until
   combined, and brush the pastry with the egg wash.

3. Place the focaccia in the oven and bake for 30 to 35 minutes,
   until golden brown. Remove from the oven and let cool
   slightly before cutting it into squares.

FOCACCIA BARESE

YIELD: **2 SMALL FOCACCIA**

ACTIVE TIME: **40 MINUTES**

TOTAL TIME: **4 HOURS**

INGREDIENTS

1 TEASPOON INSTANT YEAST OR 1⅔ TEASPOONS ACTIVE DRY YEAST

14 OZ. WATER

14 OZ. BREAD FLOUR, PLUS MORE AS NEEDED

7 OZ. SEMOLINA FLOUR

1 POTATO, BOILED, PEELED, AND MASHED

2½ TEASPOONS TABLE SALT, PLUS MORE TO TASTE

EXTRA-VIRGIN OLIVE OIL, AS NEEDED

2 VERY RIPE TOMATOES, CHOPPED

GREEN OLIVES, PITTED AND CHOPPED, TO TASTE

FRESH OREGANO, FINELY CHOPPED, TO TASTE

DIRECTIONS

1. If using active dry yeast, warm 3½ tablespoons of the water until it is about 90°F. Add the water and the yeast to a bowl and gently stir. Let the mixture sit until it starts to foam.

2. In a large bowl, combine the flours, potato, yeast, and water. Work the mixture until it just holds together. Transfer it to a flour-dusted work surface and knead the dough until it is compact, smooth, and elastic.

3. Add the salt and knead until the dough is developed, elastic, and extensible, about 5 minutes. Form the dough into a ball and place it in an airtight container that has been greased with olive oil. Let rest at room temperature until it has doubled in size, about 2 hours.

4. Generously grease two 10-inch cast-iron skillets or round cake pans with olive oil. Place the dough on a flour-dusted work surface and divide it into two pieces. Place the dough in the pans and spread it to the edge of each, making sure not to press down too hard and deflate the focaccia. Let the dough rest at room temperature for another hour.

5. Preheat the oven to its maximum temperature and place a rack in the middle position. Top the focaccia with the tomatoes, olives, and oregano, season with salt, and drizzle olive oil over everything. Place the pans directly on the bottom of the oven and bake for 10 minutes.

6. Transfer the pans to the middle rack and bake until the edges of the focaccia look brown and crunchy, 5 to 7 more minutes. Remove and let cool slightly before serving.

FOCACCIA DI ALTAMURA

YIELD: **2 SMALL FOCACCIA**

ACTIVE TIME: **40 MINUTES**

TOTAL TIME: **4 HOURS**

INGREDIENTS

1 TEASPOON INSTANT YEAST OR
1⅔ TEASPOONS ACTIVE DRY YEAST

14 OZ. WATER

21.1 OZ. SEMOLINA FLOUR, PLUS
MORE AS NEEDED

2½ TEASPOONS TABLE SALT, PLUS
MORE TO TASTE

EXTRA-VIRGIN OLIVE OIL, AS
NEEDED

1 LARGE ONION, SLICED

2 VERY RIPE TOMATOES, SLICED

FRESH OREGANO, FINELY CHOPPED,
TO TASTE

DIRECTIONS

1. If using active dry yeast, warm 3½ tablespoons of the water until it is about 90°F. Add the water and the yeast to a bowl and gently stir. Let the mixture sit until it starts to foam.

2. In a large bowl, combine the flour, yeast, and water and work the mixture until it just holds together. Transfer it to a flour-dusted work surface and knead the dough until it is compact, smooth, and elastic.

3. Add the salt and knead until the dough is developed, elastic, and extensible, about 5 minutes. Form the dough into a ball and place it in an airtight container that has been greased with olive oil. Let rest at room temperature until it has doubled in size, about 2 hours.

4. Generously grease two 10-inch cast-iron skillets or round cake pans with olive oil. Place the dough on a flour-dusted work surface and divide it into two pieces. Place a piece of dough in each pan and spread it to the edge, making sure not to press down too hard and deflate it. Let the dough rest at room temperature for another hour.

5. Preheat the oven to its maximum temperature and place a rack in the middle position. Top the focaccia with the onion and tomatoes, season with salt and oregano, and drizzle olive oil over the top. Place the pans directly on the bottom of the oven and bake for 10 minutes.

6. Transfer the pans to the middle rack and bake until the edges of the focaccia look brown and crunchy, 5 to 7 more minutes. Remove and let cool slightly before serving.

SFINCIONE PALERMITANO

YIELD: **1 LARGE FOCACCIA**

ACTIVE TIME: **1 HOUR**

TOTAL TIME: **4 HOURS AND 30 MINUTES**

INGREDIENTS

1⅓ TEASPOONS INSTANT YEAST OR
1¾ TEASPOONS ACTIVE DRY YEAST

22.5 OZ. WATER

19.75 OZ. BREAD FLOUR, PLUS MORE
AS NEEDED

8.4 OZ. SEMOLINA FLOUR

2½ TEASPOONS TABLE SALT, PLUS
MORE TO TASTE

3 TABLESPOONS EXTRA-VIRGIN
OLIVE OIL, PLUS MORE AS NEEDED

2 ONIONS, SLICED

22.9 OZ. CANNED WHOLE PEELED
TOMATOES, WITH THEIR LIQUID,
CRUSHED BY HAND

11 TO 14 ANCHOVY FILLETS, BONED
AND CHOPPED

BLACK PEPPER, TO TASTE

10.6 OZ. CACIOCAVALLO CHEESE
OR LOW-MOISTURE MOZZARELLA
CHEESE, CUBED

FRESH OREGANO, FINELY CHOPPED,
TO TASTE

5.3 OZ. LOW-MOISTURE MOZZARELLA
CHEESE, GRATED

BREAD CRUMBS, TO TASTE

DIRECTIONS

1. If using active dry yeast, warm 3½ tablespoons of the water until it is about 90°F. Add the water and the yeast to a bowl and gently stir. Let the mixture sit until it starts to foam.

2. In a large bowl, combine the flours, yeast, and water until the dough holds together. Transfer it to a flour-dusted work surface and knead the dough until it is compact, smooth, and elastic.

3. Add the salt and knead until the dough is developed, elastic, and extensible, about 5 minutes. Form the dough into a ball and cover the bowl with a damp kitchen towel. Let rest at room temperature until it has doubled in size, about 2 hours.

4. Coat the bottom of a skillet with olive oil and warm over medium-low heat. When the oil starts to shimmer, add the onions and cook, stirring frequently, until they are soft, about 12 minutes. Add the tomatoes and 3 of the anchovies, cover the skillet, reduce the heat, and simmer until the flavor is to your liking, 20 to 30 minutes. Season with salt and pepper and let cool completely.

5. Grease an 18 x 13–inch baking sheet with olive oil, place the dough on the pan, and gently stretch it until it covers the entire pan. Cover with plastic wrap and let rest for 1 hour.

6. Preheat the oven to 430°F. Top the focaccia with the cubed cheese and the remaining anchovies and press down on them until they are embedded in the dough. Cover with the tomato sauce, generously sprinkle oregano over the sauce, and drizzle with olive oil. Sprinkle the grated mozzarella and a generous handful of bread crumbs over the focaccia.

7. Place in the oven and bake for 20 minutes. Lower the temperature to 350°F and bake for another 15 to 20 minutes, until the focaccia is golden brown both on the edges and on the bottom.

RIANATA

YIELD: **1 LARGE FOCACCIA**

ACTIVE TIME: **40 MINUTES**

TOTAL TIME: **4 HOURS AND 45 MINUTES**

INGREDIENTS

1 TEASPOON INSTANT YEAST OR
1⅔ TEASPOONS ACTIVE DRY YEAST

14.8 OZ. WATER

15.8 OZ. BREAD FLOUR, PLUS MORE
AS NEEDED

8.8 OZ. SEMOLINA FLOUR

1½ TABLESPOONS EXTRA-VIRGIN
OLIVE OIL, PLUS MORE AS NEEDED

2½ TEASPOONS TABLE SALT, PLUS
MORE TO TASTE

7 TO 8 ANCHOVY FILLETS, BONED
AND CHOPPED

30 CHERRY TOMATOES, HALVED

8.8 OZ. PECORINO CHEESE, FRESHLY
GRATED

2 TEASPOONS FINELY CHOPPED
FRESH MARJORAM

DIRECTIONS

1. If using active dry yeast, warm 3½ tablespoons of the water until it is about 90°F. Add the water and the yeast to a bowl and gently stir. Let the mixture sit until it starts to foam.

2. In a large bowl, combine the flours, olive oil, yeast, and water until the dough holds together. Transfer it to a flour-dusted work surface and knead the dough until it is compact, smooth, and elastic.

3. Add the salt and knead until the dough is developed, elastic, and extensible, about 5 minutes. Form the dough into a ball and place it in an airtight container that has been greased with olive oil. Let it rest at room temperature until it has doubled in size, about 2 hours.

4. Grease an 18 x 13–inch baking sheet with olive oil, place the dough on it, and brush the dough with more olive oil. Cover with a kitchen towel and let rest for 30 minutes.

5. Gently stretch the dough until it covers the entire pan. Let rest for another hour.

6. Preheat the oven to 430°F. Press the anchovies and the tomatoes into the dough, sprinkle the pecorino over the focaccia, season with salt and the marjoram, and drizzle olive oil over everything.

7. Place in the oven and bake for 20 to 30 minutes, until the focaccia is golden brown and crisp on the edges and bottom. Remove and let cool slightly before serving.

MUSTAZZEDDU

YIELD: **1 LARGE FOCACCIA**

ACTIVE TIME: **40 MINUTES**

TOTAL TIME: **4 HOURS AND 30 MINUTES**

INGREDIENTS

28.2 OZ. CHERRY TOMATOES, CHOPPED

2 GARLIC CLOVES, CHOPPED

4 FRESH BASIL LEAVES

1 TABLESPOON EXTRA-VIRGIN OLIVE OIL, PLUS MORE AS NEEDED

1½ TEASPOONS TABLE SALT, PLUS MORE TO TASTE

1 TEASPOON INSTANT YEAST OR 1⅔ TEASPOONS ACTIVE DRY YEAST

11.6 OZ. WATER

12.3 OZ. SEMOLINA FLOUR

5.3 OZ. BREAD FLOUR, PLUS MORE AS NEEDED

BLACK PEPPER, TO TASTE

DIRECTIONS

1. Place the tomatoes, garlic, basil leaves, and a generous amount of olive oil in a bowl, season with salt, and stir to combine. Let the mixture sit for 2 hours, drain it in a colander, and let drain further for 1 hour.

2. If using active dry yeast, warm 3½ tablespoons of the water until it is about 90°F. Add the water and the yeast to a bowl and gently stir. Let the mixture sit until it starts to foam.

3. In a large bowl, combine the flours, olive oil, yeast, and water until the dough holds together. Add the salt and knead the dough until it is compact, smooth, and elastic. Cover the bowl with a damp kitchen towel and let it rest at room temperature until it has doubled in size, about 2 hours.

4. Place the dough on a flour-dusted work surface and roll it out until it is an approximately ¾-inch-thick disk. Place it on a parchment-lined 18 x 13–inch baking sheet, cover with the kitchen towel, and let rest for another hour.

5. Preheat the oven to 430°F and place a rack in the middle position. Place the tomato mixture on the focaccia, making sure to leave a border of dough at the edge. Fold the dough over the filling. You can leave the filling exposed or cover it completely, both are traditional in Sardinia, where this focaccia hails from.

6. Brush the dough with olive oil, place the pan directly on the bottom of the oven, and bake for 10 minutes. Lower the temperature to 390°F, transfer the focaccia to the middle rack, and bake for 30 to 40 minutes, until golden brown on the edges and on the bottom. Remove and let cool slightly before seasoning with pepper, slicing, and serving.

QUICK PIZZA DOUGH

YIELD: **4 BALLS OF DOUGH**

ACTIVE TIME: **20 MINUTES**

TOTAL TIME: **2 HOURS**

INGREDIENTS

2½ TEASPOONS INSTANT YEAST OR
3⅓ TEASPOONS ACTIVE DRY YEAST

15.5 OZ. WARM WATER (105°F)

23.2 OZ. BREAD FLOUR

1 TABLESPOON TABLE SALT

DIRECTIONS

1. If using active dry yeast, dissolve the yeast in the water and let the mixture rest for a few minutes, until it starts to foam.

2. In a large bowl, combine the flour, yeast, and water and work the mixture until it just holds together. Transfer it to a flour-dusted work surface and knead the dough until it is compact, smooth, and elastic.

3. Add the salt and knead until the dough is developed, elastic, and extensible, about 5 minutes. Form the dough into a ball and cover it with a damp kitchen towel. Let rest in a naturally warm spot (in the oven with the light on is a good option) until it has doubled in size, 1 hour to 1½ hours.

4. Punch the dough down, divide it into four pieces, and shape them into balls. Cover with a kitchen towel and let them rest for 5 minutes. Place the balls of dough on a flour-dusted work surface and push and roll them to increase the tension within. Cover with a kitchen towel and let rest for 40 minutes to 1 hour before using to make pizza.

NEAPOLITAN PIZZA DOUGH

YIELD: **4 BALLS OF DOUGH**

ACTIVE TIME: **30 MINUTES**

TOTAL TIME: **8 TO 12 HOURS**

INGREDIENTS

⅛ TEASPOON INSTANT YEAST OR ⅛ TEASPOON PLUS 1 PINCH ACTIVE DRY YEAST

14.8 OZ. WATER

23.9 OZ. BREAD FLOUR, PLUS MORE AS NEEDED

1 TABLESPOON TABLE SALT

EXTRA-VIRGIN OLIVE OIL, AS NEEDED

DIRECTIONS

1. If using active dry yeast, warm 3½ tablespoons of the water until it is about 105°F. Add the water and the yeast to a bowl and gently stir. Let sit until it starts to foam.

2. In a large bowl, combine the flour, yeast, and water. Work the mixture until it just holds together. Transfer it to a flour-dusted work surface and knead the dough until it is compact, smooth, and elastic.

3. Add the salt and knead until the dough is developed and elastic, meaning it pulls back energetically when pulled. Transfer the dough to an airtight container coated with olive oil, cover, and let rest for 2 to 3 hours at room temperature. For a classic Neapolitan dough, room temperature should be 77°F. If your kitchen is colder, let the dough rest longer before shaping it into rounds.

4. Divide the dough into four pieces and shape them into very tight rounds, as it is important to create tension in the outer layer of dough. Place the rounds in a baking dish with high edges, leaving enough space between rounds that they won't touch when fully risen. Cover with a kitchen towel and let rest for 6 to 8 hours depending on the temperature in the room before using to make pizza.

24-HOUR PIZZA DOUGH

YIELD: **4 BALLS OF DOUGH**

ACTIVE TIME: **20 MINUTES**

TOTAL TIME: **30 HOURS**

INGREDIENTS

1 TEASPOON INSTANT YEAST OR 1¼ TEASPOONS ACTIVE DRY YEAST

14.8 OZ. WATER

23.9 OZ. BREAD FLOUR

1 TABLESPOON TABLE SALT

EXTRA-VIRGIN OLIVE OIL, AS NEEDED

DIRECTIONS

1. If using active dry yeast, warm 3½ tablespoons of the water until it is about 105°F. Add the water and the yeast to a bowl and gently stir. Let sit until it starts to foam.

2. In a large bowl, combine the flour, yeast, and water. Work the mixture until it just holds together. Transfer it to a flour-dusted work surface and knead the dough until it is compact, smooth, and elastic.

3. Add the salt and knead until the dough is developed, elastic, and extensible, about 5 minutes. Form the dough into a ball, transfer to an airtight container coated with olive oil, cover, and let it rest at room temperature until it has doubled in size, 3 to 4 hours. The time for this first fermentation can be reduced if you place the dough in a naturally warm spot. In the oven with the light on is a good option if you're going to go this route.

4. Divide the dough into four pieces and shape them into very tight rounds, as it is important to create tension in the outer layer of dough. Place the rounds in a baking dish with high edges, leaving enough space between rounds that they won't touch when fully risen. Cover with a kitchen towel and refrigerate for 24 hours. Let sit at room temperature for 1 to 2 hours before making pizza.

NO-KNEAD PIZZA DOUGH

YIELD: **4 BALLS OF DOUGH**

ACTIVE TIME: **10 MINUTES**

TOTAL TIME: **22 HOURS**

INGREDIENTS

⅛ TEASPOON INSTANT YEAST OR ⅛ TEASPOON PLUS 1 PINCH ACTIVE DRY YEAST

16.2 OZ. WATER

22.6 OZ. BREAD FLOUR

1 TABLESPOON TABLE SALT

DIRECTIONS

1. If using active dry yeast, warm 3½ tablespoons of the water until it is about 105°F. Add the water and the yeast to a bowl and gently stir. Let sit until it starts to foam. Instant yeast does not need to be proofed.

2. In a large bowl, combine the flour, yeast, water, and salt. Work the mixture until there are no more lumps remaining in the dough. Cover the bowl with plastic wrap and let the mixture rest until it has doubled in size, 16 to 20 hours.

3. Divide the dough into four pieces and shape them into tight rounds. Cover with a damp kitchen towel and let them rest for 2 hours before making pizza.

PIZZA MARINARA

YIELD: **1 PIZZA**

ACTIVE TIME: **15 MINUTES**

TOTAL TIME: **45 MINUTES**

INGREDIENTS

SEMOLINA FLOUR, AS NEEDED

1 BALL OF PIZZA DOUGH

⅓ CUP PIZZA SAUCE (SEE PAGE 86)

1 GARLIC CLOVE, SLICED THIN

SALT, TO TASTE

DRIED OREGANO, TO TASTE

EXTRA-VIRGIN OLIVE OIL, TO TASTE

DIRECTIONS

1. Preheat the oven to the maximum temperature and place a baking stone or steel on the bottom of the oven as it warms. Dust a work surface with the semolina flour, place the dough on the surface, and gently stretch it into a round. Cover the dough with the sauce and top with the garlic.

2. Season the pizza with salt and dried oregano and drizzle olive oil over the top.

3. Dust a peel or a flat baking sheet with semolina flour and use it to transfer the pizza to the heated baking implement in the oven. Bake for about 15 minutes, until the crust is golden brown and starting to char. Remove and let cool slightly before slicing and serving.

MARGHERITA

YIELD: **1 PIZZA**

ACTIVE TIME: **15 MINUTES**

TOTAL TIME: **45 MINUTES**

INGREDIENTS

SEMOLINA FLOUR, AS NEEDED

1 BALL OF PIZZA DOUGH

⅓ CUP PIZZA SAUCE (SEE PAGE 86)

4 OZ. FRESH MOZZARELLA CHEESE, DRAINED AND CUT INTO SHORT STRIPS

FRESH BASIL LEAVES, TO TASTE

SALT, TO TASTE

EXTRA-VIRGIN OLIVE OIL, TO TASTE

DIRECTIONS

1. Preheat the oven to the maximum temperature and place a baking stone or steel on the bottom of the oven as it warms. Dust a work surface with semolina flour, place the dough on the surface, and gently stretch it into a round. Cover the dough with the sauce and top with the mozzarella and basil leaves.

2. Season the pizza with salt and drizzle olive oil over the top.

3. Dust a peel or a flat baking sheet with semolina flour and use it transfer the pizza to the heated baking implement in the oven. Bake for about 15 minutes, until the crust is golden brown and starting to char. Remove and let cool slightly before slicing and serving.

ROMANA

YIELD: **1 PIZZA**

ACTIVE TIME: **15 MINUTES**

TOTAL TIME: **45 MINUTES**

INGREDIENTS

SEMOLINA FLOUR, AS NEEDED

1 BALL OF PIZZA DOUGH

⅓ CUP PIZZA SAUCE (SEE PAGE 86)

2.5 OZ. FRESH MOZZARELLA CHEESE, DRAINED AND CUT INTO SHORT STRIPS

4 TO 5 ANCHOVY FILLETS, BONED AND CHOPPED

1 TABLESPOON CAPERS, DRAINED AND RINSED

SALT, TO TASTE

DRIED OREGANO, TO TASTE

EXTRA-VIRGIN OLIVE OIL, TO TASTE

DIRECTIONS

1. Preheat the oven to the maximum temperature and place a baking stone or steel on the bottom of the oven as it warms. Dust a work surface with semolina flour, place the dough on the surface, and gently stretch it into a round. Cover the dough with the sauce and top with the mozzarella, anchovies, and capers.

2. Season the pizza with salt and oregano and drizzle olive oil over the top.

3. Dust a peel or a flat baking sheet with semolina flour and use it to transfer the pizza to the heated baking implement in the oven. Bake for about 15 minutes, until the crust is golden brown and starting to char. Remove and let cool slightly before slicing and serving.

CAPRICCIOSA

YIELD: **1 PIZZA**

ACTIVE TIME: **15 MINUTES**

TOTAL TIME: **45 MINUTES**

INGREDIENTS

SEMOLINA FLOUR, AS NEEDED

1 BALL OF PIZZA DOUGH

⅓ CUP PIZZA SAUCE (SEE PAGE 86)

2 ARTICHOKE HEARTS, CHOPPED

¼ CUP MUSHROOMS

SALT, TO TASTE

EXTRA-VIRGIN OLIVE OIL, TO TASTE

3 OZ. FRESH MOZZARELLA CHEESE, DRAINED AND CUT INTO SHORT STRIPS

2 SLICES OF PROSCIUTTO, TORN

1 SMALL HANDFUL OF PITTED BLACK OLIVES

FRESH BASIL LEAVES, TO TASTE

DIRECTIONS

1. Preheat the oven to the maximum temperature and place a baking stone or steel on the bottom of the oven as it warms. Dust a work surface with the semolina flour, place the dough on the surface, and gently stretch it into a round. Cover the dough with the sauce and top with the artichokes and mushrooms.

2. Season the pizza with salt and drizzle olive oil over the top.

3. Dust a peel or a flat baking sheet with semolina flour and use it to transfer the pizza to the heated baking implement in the oven. Bake for about 5 minutes, until the crust starts to brown. Remove the pizza, distribute the mozzarella, prosciutto, olives, and basil over the top, and return the pizza to the oven. Bake for about 10 minutes, until the crust is golden brown and starting to char. Remove and let cool slightly before slicing and serving.

BOSCAIOLA

YIELD: **1 PIZZA**

ACTIVE TIME: **25 MINUTES**

TOTAL TIME: **55 MINUTES**

INGREDIENTS

EXTRA-VIRGIN OLIVE OIL, TO TASTE

1 LINK OF ITALIAN SAUSAGE, CHOPPED

SEMOLINA FLOUR, AS NEEDED

1 BALL OF PIZZA DOUGH

⅓ CUP PIZZA SAUCE (SEE PAGE 86)

½ CUP MUSHROOMS

SALT, TO TASTE

3 OZ. FRESH MOZZARELLA CHEESE, DRAINED AND CUT INTO SHORT STRIPS

DIRECTIONS

1. Preheat the oven to the maximum temperature and place a baking stone or steel on the bottom of the oven as it warms. Coat the bottom of a skillet with olive oil and warm it over medium-high heat. When the oil starts to shimmer, add the sausage and cook until it starts to brown, about 6 minutes. Remove from heat and set aside.

2. Dust a work surface with the semolina flour, place the dough on the surface, and gently stretch it into a round. Cover the dough with the sauce and top with the mushrooms and sausage.

3. Season the pizza with salt and drizzle olive oil over the top.

4. Dust a peel or a flat baking sheet with semolina flour and use it to transfer the pizza to the heated baking implement in the oven. Bake for about 5 minutes, until the crust starts to brown. Remove the pizza, distribute the mozzarella over the top, and return the pizza to the oven. Bake for about 10 minutes, until the crust is golden brown and starting to char. Remove and let cool slightly before slicing and serving.

DIAVOLA

YIELD: **1 PIZZA**

ACTIVE TIME: **15 MINUTES**

TOTAL TIME: **50 MINUTES**

INGREDIENTS

2 TABLESPOONS EXTRA-VIRGIN OLIVE OIL, PLUS MORE TO TASTE

RED PEPPER FLAKES, TO TASTE

SEMOLINA FLOUR, AS NEEDED

1 BALL OF PIZZA DOUGH

⅓ CUP PIZZA SAUCE (SEE PAGE 86)

2.5 OZ. CACIOCAVALLO OR PROVOLA CHEESE, CUBED

5 SLICES OF SPICY SALAMI

SALT, TO TASTE

DRIED OREGANO, TO TASTE

DIRECTIONS

1. Preheat the oven to the maximum temperature and place a baking stone or steel on the bottom of the oven as it warms. Combine the olive oil and red pepper flakes in a small bowl and set it aside.

2. Dust a work surface with the semolina flour, place the dough on the surface, and gently stretch it into a round. Cover the dough with the sauce and top with the cheese and salami. Drizzle the spicy olive oil over the top and season with salt and oregano.

3. Dust a peel or a flat baking sheet with semolina flour and use it to transfer the pizza to the heated baking implement in the oven. Bake for about 15 minutes, until the crust is golden brown and starting to char. Remove and let cool slightly before slicing and serving.

CARRETTIERA

YIELD: **1 PIZZA**

ACTIVE TIME: **25 MINUTES**

TOTAL TIME: **1 HOUR**

INGREDIENTS

EXTRA-VIRGIN OLIVE OIL, AS NEEDED

½ GARLIC CLOVE, MINCED

5 OZ. BROCCOLI RABE, TRIMMED

SALT AND PEPPER, TO TASTE

1 LINK OF SWEET ITALIAN SAUSAGE, CHOPPED

SEMOLINA FLOUR, AS NEEDED

1 BALL OF PIZZA DOUGH

3 OZ. FRESH MOZZARELLA CHEESE, DRAINED AND CUT INTO SHORT STRIPS

DIRECTIONS

1. Preheat the oven to the maximum temperature and place a baking stone or steel on the bottom of the oven as it warms. Coat the bottom of a skillet with olive oil and warm it over medium-high heat. When the oil starts to shimmer, add the garlic and broccoli rabe and cook, stirring frequently, until the broccoli rabe has softened, about 8 minutes. Season with salt and pepper, add the sausage, and cook until the sausage is browned, about 6 minutes. Remove from heat and let cool.

2. Dust a work surface with the semolina flour, place the dough on the surface, and gently stretch it into a round. Spread the sautéed broccoli rabe and sausage over the pizza and top with the mozzarella. Drizzle olive oil over the pizza.

3. Dust a peel or a flat baking sheet with semolina flour and use it to transfer the pizza to the heated baking implement in the oven. Bake for about 15 minutes, until the crust is golden brown and starting to char. Remove and let cool slightly before slicing and serving.

QUATTRO FORMAGGI

YIELD: **1 PIZZA**

ACTIVE TIME: **15 MINUTES**

TOTAL TIME: **45 MINUTES**

INGREDIENTS

SEMOLINA FLOUR, AS NEEDED

1 BALL OF PIZZA DOUGH

2 OZ. FRESH MOZZARELLA CHEESE, DRAINED AND CUT INTO SHORT STRIPS

2 OZ. FONTINA OR PROVOLONE CHEESE, SHREDDED

2 OZ. GORGONZOLA CHEESE, CRUMBLED

2 OZ. PECORINO OR PARMESAN CHEESE, GRATED

SALT AND PEPPER, TO TASTE

EXTRA-VIRGIN OLIVE OIL, TO TASTE

DIRECTIONS

1. Preheat the oven to the maximum temperature and place a baking stone or steel on the bottom of the oven as it warms. Dust a work surface with the semolina flour, place the dough on the surface, and gently stretch it into a round. Distribute the cheeses over the dough.

2. Season the pizza with salt and pepper and drizzle olive oil over the top.

3. Dust a peel or a flat baking sheet with semolina flour and use it to transfer the pizza to the heated baking implement in the oven. Bake for about 15 minutes, until the crust is golden brown and starting to char. Remove and let cool slightly before slicing and serving.

PESCATORA

YIELD: **1 PIZZA**

ACTIVE TIME: **25 MINUTES**

TOTAL TIME: **1 HOUR**

INGREDIENTS

EXTRA-VIRGIN OLIVE OIL, AS NEEDED

5 LARGE SHRIMP, SHELLED AND DEVEINED

HANDFUL OF CALAMARI RINGS

6 MUSSELS, DEBEARDED AND RINSED WELL

HANDFUL OF BABY OCTOPUS

½ GARLIC CLOVE, MINCED

SALT AND PEPPER, TO TASTE

RED PEPPER FLAKES, TO TASTE

SEMOLINA FLOUR, AS NEEDED

1 BALL OF PIZZA DOUGH

½ CUP PIZZA SAUCE (SEE PAGE 86)

DRIED OREGANO, TO TASTE

FRESH PARSLEY, FOR GARNISH

DIRECTIONS

1. Preheat the oven to the maximum temperature and place a baking stone or steel on the bottom of the oven as it warms. Coat the bottom of a skillet with olive oil and warm it over medium-high heat. When the oil starts to shimmer, add all of the seafood and the garlic. Season with salt and red pepper flakes and cook until most of the mussels have opened and the rest of the seafood is just cooked through, about 4 minutes. Remove from heat, discard any mussels that do not open, and remove the meat from those that have opened.

2. Dust a work surface with the semolina flour, place the dough on the surface, and gently stretch it into a round. Cover the dough with the sauce and season with oregano and pepper.

3. Dust a peel or a flat baking sheet with semolina flour and use it to transfer the pizza to the heated baking implement in the oven. Bake for about 5 minutes, until the crust starts to brown. Remove the pizza, distribute the seafood over it, drizzle olive oil on top, and return the pizza to the oven. Bake for about 10 minutes, until the crust is golden brown and starting to char. Remove and let cool slightly before garnishing with the parsley, slicing, and serving.

CAPRESE

INGREDIENTS

SEMOLINA FLOUR, AS NEEDED

1 BALL OF PIZZA DOUGH

⅓ CUP PIZZA SAUCE (SEE PAGE 86)

4.5 OZ. FRESH MOZZARELLA CHEESE, DRAINED AND SLICED

1 TOMATO, SLICED

SALT AND PEPPER, TO TASTE

DRIED OREGANO, TO TASTE

EXTRA-VIRGIN OLIVE OIL, TO TASTE

FRESH BASIL LEAVES, FOR GARNISH

DIRECTIONS

1. Preheat the oven to the maximum temperature and place a baking stone or steel on the bottom of the oven as it warms. Dust a work surface with the semolina flour, place the dough on the surface, and gently stretch it into a round. Cover the dough with the sauce and top with the mozzarella and tomato.

2. Season the pizza with salt, pepper, and oregano and drizzle olive oil over the top.

3. Dust a peel or a flat baking sheet with semolina flour and use it to transfer the pizza to the heated baking implement in the oven. Bake for about 15 minutes, until the crust is golden brown and starting to char. Remove and let cool slightly before garnishing with the basil, slicing, and serving.

ORTOLANA

YIELD: **1 PIZZA**

ACTIVE TIME: **30 MINUTES**

TOTAL TIME: **1 HOUR AND 15 MINUTES**

INGREDIENTS

¼ CUP MUSHROOMS, CHOPPED

SALT AND PEPPER, TO TASTE

EXTRA-VIRGIN OLIVE OIL, TO TASTE

½ BELL PEPPER, SLICED

½ SMALL EGGPLANT, SLICED

SEMOLINA FLOUR, AS NEEDED

1 BALL OF PIZZA DOUGH

⅓ CUP PIZZA SAUCE (SEE PAGE 86)

¼ ONION, SLICED

FRESH BASIL LEAVES, TO TASTE

DRIED OREGANO, TO TASTE

DIRECTIONS

1. Preheat the oven to the maximum temperature and place a baking stone or steel on the bottom of the oven as it warms. Place the mushrooms in a bowl, season with salt and pepper, and generously drizzle olive oil over them. Stir to combine and let the mixture sit for 10 minutes. Drain and set aside.

2. Place the bell pepper and eggplant on an aluminum foil–lined baking sheet, season with salt and pepper, drizzle olive oil over the vegetables, and place in the oven. Roast until they are tender and browned, about 25 minutes. Remove from the oven and let cool.

3. Dust a work surface with the semolina flour, place the dough on the surface, and gently stretch it into a round. Cover the dough with the sauce and top with the mushrooms, eggplant, peppers, onion, and basil leaves.

4. Season the pizza with salt and oregano and drizzle olive oil over the top.

5. Dust a peel or a flat baking sheet with semolina and use it to transfer the pizza to the heated baking implement in the oven. Bake for about 15 minutes, until the crust is golden brown and starting to char. Remove and let cool slightly before slicing and serving.

ROASTED FENNEL & SAUSAGE PIZZA

YIELD: **1 PIZZA**

ACTIVE TIME: **25 MINUTES**

TOTAL TIME: **1 HOUR AND 15 MINUTES**

INGREDIENTS

½ BULB OF FENNEL, TRIMMED AND SLICED

SALT AND PEPPER, TO TASTE

EXTRA-VIRGIN OLIVE OIL, AS NEEDED

SEMOLINA FLOUR, AS NEEDED

1 BALL OF PIZZA DOUGH

⅓ CUP PIZZA SAUCE (SEE PAGE 86)

2 LINKS OF SWEET ITALIAN SAUSAGE, BROWNED AND CHOPPED

½ ONION, SLICED

4 OZ. FRESH MOZZARELLA CHEESE, DRAINED AND TORN

DIRECTIONS

1. Preheat the oven to 430°F. Place the fennel in a baking dish, season with salt, and drizzle olive oil over the fennel, and place in the oven. Roast until it is tender and just starting to caramelize, 30 to 35 minutes. Remove from the oven and let cool completely.

2. Preheat the oven to the maximum temperature and place a baking stone or steel on the bottom of the oven as it warms. Dust a work surface with the semolina flour, place the dough on the surface, and gently stretch it into a round. Cover the dough with the sauce and top with the sausage, roasted fennel, and the onion.

3. Season the pizza with salt and pepper and drizzle olive oil over the top.

4. Dust a peel or a flat baking sheet with semolina and use it to transfer the pizza to the heated baking implement surface in the oven. Bake for about 5 minutes, until the crust starts to brown. Remove the pizza, distribute the mozzarella over the top, and return the pizza to the oven. Bake for about 10 minutes, until the crust is golden brown and starting to char. Remove and let cool slightly before slicing and serving.

PIZZA WITH PROSCIUTTO, ARUGULA & PARMESAN

YIELD: **1 PIZZA**

ACTIVE TIME: **15 MINUTES**

TOTAL TIME: **45 MINUTES**

INGREDIENTS

SEMOLINA FLOUR, AS NEEDED

1 BALL OF PIZZA DOUGH

⅓ CUP PIZZA SAUCE (SEE PAGE 86)

SALT AND PEPPER, TO TASTE

EXTRA-VIRGIN OLIVE OIL, TO TASTE

4 OZ. FRESH MOZZARELLA CHEESE, DRAINED AND CHOPPED

4 OZ. PROSCIUTTO, TORN

GENEROUS HANDFUL OF ARUGULA

2 OZ. PARMESAN CHEESE, SHAVED

DIRECTIONS

1. Preheat the oven to the maximum temperature and place a baking stone or steel on the bottom of the oven as it warms. Dust a work surface with semolina flour, place the dough on the surface, and gently stretch it into a round. Cover the dough with the sauce, season with salt and pepper, and drizzle olive oil over the top.

2. Dust a peel or a flat baking sheet with semolina and use it to transfer the pizza to the heated baking implement in the oven. Bake for about 5 minutes, until the crust starts to brown. Remove the pizza, distribute the mozzarella over the top, and return the pizza to the oven. Bake for about 10 minutes, until the crust is golden brown and starting to char. Remove and top with the prosciutto, the arugula, and the Parmesan. Season with salt and pepper, drizzle olive oil over the pizza, and serve.

SQUASH BLOSSOM & RICOTTA PIZZA

YIELD: **1 PIZZA**

ACTIVE TIME: **15 MINUTES**

TOTAL TIME: **45 MINUTES**

INGREDIENTS

SEMOLINA FLOUR, AS NEEDED

1 BALL OF PIZZA DOUGH

EXTRA-VIRGIN OLIVE OIL, TO TASTE

4 OZ. LOW-MOISTURE MOZZARELLA CHEESE, SHREDDED

3 SQUASH BLOSSOMS, STAMENS REMOVED, SLICED LENGTHWISE

3 OZ. RICOTTA CHEESE

SALT AND PEPPER, TO TASTE

ZEST OF 1 LEMON

DIRECTIONS

1. Preheat the oven to the maximum temperature and place a baking stone or steel on the bottom of the oven as it warms. Dust a work surface with semolina flour, place the dough on the surface, and gently stretch it into a round.

2. Drizzle olive oil over the dough, cover with the shredded mozzarella, and distribute the squash blossoms over the cheese. You want to open the squash blossoms up so that they cover as much of the pizza as possible. Distribute dollops of the ricotta over the pizza, season with salt and pepper, and drizzle more olive oil over the top.

3. Dust a peel or a flat baking sheet with semolina and use it to transfer the pizza to the heated baking implement in the oven. Bake for 15 minutes, until the crust is golden brown and starting to char. Remove, sprinkle the lemon zest over the pizza, and let it cool slightly before serving.

ARTICHOKE & POTATO PIZZA

YIELD: **1 PIZZA**

ACTIVE TIME: **20 MINUTES**

TOTAL TIME: **1 HOUR**

INGREDIENTS

SALT AND PEPPER, TO TASTE

1 POTATO, PEELED AND SLICED THIN

SEMOLINA FLOUR, AS NEEDED

1 BALL OF PIZZA DOUGH

EXTRA-VIRGIN OLIVE OIL, TO TASTE

3 OZ. LOW-MOISTURE MOZZARELLA CHEESE, SHREDDED

4 ARTICHOKE HEARTS IN OLIVE OIL, DRAINED AND CHOPPED

FRESH ROSEMARY, TO TASTE

DIRECTIONS

1. Preheat the oven to the maximum temperature and place a baking stone or steel on the bottom of the oven as it warms. Bring a pot of salted water to a boil and prepare an ice water bath. Add the potato to the boiling water and cook until it is translucent, 2 to 4 minutes. Drain, transfer the potato to the ice water bath, and let sit for 2 minutes. Drain again and pat dry.

2. Dust a work surface with the semolina flour, place the dough on the surface, and gently stretch it into a round. Drizzle olive oil over the dough, cover with the shredded mozzarella, and distribute the potato and artichoke over the cheese. Season with salt and pepper, drizzle olive oil over the pizza, and sprinkle a generous amount of rosemary on top.

3. Dust a peel or a flat baking sheet with semolina and use it to transfer the pizza to the heated baking implement in the oven. Bake for about 15 minutes, until the crust is golden brown and starting to char. Remove and let the pizza cool slightly before slicing and serving.

HAM & MUSHROOM PIZZA

YIELD: **1 PIZZA**

ACTIVE TIME: **15 MINUTES**

TOTAL TIME: **45 MINUTES**

INGREDIENTS

¾ CUP BUTTON MUSHROOMS, SLICED

½ GARLIC CLOVE, MINCED

SALT AND PEPPER, TO TASTE

EXTRA-VIRGIN OLIVE OIL, AS NEEDED

SEMOLINA FLOUR, AS NEEDED

1 BALL OF PIZZA DOUGH

⅓ CUP PIZZA SAUCE (SEE PAGE 86)

4 OZ. FRESH MOZZARELLA CHEESE, DRAINED AND TORN

2.4 OZ. HAM, CHOPPED

DIRECTIONS

1. Preheat the oven to the maximum temperature and place a baking stone or steel on the bottom of the oven as it warms. Place the mushrooms and garlic in a bowl, season with salt, and drizzle olive oil over the mixture. Stir to combine and let the mushrooms marinate for 10 minutes.

2. Dust a work surface with the semolina flour, place the dough on the surface, and gently stretch it into a round. Cover the dough with the sauce, drain the mushrooms, and distribute them on top. Season the pizza with salt and pepper and drizzle olive oil over the top.

3. Dust a peel or a flat baking sheet with semolina and use it to transfer the pizza to the heated baking implement in the oven. Bake for about 5 minutes, until the crust starts to brown. Remove, distribute the mozzarella and ham over the top, and return the pizza to the oven. Bake for about 10 minutes, until the crust is golden brown and starting to char. Remove and let cool slightly before slicing and serving.

SPINACH & RICOTTA PIZZA

YIELD: **1 PIZZA**

ACTIVE TIME: **20 MINUTES**

TOTAL TIME: **1 HOUR**

INGREDIENTS

EXTRA-VIRGIN OLIVE OIL, AS NEEDED

3 OZ. FRESH SPINACH

½ GARLIC CLOVE, CHOPPED

DASH OF FRESHLY GRATED NUTMEG

SALT AND PEPPER, TO TASTE

SEMOLINA FLOUR, AS NEEDED

1 BALL OF PIZZA DOUGH

3 OZ. RICOTTA CHEESE

2 OZ. PROVOLONE CHEESE, GRATED

DIRECTIONS

1. Preheat the oven to the maximum temperature and place a baking stone or steel on the bottom of the oven as it warms. Coat the bottom of a skillet with olive oil and warm it over medium heat. When the oil starts to shimmer, add the spinach, cover the pan, and cook until the spinach has wilted, about 2 minutes. Uncover the pan, add the garlic and nutmeg, and season with salt and pepper. Raise the heat to medium-high and cook, stirring frequently, until all of the liquid has evaporated from the pan. Remove from heat and let cool.

2. Dust a work surface with the semolina flour, place the dough on the surface, and gently stretch it into a round. Drizzle olive oil over the dough and distribute half of the spinach over it.

3. Dust a peel or a flat baking sheet with semolina and use it to transfer the pizza to the heated baking implement in the oven. Bake for about 5 minutes, until the crust starts to brown. Remove the pizza, distribute the ricotta, provolone, and the rest of the spinach over it, and drizzle olive oil over the top. Return the pizza to the oven and bake for about 10 minutes, until the crust is golden brown and starting to char. Remove and let cool slightly before slicing and serving.

POTATO & PESTO PIZZA

YIELD: **1 PIZZA**

ACTIVE TIME: **20 MINUTES**

TOTAL TIME: **1 HOUR**

INGREDIENTS

SALT AND PEPPER, TO TASTE

1 SMALL POTATO, SLICED

SEMOLINA FLOUR, AS NEEDED

1 BALL OF PIZZA DOUGH

3 OZ. CACIOCAVALLO CHEESE, SLICED

2 TABLESPOONS BASIL PESTO (SEE PAGE 78)

EXTRA-VIRGIN OLIVE OIL, AS NEEDED

DIRECTIONS

1. Preheat the oven to the maximum temperature and place a baking stone or steel on the bottom of the oven as it warms. Bring salted water to a boil in a saucepan and prepare an ice water bath. Add the potato to the boiling water, cook until it is translucent, 2 to 4 minutes, drain, and place it in the ice water bath. Let it sit for 2 minutes, drain, and pat dry with paper towels.

2. Dust a work surface with the semolina flour, place the dough on the surface, and gently stretch it into a round. Distribute the cheese, potato, and pesto over the dough, drizzle olive oil over everything, and season the pizza with salt and pepper.

3. Dust a peel or a flat baking sheet with semolina and use it to transfer the pizza to the heated baking implement in the oven. Bake for about 15 minutes, until the crust is golden brown and starting to char. Remove and let cool slightly before slicing and serving.

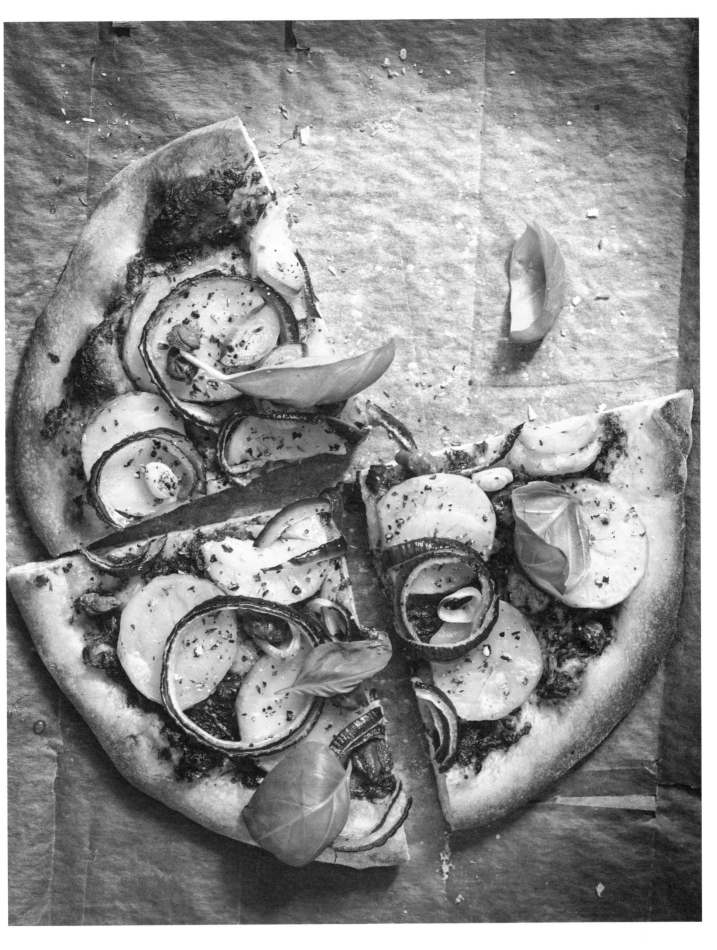

PIZZA WITH SAUSAGE, BROCCOLI RABE & CHERRY TOMATOES

YIELD: **1 PIZZA**

ACTIVE TIME: **25 MINUTES**

TOTAL TIME: **1 HOUR**

INGREDIENTS

EXTRA-VIRGIN OLIVE OIL, AS NEEDED

3 OZ. BROCCOLI RABE, TRIMMED

1 GARLIC CLOVE

1 LINK OF SWEET ITALIAN SAUSAGE, SLICED

SALT AND PEPPER, TO TASTE

SEMOLINA FLOUR, AS NEEDED

1 BALL OF PIZZA DOUGH

3 OZ. FRESH MOZZARELLA CHEESE, DRAINED AND TORN

HANDFUL OF CHERRY TOMATOES

DIRECTIONS

1. Preheat the oven to the maximum temperature and place a baking stone or steel on the bottom of the oven as it warms. Coat the bottom of a skillet with olive oil and warm it over medium-high heat. When the oil starts to shimmer, add the broccoli rabe and garlic and cook, stirring frequently, until the broccoli rabe has softened, about 8 minutes. Add the sausage to pan and cook until it is browned and all of the liquid in the pan has evaporated, about 5 minutes. Remove the pan from heat, remove the garlic and discard it, season the mixture with salt and pepper, and let it cool.

2. Dust a work surface with the semolina flour, place the dough on the surface, and gently stretch it into a round. Drizzle olive oil over the dough and distribute the mozzarella over it. Top with the sausage mixture and cherry tomatoes. Season the pizza with salt and drizzle olive oil over the top.

3. Dust a peel or a flat baking sheet with semolina and use it to transfer the pizza to the heated baking implement in the oven. Bake for about 15 minutes, until the crust is golden brown and starting to char. Remove and let cool slightly before slicing and serving.

SAUSAGE & BROCCOLI PIZZA

YIELD: **1 PIZZA**

ACTIVE TIME: **20 MINUTES**

TOTAL TIME: **1 HOUR**

INGREDIENTS

SALT AND PEPPER, TO TASTE

1 CUP BROCCOLI FLORETS

SEMOLINA FLOUR, AS NEEDED

1 BALL OF PIZZA DOUGH

⅓ CUP PIZZA SAUCE (SEE PAGE 86)

2 LINKS OF HOT ITALIAN SAUSAGE, BROWNED AND CHOPPED

4 OZ. FRESH MOZZARELLA CHEESE, DRAINED AND CHOPPED

EXTRA-VIRGIN OLIVE OIL, AS NEEDED

DIRECTIONS

1. Preheat the oven to the maximum temperature and place a baking stone or steel on the bottom of the oven as it warms. Bring salted water to a boil in a saucepan and prepare an ice water bath. Add the broccoli, cook for 1 minute, and transfer to the ice water bath. Let it sit for 2 minutes, drain, and pat dry with paper towels.

2. Dust a work surface with the semolina flour, place the dough on the surface, and gently stretch it into a round. Cover the dough with the sauce and top with the sausage and broccoli.

3. Season the pizza with salt and pepper and drizzle olive oil over the top.

4. Dust a peel or a flat baking sheet with semolina and use it to transfer the pizza to the heated baking implement in the oven. Bake for about 5 minutes, until the crust starts to brown. Remove the pizza, distribute the mozzarella over the top, and return the pizza to the oven. Bake for about 10 minutes, until the crust is golden brown and starting to char. Remove and let cool slightly before slicing and serving.

PIZZA WITH GARDEN VEGETABLES, ARTICHOKES & SALAMI

YIELD: **1 PIZZA**

ACTIVE TIME: **15 MINUTES**

TOTAL TIME: **1 HOUR AND 15 MINUTES**

INGREDIENTS

¼ EGGPLANT, SLICED THIN

½ BELL PEPPER, SLICED

SALT AND PEPPER, TO TASTE

EXTRA-VIRGIN OLIVE OIL, AS NEEDED

SEMOLINA FLOUR, AS NEEDED

1 BALL OF PIZZA DOUGH

⅓ CUP PIZZA SAUCE (SEE PAGE 86)

4 ARTICHOKE HEARTS IN OLIVE OIL, DRAINED AND CHOPPED

6 SLICES OF SALAMI

3 OZ. FRESH MOZZARELLA CHEESE, DRAINED AND SLICED

DIRECTIONS

1. Preheat the oven to the maximum temperature and place a baking stone or steel on the bottom of the oven as it warms. Place the eggplant and bell pepper on an aluminum foil–lined baking sheet, season with salt and pepper, drizzle olive oil over the vegetables, and place in the warming oven. Roast until they are tender and browned, about 25 minutes. Remove from the oven and let cool.

2. Dust a work surface with the semolina flour, place the dough on the surface, and gently stretch it into a round. Cover the dough with the sauce and top with the artichokes, eggplant, bell pepper, salami, and mozzarella.

3. Season the pizza with salt and drizzle olive oil over the top.

4. Dust a peel or a flat baking sheet with semolina and use it to transfer the pizza to the heated baking implement in the oven. Bake for about 15 minutes, until the crust is golden brown and starting to char. Remove and let cool slightly before slicing and serving.

PIZZA WITH PROSCIUTTO & ASPARAGUS

YIELD: **1 PIZZA**

ACTIVE TIME: **20 MINUTES**

TOTAL TIME: **1 HOUR**

INGREDIENTS

SALT AND PEPPER, TO TASTE

6 SPEARS OF ASPARAGUS, TRIMMED

SEMOLINA FLOUR, AS NEEDED

1 BALL OF PIZZA DOUGH

EXTRA-VIRGIN OLIVE OIL, AS NEEDED

3 OZ. FRESH MOZZARELLA CHEESE, SLICED

4 SLICES OF PROSCIUTTO, TORN

BALSAMIC GLAZE, FOR GARNISH

DIRECTIONS

1. Preheat the oven to the maximum temperature and place a baking stone or steel on the bottom of the oven as it warms. Bring salted water to a boil in a saucepan and add the asparagus. Cook until just tender, 2 to 3 minutes, drain, and pat dry. Chop the asparagus into large pieces and set it aside.

2. Dust a work surface with the semolina flour, place the dough on the surface, and gently stretch it into a round. Drizzle olive oil over the dough, top it with the mozzarella, and season with salt and pepper.

3. Dust a peel or a flat baking sheet with semolina and use it to transfer the pizza to the heated baking implement in the oven. Bake for about 15 minutes, until the crust is golden brown and starting to char. Remove, top with the prosciutto and asparagus, and drizzle olive oil and the balsamic glaze over the pizza.

    NOTE: You can purchase a balsamic glaze, but it is just as easy to make at home. Simply place 4 parts balsamic vinegar to 1 part brown sugar in a saucepan and simmer it, stirring occasionally, until it has thickened. Remove the pan from heat and let the glaze rest for 15 minutes before using.

PIZZA WITH BROCCOLI & BACON

YIELD: **1 PIZZA**

ACTIVE TIME: **15 MINUTES**

TOTAL TIME: **50 MINUTES**

INGREDIENTS

SALT AND PEPPER, TO TASTE

1 CUP BROCCOLI FLORETS

SEMOLINA FLOUR, AS NEEDED

1 BALL OF PIZZA DOUGH

4 OZ. LOW-MOISTURE MOZZARELLA CHEESE, SHREDDED

3 SLICES OF BACON, COOKED AND CHOPPED

4 SUN-DRIED TOMATOES IN OLIVE OIL, DRAINED AND HALVED

EXTRA-VIRGIN OLIVE OIL, TO TASTE

DIRECTIONS

1. Preheat the oven to the maximum temperature and place a baking stone or steel on the bottom of the oven as it warms. Bring salted water to a boil in a saucepan and add the broccoli. Cook until just tender, about 4 minutes, drain, and set aside.

2. Dust a work surface with the semolina flour, place the dough on the surface, and gently stretch it into a round. Sprinkle half of the cheese over the dough and top with the broccoli, bacon, and sun-dried tomatoes. Season with salt and pepper, drizzle olive oil over the pizza, and sprinkle the rest of the cheese on top.

3. Dust a peel or a flat baking sheet with semolina and use it to transfer the pizza to the heated baking implement in the oven. Bake for about 15 minutes, until the crust is golden brown and starting to char. Remove and let cool slightly before slicing and serving.

PIZZA WITH ZUCCHINI CREAM, BACON & BUFFALO MOZZARELLA

YIELD: **1 PIZZA**

ACTIVE TIME: **15 MINUTES**

TOTAL TIME: **45 MINUTES**

INGREDIENTS

SEMOLINA FLOUR, AS NEEDED

1 BALL OF PIZZA DOUGH

3 TABLESPOONS ZUCCHINI CREAM (SEE SIDEBAR)

3.5 OZ. FRESH BUFFALO MOZZARELLA CHEESE, DRAINED AND CHOPPED

EXTRA-VIRGIN OLIVE OIL, TO TASTE

2 SLICES OF BACON, COOKED AND CRUMBLED

DIRECTIONS

1. Preheat the oven to the maximum temperature and place a baking stone or steel on the bottom of the oven as it warms. Dust a work surface with the semolina flour, place the dough on the surface, and gently stretch it into a round.

2. Cover the dough with the Zucchini Cream, distribute the mozzarella over it, and drizzle olive oil on top.

3. Dust a peel or a flat baking sheet with semolina and use it to transfer the pizza to the heated baking implement in the oven. Bake for about 15 minutes, until the crust is golden brown and starting to char. Remove and let cool slightly before sprinkling the bacon over the pizza, slicing, and serving.

ZUCCHINI CREAM

Coat the bottom of a skillet with olive oil and warm it over medium heat. When the oil starts to shimmer, add 1 chopped zucchini and ½ chopped onion and cook, stirring occasionally, until they are soft, about 10 minutes. Season with salt and pepper, raise the heat to medium-high, and cook until all of the liquid in the pan has evaporated. Place the sautéed vegetables in a blender or food processor, add a tablespoon of extra-virgin olive oil, and blitz until smooth.

CALAMARI, SHRIMP & PESTO PIZZA

YIELD: **1 PIZZA**

ACTIVE TIME: **15 MINUTES**

TOTAL TIME: **45 MINUTES**

INGREDIENTS

SEMOLINA FLOUR, AS NEEDED

1 BALL OF PIZZA DOUGH

⅓ CUP PIZZA SAUCE (SEE PAGE 86)

HANDFUL OF BLACK OR GREEN OLIVES, PITTED AND HALVED

SALT AND PEPPER, TO TASTE

EXTRA-VIRGIN OLIVE OIL, TO TASTE

3 OZ. CALAMARI RINGS, COOKED

5 SHRIMP, PEELED, DEVEINED, AND COOKED

2 TABLESPOONS BASIL PESTO (SEE PAGE 78)

DIRECTIONS

1. Preheat the oven to the maximum temperature and place a baking stone or steel on the bottom the oven as it warms. Dust a work surface with the semolina flour, place the dough on the surface, and gently stretch it into a round. Cover the dough with the Pizza Sauce and top with the olives. Season with salt and pepper and drizzle olive oil over the pizza.

2. Dust a peel or a flat baking sheet with semolina and use it to transfer the pizza to the heated baking implement in the oven. Bake for about 5 minutes, until the crust starts to brown. Remove the pizza, distribute the calamari, shrimp, and pesto over the top, and return the pizza to the oven. Bake for about 10 minutes, until the crust is golden brown and starting to char. Remove and let cool slightly before slicing and serving.

PIZZA WITH PUMPKIN, FETA & ARUGULA

YIELD: **1 PIZZA**

ACTIVE TIME: **15 MINUTES**

TOTAL TIME: **45 MINUTES**

INGREDIENTS

SEMOLINA FLOUR, AS NEEDED

1 BALL OF PIZZA DOUGH

3 OZ. LOW-MOISTURE MOZZARELLA CHEESE, SHREDDED

3.5 OZ. ROASTED PUMPKIN, DICED

SALT AND PEPPER, TO TASTE

EXTRA-VIRGIN OLIVE OIL, TO TASTE

3 OZ. FETA CHEESE, CRUMBLED

½ CUP ARUGULA

PARMESAN CHEESE, GRATED, TO TASTE

BALSAMIC VINEGAR, TO TASTE

DIRECTIONS

1. Preheat the oven to the maximum temperature and place a baking stone or steel on the bottom of the oven as it warms. Dust a work surface with the semolina flour, place the dough on the surface, and gently stretch it into a round. Cover the dough with the mozzarella and top with the pumpkin. Season with salt and pepper and drizzle olive oil over the pizza.

2. Dust a peel or a flat baking sheet with semolina and use it to transfer the pizza to the heated baking implement in the oven. Bake for about 5 minutes, until the crust starts to brown. Remove the pizza, top with the feta, arugula, Parmesan, and balsamic vinegar, drizzle olive oil over the pizza, and return it to the oven. Bake for about 10 minutes, until the crust is golden brown and starting to char. Remove and let cool slightly before slicing and serving.

PIZZA WITH BRIE & PEAR

YIELD: **1 PIZZA**

ACTIVE TIME: **15 MINUTES**

TOTAL TIME: **45 MINUTES**

INGREDIENTS

SEMOLINA FLOUR, AS NEEDED

1 BALL OF PIZZA DOUGH

2 OZ. LOW-MOISTURE MOZZARELLA CHEESE, SHREDDED

2 OZ. BRIE CHEESE, RIND REMOVED AND CHOPPED

½ SMALL PEAR, CUBED

EXTRA-VIRGIN OLIVE OIL, TO TASTE

FRESH THYME, FOR GARNISH

DIRECTIONS

1. Preheat the oven to the maximum temperature and place a baking stone or steel on the bottom of the oven as it warms. Dust a work surface with the semolina flour, place the dough on the surface, and gently stretch it into a round. Cover the dough with the mozzarella, top with the Brie and the pear, and drizzle olive oil over the pizza.

2. Dust a peel or a flat baking sheet with semolina and use it to transfer the pizza to the heated baking implement in the oven. Bake for about 15 minutes, until the crust is golden brown and starting to char. Remove and let cool slightly before garnishing with the thyme, slicing, and serving.

FIG, PROSCIUTTO & BALSAMIC PIZZA

YIELD: **1 PIZZA**

ACTIVE TIME: **15 MINUTES**

TOTAL TIME: **45 MINUTES**

INGREDIENTS

SEMOLINA FLOUR, AS NEEDED

1 BALL OF PIZZA DOUGH

2.5 OZ. LOW-MOISTURE MOZZARELLA CHEESE, SHREDDED

1 TABLESPOON BASIL PESTO (SEE PAGE 78)

2 OZ. GORGONZOLA CHEESE, CRUMBLED

EXTRA-VIRGIN OLIVE OIL, TO TASTE

2 TO 3 FIGS, CHOPPED

3 SLICES OF PROSCIUTTO, TORN

HANDFUL OF ARUGULA

PARMESAN CHEESE, FRESHLY GRATED, TO TASTE

BALSAMIC GLAZE, TO TASTE

DIRECTIONS

1. Preheat the oven to the maximum temperature and place a baking stone or steel on the bottom of the oven as it warms. Dust a work surface with the semolina flour, place the dough on the surface, and gently stretch it into a round. Cover the dough with the mozzarella, pesto, and gorgonzola and drizzle olive oil over the pizza.

2. Dust a peel or a flat baking sheet with semolina and use it to transfer the pizza to the heated baking implement in the oven. Bake for about 5 minutes, until the crust starts to brown. Remove the pizza, top with the figs and prosciutto, and return the pizza to the oven. Bake for about 10 minutes, until the crust is golden brown and starting to char. Remove and let cool slightly before topping with the arugula, Parmesan, and balsamic, slicing, and serving.

PIZZA WITH HAM, GORGONZOLA, PEARS & WALNUTS

YIELD: **1 PIZZA**

ACTIVE TIME: **15 MINUTES**

TOTAL TIME: **45 MINUTES**

INGREDIENTS

SEMOLINA FLOUR, AS NEEDED

1 BALL OF PIZZA DOUGH

2 OZ. LOW-MOISTURE MOZZARELLA CHEESE, SHREDDED

½ SMALL PEAR, SLICED THIN

2 OZ. GORGONZOLA CHEESE, CRUMBLED

EXTRA-VIRGIN OLIVE OIL, TO TASTE

2 TO 3 FIGS, CHOPPED

3 SLICES OF SERRANO HAM, TORN

¼ CUP WALNUTS, CHOPPED

BLACK PEPPER, TO TASTE

DIRECTIONS

1. Preheat the oven to the maximum temperature and place a baking stone or steel on the bottom of the oven as it warms. Dust a work surface with the semolina flour, place the dough on the surface, and gently stretch it into a round. Cover the dough with the mozzarella, pear, and gorgonzola and drizzle olive oil over the pizza.

2. Dust a peel or a flat baking sheet with semolina and use it to transfer the pizza to the heated baking implement in the oven. Bake for about 5 minutes, until the crust starts to brown. Remove the pizza, top with the figs, ham, and walnuts, season with pepper, drizzle olive oil over the top, and return the pizza to the oven. Bake for about 10 minutes, until the crust is golden brown and starting to char. Remove and let cool slightly before slicing and serving.

CHICKEN, SPINACH & PINE NUT PIZZA

YIELD: **1 PIZZA**

ACTIVE TIME: **20 MINUTES**

TOTAL TIME: **50 MINUTES**

INGREDIENTS

EXTRA-VIRGIN OLIVE OIL, TO TASTE

1 CUP BABY SPINACH

SALT AND PEPPER, TO TASTE

SEMOLINA FLOUR, AS NEEDED

1 BALL OF PIZZA DOUGH

3 OZ. LOW-MOISTURE MOZZARELLA CHEESE, SHREDDED

1 CUP COOKED CHICKEN BREAST, CUBED

2 TABLESPOONS PINE NUTS

DIRECTIONS

1. Preheat the oven to the maximum temperature and place a baking stone or steel on the bottom of the oven as it warms. Coat the bottom of a skillet with olive oil and warm over medium-high heat. When the oil starts to shimmer, add the spinach, season with salt and pepper, and cook until it is wilted, about 2 minutes. Remove the pan from heat and set aside.

2. Dust a work surface with the semolina flour, place the dough on the surface, and gently stretch it into a round. Cover the dough with half of the mozzarella and top with the chicken, pine nuts, and spinach. Season with salt and pepper, drizzle olive oil over the pizza, and distribute the remaining mozzarella over the top.

3. Dust a peel or a flat baking sheet with semolina and use it to transfer the pizza to the heated baking implement in the oven. Bake for about 15 minutes, until the crust is golden brown and starting to char. Remove and let cool slightly before slicing and serving.

CHAPTER 6

ENTREES

Beloved dishes like Pasta Primavera, Lasagna, and Penne alla Vodka can be found in this chapter, but so can lesser-known and no-less-exceptional recipes such as Porchetta and Chicken Cacciatore. Featuring a balance of Old World simplicity and modern decadence, these preparations foster the celebration of life with family and friends that Italy and its people are famed for.

LAMB SCOTTADITO

YIELD: **6 SERVINGS**

ACTIVE TIME: **20 MINUTES**

TOTAL TIME: **2 HOURS AND 30 MINUTES**

INGREDIENTS

4 GARLIC CLOVES, MINCED

½ CUP ROSEMARY, FINELY CHOPPED

¼ CUP EXTRA-VIRGIN OLIVE OIL, PLUS MORE TO TASTE

2¼ LBS. LAMB CHOPS, POUNDED THIN AND TRIMMED

SALT AND PEPPER, TO TASTE

DIRECTIONS

1. Place the garlic, rosemary, and olive oil in a large bowl and stir to combine. Set the marinade aside.

2. Season the lamb chops with salt and pepper, add them to the marinade, and turn them until evenly coated. Cover the bowl with plastic wrap, place it in the refrigerator, and chill for 2 hours.

3. Preheat your gas or charcoal grill to medium-high heat (about 450°F). Remove the lamb chops from the marinade, wipe off the marinade, and let them sit at room temperature.

4. Place the lamb chops on the grill and cook until charred on both sides, about 3 minutes per side. Transfer the lamb chops to a platter and let them rest for 10 minutes before serving.

BISTECCA ALLA FIORENTINA

YIELD: **4 SERVINGS**

ACTIVE TIME: **20 MINUTES**

TOTAL TIME: **2 HOURS AND 30 MINUTES**

INGREDIENTS

2 TEASPOONS ONION POWDER

2 TEASPOONS GARLIC POWDER

1 TABLESPOON KOSHER SALT

1 TEASPOON BLACK PEPPER

2½ TO 3 LBS. PORTERHOUSE STEAKS,
AT ROOM TEMPERATURE

2 TABLESPOONS EXTRA-VIRGIN
OLIVE OIL

2 SPRIGS OF FRESH ROSEMARY

2 SPRIGS OF FRESH SAGE

2 SPRIGS OF FRESH THYME

3 TABLESPOONS UNSALTED BUTTER,
MELTED

DIRECTIONS

1. Combine the onion powder, garlic powder, salt, and pepper in a small bowl and set the mixture aside.

2. Brush the steaks with the olive oil and then generously sprinkle the spice mixture over the steaks. Let the steaks sit at room temperature for 2 hours.

3. Preheat your gas or charcoal grill to high heat (about 500°F). Place the steaks on the grill and cook, turning them over once, until their interiors are about 125°F, about 10 minutes. Remove the steaks from the grill and let them rest for 10 minutes before carving and serving. While resting, they will come up to 130°F, which is a perfect medium-rare.

4. Place the fresh herbs and butter in a skillet and melt the butter over medium heat. To serve, pour some of the herb butter over each of the steaks.

PORCHETTA

YIELD: **6 SERVINGS**

ACTIVE TIME: **30 MINUTES**

TOTAL TIME: **2 DAYS**

INGREDIENTS

5- TO 6-LB. SKIN-ON PORK BELLY

1 TABLESPOON FINELY CHOPPED FRESH ROSEMARY

1 TABLESPOON FINELY CHOPPED FRESH THYME

1 TABLESPOON FINELY CHOPPED FRESH SAGE

2 TEASPOONS GARLIC POWDER

SALT, TO TASTE

1-LB. CENTER-CUT PORK TENDERLOIN

DIRECTIONS

1. Place the pork belly skin side down on a cutting board. Using a sharp knife, score the flesh in a cross-hatch pattern, cutting about ¼ inch deep. Flip the pork belly over and poke small holes in the skin. Turn the pork belly back over and rub the herbs, garlic powder, and salt into the scored flesh. Place the pork tenderloin in the center of the pork belly and then roll the pork belly up so that it retains its length. Tie the rolled pork belly securely with kitchen twine every ½ inch.

2. Transfer the pork belly to a rack with a large pan underneath, place it in the fridge, and leave uncovered for 2 days. This allows the skin to dry out a bit. Blot the pork belly occasionally with paper towels to remove excess moisture.

3. Remove the pork belly from the refrigerator and let it stand at room temperature for 1 hour. Preheat the oven to 480°F. When the pork belly is room temperature, place the rack and the pan in the oven and roast for 35 minutes, turning the porchetta occasionally to ensure even cooking.

4. Reduce the oven temperature to 300°F and cook the porchetta until a meat thermometer inserted into the center reaches 145°F, about 1 to 2 hours. The porchetta's skin should be crispy. If it is not as crispy as you'd like, raise the oven's temperature to 500°F and cook until crispy. Remove from the oven and let the porchetta rest for 15 minutes before slicing.

CHICKEN CACCIATORE

YIELD: **6 SERVINGS**

ACTIVE TIME: **25 MINUTES**

TOTAL TIME: **1 HOUR AND 45 MINUTES**

INGREDIENTS

2 LBS. BONE-IN, SKIN-ON CHICKEN THIGHS

SALT AND PEPPER, TO TASTE

2 TABLESPOONS EXTRA-VIRGIN OLIVE OIL

1 LARGE ONION, CHOPPED

1 LB. CANNED, PEELED, AND WHOLE SAN MARZANO TOMATOES, WITH THEIR LIQUID, CRUSHED BY HAND

2 CARROTS, PEELED AND GRATED

4 OZ. BUTTON MUSHROOMS, STEMMED AND CHOPPED

1 CUP MARINARA SAUCE (SEE PAGE 77)

½ CUP DRY WHITE WINE

1 BAY LEAF

1 TEASPOON FRESH THYME

1 TEASPOON CHOPPED FRESH MARJORAM

4 GARLIC CLOVES, MINCED

DIRECTIONS

1. Season the chicken thighs with salt and pepper.

2. Place the olive oil in a large skillet and warm it over medium heat. When the oil starts to shimmer, add the chicken thighs, skin side down, and cook until browned on both sides, about 8 minutes.

3. Add the remaining ingredients and stir to combine. Let the cacciatore simmer until the chicken is very tender and the flavor is to your liking, at least 1 hour.

4. Remove the bay leaf, discard it, and serve the cacciatore.

CHICKEN PARMESAN

YIELD: **6 SERVINGS**

ACTIVE TIME: **25 MINUTES**

TOTAL TIME: **1 HOUR AND 30 MINUTES**

INGREDIENTS

2 LBS. BONELESS, SKINLESS CHICKEN CUTLETS, POUNDED THIN, AT ROOM TEMPERATURE

SALT AND PEPPER, TO TASTE

½ CUP ALL-PURPOSE FLOUR

3 LARGE EGGS

2 CUPS PANKO

½ CUP EXTRA-VIRGIN OLIVE OIL

5 CUPS MARINARA SAUCE (SEE PAGE 77)

1 CUP FRESHLY GRATED PARMESAN CHEESE

½ LB. FRESH MOZZARELLA CHEESE, CHOPPED

DIRECTIONS

1. Preheat the oven to 400°F. Season the chicken breasts with salt and pepper. Place the flour, eggs, and panko in their own shallow bowl. Dip the cutlets in each until evenly coated and then set them aside.

2. Place the oil in a large skillet and warm it over medium-high heat. When the oil starts to shimmer, add the chicken and cook, turning as needed, until browned all over, about 8 minutes. Work in batches if necessary to avoid crowding the skillet. Transfer the browned cutlets to a paper towel–lined plate.

3. Coat the bottom of a 9 x 13–inch baking pan with a thin layer of sauce. Sprinkle one-third of the Parmesan over the sauce, layer half of the cutlets over the cheese, and top them with half of the mozzarella. Spread half of the remaining sauce over the mozzarella, sprinkle another third of the Parmesan over the sauce, and repeat the layering process, ending with a layer of Parmesan on top.

4. Place the pan in the oven and bake until the chicken is cooked through and the cheese is golden brown, about 40 minutes. Remove from the oven and let cool briefly before serving.

SPAGHETTI ALLA GRICIA

YIELD: **4 SERVINGS**

ACTIVE TIME: **10 MINUTES**

TOTAL TIME: **30 MINUTES**

INGREDIENTS

½ LB. GUANCIALE, DICED

½ TEASPOON BLACK PEPPER, PLUS MORE TO TASTE

SALT, TO TASTE

¾ LB. SPAGHETTI

1 TEASPOON EXTRA-VIRGIN OLIVE OIL

⅓ CUP FRESHLY GRATED PECORINO ROMANO CHEESE, PLUS MORE FOR GARNISH

DIRECTIONS

1. Place the guanciale in a large, deep skillet and cook over medium heat, stirring occasionally, until the fat renders and the edges start to brown, about 20 minutes. Stir in the pepper and remove the skillet from the heat.

2. Bring a large pot of water to a boil. Add salt and the pasta and cook 1 minute less than the directed time. Reserve ¾ cup of pasta water, drain the pasta, and return the pot to the stove. Add reserved pasta water and the olive oil, raise the heat to high, add the pasta, and toss to combine.

3. Stir in the guanciale, its rendered fat, and the pecorino and cook, tossing constantly, for 2 minutes. Season with salt and pepper and garnish with additional pecorino.

BUCATINI ALL'AMATRICIANA

YIELD: **4 SERVINGS**

ACTIVE TIME: **15 MINUTES**

TOTAL TIME: **40 MINUTES**

INGREDIENTS

1 TABLESPOON EXTRA-VIRGIN OLIVE OIL, PLUS MORE AS NEEDED

2½ LBS. RIPE PLUM TOMATOES, PEELED, SEEDED, AND CHOPPED

4 OZ. GUANCIALE OR PANCETTA, SLICED

2 DRIED RED CHILI PEPPERS, SEEDED TO TASTE AND CHOPPED

SALT AND PEPPER, TO TASTE

¾ LB. BUCATINI

½ CUP DRY WHITE WINE

2 PINCHES OF SUGAR

½ CUP FRESHLY GRATED PECORINO ROMANO CHEESE, PLUS MORE FOR GARNISH

HANDFUL OF FRESH PARSLEY, CHOPPED, FOR GARNISH

DIRECTIONS

1. Bring a large pot of water to a boil. Place the olive oil in a large, deep skillet and warm it over medium heat. When the oil starts to shimmers, add the tomatoes, guanciale or pancetta, and the chilies and cook until the meat starts to brown, about 6 minutes. Transfer the meat to a small bowl and set it aside.

2. Add salt and the bucatini to the boiling water and cook the pasta 2 minutes less than the directed cooking time.

3. While the pasta is cooking, set the heat under the skillet to medium-high and add the wine. Scrape up all the browned bits stuck to bottom of the pan with a wooden spoon. Cook for 5 minutes, add the sugar, and season with salt and pepper. Cook for 10 minutes, adding a few spoonfuls of the pasta water if the sauce looks too thick.

4. Reserve ¼ cup of the pasta water and drain the pasta. Return the pot to the stove. Add the reserved pasta water, set the heat to high, add the pasta, drizzle it with olive oil, and toss for 1 minute. Transfer the pasta to skillet, sprinkle the pecorino and guanciale or pancetta over it, and cook, tossing to distribute, for 2 minutes. Season the dish with salt and pepper and garnish it with parsley and additional pecorino.

ORECCHIETTE WITH GREENS & POTATOES

YIELD: **4 SERVINGS**

ACTIVE TIME: **20 MINUTES**

TOTAL TIME: **30 MINUTES**

INGREDIENTS

6 TABLESPOONS EXTRA-VIRGIN OLIVE OIL, PLUS 1 TEASPOON

2 GARLIC CLOVES, HALVED

1 TEASPOON CAPERS, RINSED, DRAINED, AND MINCED

½ CUP GREEN OLIVES, PITTED AND MINCED

⅛ TEASPOON CAYENNE PEPPER

2 LARGE RUSSET POTATOES, PEELED AND CHOPPED

SALT AND BLACK PEPPER, TO TASTE

¾ LB. ORECCHIETTE (SEE PAGE 169)

½ LB. FRESH GREENS

¼ CUP FRESHLY GRATED PECORINO ROMANO CHEESE, PLUS MORE FOR GARNISH

DIRECTIONS

1. Place 6 tablespoons of the olive oil in a large, deep skillet and warm it over low heat. When the oil starts to shimmer, add the garlic, capers, olives, and cayenne and sauté until the garlic starts to brown, about 3 minutes. Discard the garlic and remove the pan from heat.

2. Bring a pot of water to a boil and add salt and the potatoes. Boil for 10 minutes, add the pasta and greens, and cook for 2 minutes. Reserve ½ cup of the pasta water, drain, and return the pot to the stove.

3. Set the skillet containing the sauce over medium-high heat. Add reserved pasta water to the pan, turn heat to high, and add the pasta, potatoes, greens, and the remaining olive oil. Toss until the water has been absorbed. Add the pecorino and toss until distributed. Season the dish with salt and pepper and garnish with additional pecorino before serving.

SPAGHETTI & MEATBALLS

YIELD: **6 SERVINGS**

ACTIVE TIME: **40 MINUTES**

TOTAL TIME: **1 HOUR**

INGREDIENTS

2 TABLESPOONS EXTRA-VIRGIN OLIVE OIL

1 SMALL ONION, MINCED

3 GARLIC CLOVES, MINCED

¼ TEASPOON RED PEPPER FLAKES

1 LARGE EGG

2 TABLESPOONS WHOLE MILK

½ CUP ITALIAN BREAD CRUMBS

¼ CUP FRESHLY GRATED PARMESAN CHEESE

¼ CUP GRATED FRESH MOZZARELLA CHEESE

2 TABLESPOONS FINELY CHOPPED FRESH PARSLEY

1 TEASPOON ITALIAN SEASONING

½ LB. GROUND PORK

½ LB. GROUND BEEF

¼ LB. GROUND VEAL

SALT AND PEPPER, TO TASTE

1 LB. SPAGHETTI

2 CUPS MARINARA SAUCE (SEE PAGE 77)

DIRECTIONS

1. Preheat the broiler to high, position a rack so that the tops of the meatballs will be approximately 6 inches below the broiler, and line a rimmed baking sheet with aluminum foil.

2. Place the oil in a large skillet and warm over medium-high heat. When it starts to shimmer, add the onion, garlic, and red pepper flakes and sauté until the onion is translucent, about 3 minutes. Remove the pan from heat and set it aside.

3. Place the egg, milk, bread crumbs, Parmesan, mozzarella, parsley, and Italian seasoning in a mixing bowl and stir until combined. Add the pork, beef, veal, and the onion mixture, season with salt and pepper, and stir until thoroughly combined. Working with wet hands, form the mixture into 1½-inch meatballs, arrange them on the baking sheet, and spray the tops with cooking spray.

4. Place the meatballs in the oven and broil until browned all over, turning them as they cook. Remove the meatballs from the oven and set them aside.

5. While the meatballs are in the oven, bring water to a boil in a large saucepan. Add salt and the spaghetti and cook until the pasta is al dente, about 8 minutes.

6. Place the sauce in the skillet and warm it over medium heat. Add the meatballs to the sauce, reduce the heat to low, cover the pan, and simmer, turning the meatballs occasionally, until they are cooked through, about 15 minutes.

7. Drain the pasta and divide it between the serving plates. Ladle the sauce and meatballs over the top and serve.

BUTTERNUT SQUASH RAVIOLI

YIELD: **4 SERVINGS**

ACTIVE TIME: **30 MINUTES**

TOTAL TIME: **1 HOUR AND 30 MINUTES**

INGREDIENTS

1½ LBS. BUTTERNUT SQUASH, HALVED LENGTHWISE AND SEEDED

EXTRA-VIRGIN OLIVE OIL, AS NEEDED

¼ CUP FRESH BREAD CRUMBS

½ CUP FRESHLY GRATED PARMESAN CHEESE, PLUS MORE FOR GARNISH

¼ CUP CRUMBLED GORGONZOLA CHEESE

2 EGG YOLKS, BEATEN

1 TEASPOON FRESHLY GRATED NUTMEG

10 FRESH ROSEMARY LEAVES, FINELY CHOPPED

RAVIOLI (SEE PAGE 162)

SALT, TO TASTE

FONTINA SAUCE (SEE PAGE 90), FOR SERVING

DIRECTIONS

1. Preheat the oven to 375°F. Brush the flesh of the squash with olive oil and place them, cut side up, on parchment-lined baking sheets. Place the squash in the oven and roast until fork-tender, 40 to 45 minutes. Remove from the oven and let cool, then scoop the flesh into a bowl and mash until smooth. Add the bread crumbs, cheeses, egg yolks, nutmeg, and rosemary to the squash and stir until thoroughly combined.

2. Bring a large saucepan of water to a boil and make the ravioli as instructed, filling the depressions with the butternut squash mixture.

3. When the water is boiling, add salt and the ravioli, stir to make sure they do not stick to the bottom, and cook until tender but still chewy, about 2 minutes. Drain, divide them between the serving plates, drizzle the Fontina Sauce over the top, and garnish with additional Parmesan.

344

YIELD: **6 SERVINGS**

ACTIVE TIME: **35 MINUTES**

TOTAL TIME: **1 HOUR**

INGREDIENTS

5 TABLESPOONS EXTRA-VIRGIN OLIVE OIL, PLUS MORE AS NEEDED

10 SCALLIONS, TRIMMED AND SLICED THIN

SALT, TO TASTE

1 LB. CREMINI MUSHROOMS, STEMMED AND MINCED

1 LB. EXTRA-FIRM TOFU, DRAINED AND CUT INTO ½-INCH SLICES

4 CUPS SHREDDED CABBAGE

4 CARROTS, PEELED AND GRATED

3 TABLESPOONS WATER

2 TABLESPOONS SUGAR

1 TEASPOON WHITE PEPPER

4 TEASPOONS CORNSTARCH

ALL-YOLK PASTA DOUGH (SEE PAGES 158–159), ROLLED ¹⁄₁₆ INCH THICK AND CUT INTO 15-INCH SHEETS

2 HANDFULS OF FRESH PARSLEY, CHOPPED, PLUS MORE FOR GARNISH

2 CUPS MARINARA SAUCE (SEE PAGE 77), WARMED

VEGETARIAN ROTOLO

DIRECTIONS

1. Place the olive oil in a large skillet and warm it over medium heat. When it begins to shimmer, add the scallions and a pinch of salt and sauté until the scallions are translucent, about 3 minutes. Raise the heat to medium-high, add the mushrooms, tofu, cabbage, and carrots and sauté until all the vegetables start to soften, about 5 minutes.

2. Place 2 tablespoons of the water, the sugar, and pepper in a small bowl. Place the cornstarch and the remaining water in another bowl, whisk it until smooth, and then whisk it into the water-and-sugar mixture. Stir the resulting mixture into the skillet and raise the heat to high. Cook until the liquid has evaporated and the vegetables are cooked through, about 2 minutes. Remove the pan from heat and let the mixture cool slightly. Transfer it to a food processor and pulse until it is a chunky puree. Season with salt and set it aside.

3. Bring a large pot of water to a boil. Once it's boiling, add salt and add a single sheet of pasta. Cook for 1 minute, retrieve the sheet using two large slotted spoons, transfer to a kitchen towel and let it cool. Repeat until all the pasta sheets have been cooked.

4. Preheat the oven to 475°F. Generously grease a 15 x 10–inch baking pan with olive oil. Working with one pasta sheet at a time, lay it on a work surface covered with parchment paper. Using a rubber spatula, spread some of the puree over the sheet and sprinkle some of the parsley on top. Starting at one short end, roll the sheet up tightly. Once you are done rolling, rest it on its seam to keep it from unrolling, or secure the roll with toothpicks. When all of the pasta sheets and filling have been used up, slice each roll into 1¼-inch-thick rounds. Place them, cut side down, in the baking dish, making sure to leave space between. Place the pan in the oven and bake until lightly browned on top and heated through, 10 to 12 minutes.

5. To serve, place 2 to 3 tablespoons of the sauce on a warm plate, arrange three rotolo slices on top, and garnish with additional parsley.

ROASTED CHICKEN, ITALIAN STYLE

YIELD: **4 SERVINGS**

ACTIVE TIME: **10 MINUTES**

TOTAL TIME: **1 HOUR**

INGREDIENTS

3 TO 4 LB. CHICKEN

SALT AND PEPPER, TO TASTE

EXTRA-VIRGIN OLIVE OIL, AS NEEDED

3 SPRIGS OF FRESH ROSEMARY

3 SPRIGS OF FRESH THYME

3 SPRIGS OF FRESH MARJORAM

1 LEMON, HALVED

DIRECTIONS

1. Preheat the oven to 450°F and place a cast-iron skillet in the oven as it warms. Rinse the chicken, inside and outside, and pat it dry with paper towels. This step is important because it ensures that the chicken roasts rather than steams.

2. Season with chicken generously, inside and outside, with salt and pepper. Drizzle olive oil over the chicken and rub it over the exterior. Place the fresh herbs and lemon in the chicken's cavity.

3. Put on oven mitts, remove the skillet from the oven, and place the chicken, breast side down, in the pan.

4. Place the pan in the oven and roast for 20 minutes. Reduce the oven's temperature to 350°F and roast until a meat thermometer inserted in the breast registers 165°F, about 35 minutes. Remove from the oven, baste the chicken with the pan juices, and let it rest for 15 minutes before carving and serving.

EGGPLANT PARMESAN

YIELD: **4 SERVINGS**

ACTIVE TIME: **20 MINUTES**

TOTAL TIME: **1 HOUR**

INGREDIENTS

1 LARGE EGGPLANT

SALT, TO TASTE

2 TABLESPOONS EXTRA-VIRGIN OLIVE OIL

1 CUP ITALIAN BREAD CRUMBS

¼ CUP FRESHLY GRATED PARMESAN CHEESE

1 EGG, BEATEN

MARINARA SAUCE (SEE PAGE 77), AS NEEDED

2 GARLIC CLOVES, MINCED

½ LB. SHREDDED MOZZARELLA CHEESE

FRESH BASIL, FINELY CHOPPED, FOR GARNISH

DIRECTIONS

1. Preheat the oven to 350°F. Trim the top and bottom off the eggplant and slice it into ¼-inch-thick slices. Put the slices on paper towels in a single layer, sprinkle salt over them, and let rest for about 15 minutes. Turn the slices over, salt the other side, and let them rest for another 15 minutes. Rinse the eggplant and pat dry with paper towels.

2. Drizzle the oil over a baking sheet. In a shallow bowl, combine the bread crumbs and Parmesan cheese. Put the beaten egg in another shallow bowl. Dip the slices of eggplant in the egg and then in the bread crumb-and-cheese mixture until both sides are coated. Place the breaded slices on the baking sheet.

3. When all of the eggplant has been breaded, place it in the oven and bake for 10 minutes. Remove, turn the slices over, and bake for another 10 minutes. Remove the eggplant from the oven and let it cool slightly.

4. Place a layer of sauce in a square 8-inch baking dish or a cast-iron skillet and stir in the garlic. Lay some of the eggplant slices on top of the sauce, top them with more sauce, and then arrange the remaining eggplant on top. Sprinkle the mozzarella over the eggplant.

5. Place the dish in the oven and bake for about 30 minutes, until the sauce is bubbling and the cheese is golden brown. Remove from the oven and let cool for 10 minutes before topping with additional Marinara Sauce and fresh basil.

RIGATONI WITH CHICKPEAS

YIELD: **4 SERVINGS**

ACTIVE TIME: **20 MINUTES**

TOTAL TIME: **1 HOUR**

INGREDIENTS

3 TABLESPOONS OLIVE OIL,
PLUS 1 TEASPOON

¼ CUP DICED PANCETTA

4 YELLOW ONIONS, SLICED THIN

SALT AND PEPPER, TO TASTE

1 TABLESPOON BALSAMIC VINEGAR

¾ LB. RIGATONI

1 (14 OZ.) CAN OF CHICKPEAS,
DRAINED AND RINSED

FRESH ROSEMARY, FINELY CHOPPED,
FOR GARNISH

DIRECTIONS

1. Add the 3 tablespoons of olive oil to a large skillet and warm over medium heat. When the oil starts to shimmer, add the pancetta and sauté until it begins to brown, about 5 minutes. Transfer the pancetta to a bowl and set it aside. Reduce the heat to medium-low, add the onions, and cook, stirring frequently, until the onions are caramelized, about 40 minutes. Season with salt and pepper and stir in the balsamic vinegar. Remove the pan from heat and cover it.

2. Bring a large pot of water to a boil. Add salt, the pasta, and chickpeas and cook 2 minutes short of the directed cooking time for the pasta. Reserve ¼ cup of the pasta water and drain the pasta and chickpeas. Return the empty pot to the stove, turn the heat to high, add the remaining olive oil and the reserved pasta water. Add the pasta and chickpeas and toss to combine. Stir in the pancetta and the onions and cook until the water has been absorbed, about 2 minutes. Garnish with the rosemary before serving.

SPAGHETTI ALLA SERENA

YIELD: **4 SERVINGS**

ACTIVE TIME: **45 MINUTES**

TOTAL TIME: **1 HOUR AND 15 MINUTES**

INGREDIENTS

⅔ CUP MADEIRA WINE

8½ TABLESPOONS UNSALTED BUTTER

1 LB. CREMINI MUSHROOMS, QUARTERED

SALT AND WHITE PEPPER, TO TASTE

2 TABLESPOONS EXTRA-VIRGIN OLIVE OIL

1 SMALL YELLOW ONION, GRATED

1 RED BELL PEPPER, STEMMED, SEEDS AND RIBS REMOVED, AND SLICED THIN

1 CUP WHOLE MILK

1½ CUPS GRATED GRUYÈRE CHEESE

2 CUPS COOKED CHICKEN BREAST, SHREDDED

HANDFUL OF FRESH PARSLEY LEAVES, CHOPPED, PLUS MORE FOR GARNISH

¾ LB. SPAGHETTI

PARMESAN CHEESE, FRESHLY GRATED, FOR GARNISH

DIRECTIONS

1. Place the wine in a small saucepan, bring it to a boil, and cook until reduced by half, about 5 minutes. Remove pan from the stove and set the reduced wine aside.

2. Place 2 tablespoons of the butter in a large skillet and melt it over medium-high heat. Add half of the mushrooms and a pinch of salt and sauté until the mushrooms have softened and started to brown, about 8 minutes. Transfer to a bowl and cover it with aluminum foil. Melt another 2 tablespoons of the butter in the pan, add the remaining mushrooms, season them with salt, and sauté until they have softened and started to brown. Transfer them to the bowl containing the other mushrooms.

3. Bring a large pot of water to a boil. Add the olive oil to the skillet, reduce the heat to medium, and warm for 1 minute. Add the onion and sauté until it is translucent, about 3 minutes. Add the bell pepper and sauté until it is soft, about 10 minutes. Raise the heat to medium-high and cook until the bell pepper starts to brown, about 4 minutes.

4. Stir in the mushrooms, reduced wine, and the milk, bring to a boil, and reduce the heat to low. Add the remaining butter and the Gruyère and stir until melted. Add the chicken and parsley, season with salt and pepper, and cook, stirring occasionally, until the chicken is heated through.

5. Add salt and the pasta to the boiling water and cook 1 minute short of the directed time. Reserve ½ cup of pasta water, drain the pasta, and return the pot to the stove. Add the reserved pasta water, turn the heat to high, add the pasta, and cook until it has absorbed the water. Transfer the pasta to the skillet and toss to combine. Season to taste and garnish with additional parsley and Parmesan.

PENNE WITH CLAMS & CALAMARI

YIELD: **4 SERVINGS**

ACTIVE TIME: **25 MINUTES**

TOTAL TIME: **30 MINUTES**

INGREDIENTS

¾ LB. SQUID BODIES AND TENTACLES, SLICED THIN

SALT AND PEPPER, TO TASTE

¼ CUP EXTRA-VIRGIN OLIVE OIL, PLUS 1 TEASPOON

3 LARGE, RIPE PLUM TOMATOES, PEELED, SEEDED, AND CHOPPED

2 GARLIC CLOVES, SLICED THIN

3½ LBS. SMALL HARD-SHELL CLAMS, SCRUBBED AND RINSED

¾ LB. PENNE

2 HANDFULS OF FRESH PARSLEY, CHOPPED, FOR GARNISH

DIRECTIONS

1. Place the squid in a colander, rinse it, let it drain, and pat dry. Season with salt and pepper, toss, and set it aside.

2. Bring a large pot of water to a boil. Place the ¼ cup of olive oil in a large, deep skillet and warm it over medium-high heat. When the oil starts to shimmer, add the tomatoes and garlic, season with salt, and cook for 5 minutes. Add the squid and clams and cook, stirring occasionally, until a few of the clams open. Remove the pan from heat and cover it. Let it sit for 5 minutes, remove the cover, and discard any clams that did not open.

3. Add salt and the penne to the boiling water and cook 2 minutes less than the directed cooking time. Reserve ½ cup of the pasta water, drain the pasta, and return the pot to the stove. Raise the heat to high and add the remaining oil and the reserved pasta water. Add the pasta, toss to combine, and then add the contents of the skillet. Cook, tossing to distribute, for 2 minutes and garnish with the parsley before serving.

PASTA PRIMAVERA

YIELD: **6 SERVINGS**

ACTIVE TIME: **35 MINUTES**

TOTAL TIME: **1 HOUR**

INGREDIENTS

6½ TABLESPOONS UNSALTED BUTTER

1 CUP PANKO

SALT AND PEPPER, TO TASTE

1 YELLOW BELL PEPPER, STEMMED, SEEDS AND RIBS REMOVED, AND SLICED

3 TABLESPOONS EXTRA-VIRGIN OLIVE OIL

2 MEDIUM CARROTS, PEELED AND SLICED THIN

1½ CUPS HEAVY CREAM

¼ TEASPOON WORCESTERSHIRE SAUCE

1 CUP PEAS

1½ CUPS FRESHLY GRATED PARMESAN CHEESE, PLUS MORE FOR GARNISH

1 TEASPOON FRESHLY GRATED NUTMEG

¾ LB. PASTA

1 CUP CHERRY TOMATOES, HALVED

2 HANDFULS OF FRESH PARSLEY, CHOPPED, FOR GARNISH

2 HANDFULS OF FRESH BASIL, CHOPPED, FOR GARNISH

DIRECTIONS

1. Preheat the oven to 400°F. Place 2 tablespoons of the butter in a large skillet and melt it over medium heat. Add the panko and cook, stirring constantly, until they are a dark golden brown, 4 to 5 minutes. Transfer the panko to a bowl, season with salt and pepper, and stir to combine.

2. Place the bell pepper in a large bowl, drizzle with 2 tablespoons of the oil, and toss until evenly coated. Transfer to a parchment-lined baking sheet and spread it out in a single layer. Add the carrots to the same large bowl, drizzle with the remaining oil, and toss until evenly coated. Transfer to another parchment-lined baking sheet and spread them out in a single layer. Place both baking sheets in the oven. Roast the pepper, stirring once about halfway through, until softened and browned, 10 to 12 minutes. Roast the carrots, stirring once about halfway through, until fork-tender and lightly browned, 15 to 18 minutes. Remove from the oven, season with salt and pepper, and set the vegetables aside.

3. While the vegetables are roasting, bring a large pot of water to a boil. Combine the cream, Worcestershire sauce, and 4 tablespoons of the butter in a medium saucepan and warm over medium-low heat until the butter melts. Gently stir in the peas and Parmesan, season with salt and pepper, and add the nutmeg. Bring to a gentle simmer and cook until the sauce thickens slightly, about 2 to 3 minutes. Remove from the heat, cover the pan, and set it aside.

4. Once the water is boiling, add salt and the pasta and cook 2 minutes short of the directed time. Reserve ¼ cup of pasta water, drain the pasta, and return the pot to the stove. Add reserved pasta water and the remaining butter, raise the heat to high, add the pasta, and cook, tossing to combine, until the water has been absorbed. Stir in the cherry tomatoes, the contents of the skillet, and the roasted vegetables and cook, while gently tossing to combine, for 2 minutes. Top the dish with the toasted panko and garnish with the parsley, basil, and additional Parmesan.

SPAGHETTI ALLA CARBONARA

YIELD: **4 SERVINGS**

ACTIVE TIME: **15 MINUTES**

TOTAL TIME: **30 MINUTES**

INGREDIENTS

2½ TABLESPOONS EXTRA-VIRGIN OLIVE OIL

4 OZ. PANCETTA, DICED

SALT AND PEPPER, TO TASTE

2 LARGE EGGS, AT ROOM TEMPERATURE

¾ CUP FRESHLY GRATED PARMESAN CHEESE, PLUS MORE FOR GARNISH

1 LB. SPAGHETTI

DIRECTIONS

1. Bring a large saucepan of water to a boil. Add 2 tablespoons of the olive oil to a large skillet and warm it over medium heat. When the oil starts to shimmer, add the pancetta, and season it with pepper. Sauté the pancetta until its fat renders and the meat starts turning golden brown, about 5 minutes. Remove the skillet from heat and cover it partially.

2. Place the eggs in a small bowl and whisk until scrambled. Add the Parmesan, season with salt and pepper, and stir until combined.

3. Add salt and the pasta to the boiling water. Cook 2 minutes short of the directed cooking time, reserve ¼ cup of the pasta water, and drain the pasta. Return the pot to the stove, raise the heat to high, and add the remaining olive oil and the reserved pasta water. Add the drained pasta and toss to combine. Cook until the pasta has absorbed the water. Remove the pot from heat, add the pancetta and the egg-and-Parmesan mixture, and toss to coat the pasta. Divide the pasta between the serving bowls, season with pepper, and top each portion with additional Parmesan.

PENNE ALLA VODKA

YIELD: **6 SERVINGS**

ACTIVE TIME: **40 MINUTES**

TOTAL TIME: **1 HOUR**

INGREDIENTS

2½ TABLESPOONS UNSALTED BUTTER

4 OZ. PANCETTA, DICED

3 SHALLOTS, MINCED

SALT, TO TASTE

1 (28 OZ.) CAN OF PEELED WHOLE SAN MARZANO TOMATOES, DRAINED AND PUREED

1 TEASPOON RED PEPPER FLAKES

1 CUP HEAVY CREAM

1¼ LBS. PENNE

½ CUP VODKA, AT ROOM TEMPERATURE

1 CUP FRESHLY GRATED PARMESAN CHEESE, PLUS MORE FOR GARNISH

2 HANDFULS OF FRESH PARSLEY, CHOPPED, FOR GARNISH

DIRECTIONS

1. Place 2 tablespoons of the butter in a large skillet and melt it over medium heat. Add the pancetta and sauté until the pieces are browned and crispy, 8 to 10 minutes. Transfer to a small bowl and set aside. Add the shallots and a pinch of salt, reduce the heat to low, cover the pan, and cook, stirring occasionally, until the shallots are soft, about 10 minutes.

2. Add the tomatoes and red pepper flakes to the skillet, season with salt, and raise the heat to medium-high. Once the mixture begins to boil, reduce the heat to low, partially cover the pan, and cook until the sauce thickens slightly, 15 to 20 minutes. Add the cream and heat through until the sauce gently bubbles. Remove from heat and cover the pan.

3. Bring a large pot of water to a boil, add salt and the pasta, and cook 2 minutes short of the directed time. Reserve ¼ cup of pasta water, drain, and return the pot to the stove. Add the reserved pasta water and remaining butter, turn heat to high, add the pasta, and cook, tossing to combine, until the pasta has absorbed the water. Add the sauce and the Parmesan to the pot and toss to combine. Top the dish with the pancetta and garnish with the parsley and additional Parmesan.

SWEET POTATO GNOCCHI WITH SAGE BROWN BUTTER

YIELD: **6 SERVINGS**

ACTIVE TIME: **20 MINUTES**

TOTAL TIME: **40 MINUTES**

INGREDIENTS

SWEET POTATO GNOCCHI
(SEE PAGE 185)

EXTRA-VIRGIN OLIVE OIL, AS
NEEDED

1 STICK OF UNSALTED BUTTER

1 TABLESPOON FINELY CHOPPED
FRESH SAGE

2 CUPS ARUGULA

½ CUP WALNUTS, TOASTED AND
CHOPPED

DIRECTIONS

1. Bring a large pot of water to a boil. Working in small batches, add the gnocchi to the boiling water and stir to keep them from sticking to the bottom. The gnocchi will eventually float to the surface. Cook for 1 more minute, remove, and transfer to a bowl coated with the olive oil. Toss to coat and transfer to a parchment-lined baking sheet to cool.

2. Place the butter in a skillet and warm over medium heat until it begins to brown. Add the sage and cook until the bubbles start to dissipate. Place the arugula in a bowl and set it aside.

3. Working in batches, add the gnocchi to the skillet, stir to coat, and cook until they have a nice sear on one side. Transfer to the bowl of arugula and toss to combine. Serve and top each portion with the toasted walnuts.

TAGLIATELLE WITH ASPARAGUS & PEAS

YIELD: **4 SERVINGS**

ACTIVE TIME: **15 MINUTES**

TOTAL TIME: **25 MINUTES**

INGREDIENTS

SALT, TO TASTE

1 BUNCH OF ASPARAGUS, TRIMMED AND CHOPPED

½ LB. SNAP PEAS, TRIMMED AND CHOPPED

TAGLIATELLE (SEE PAGES 156–157)

4 TABLESPOONS UNSALTED BUTTER

¼ CUP FRESHLY GRATED PARMESAN CHEESE

½ TEASPOON RED PEPPER FLAKES

DIRECTIONS

1. Bring water to a boil in a medium saucepan and also in a large saucepan. Add salt to each of the saucepans once the water is boiling. Place the asparagus and peas in the medium saucepan and cook for 1 minute. Drain and set aside.

2. Place the pasta in the large saucepan and cook for 3 to 4 minutes, stirring constantly. Reserve ¼ cup of the pasta water and then drain the pasta.

3. Place the butter in a large skillet and melt over medium heat. Add the pasta and vegetables and toss to combine. Add the reserved pasta water, Parmesan, and red pepper flakes and toss to evenly coat. Season to taste and serve.

BUTTERNUT SQUASH CANNELLONI

YIELD: **8 SERVINGS**

ACTIVE TIME: **1 HOUR**

TOTAL TIME: **1 HOUR AND 30 MINUTES**

INGREDIENTS

FOR THE FILLING

2 LBS. BUTTERNUT SQUASH, HALVED AND SEEDED

5 TABLESPOONS EXTRA-VIRGIN OLIVE OIL

5 GARLIC CLOVES, MINCED

1½ CUPS RICOTTA CHEESE

1 CUP FRESHLY GRATED PARMESAN CHEESE

12 FRESH SAGE LEAVES, SLICED THIN

1 TEASPOON FRESHLY GRATED NUTMEG

SALT AND WHITE PEPPER, TO TASTE

FOR THE CANNELLONI

ALL-YOLK PASTA DOUGH (SEE PAGES 158–159)

SEMOLINA FLOUR, FOR DUSTING

SALT, TO TASTE

1½ TEASPOONS EXTRA-VIRGIN OLIVE OIL, PLUS MORE AS NEEDED

DIRECTIONS

1. To begin preparations for the filling, preheat the oven to 375°F. Brush the flesh of the squash with 1 tablespoon of the olive oil and place the squash on a parchment-lined baking sheet, cut side down. Place the baking sheet in the oven and roast until the squash is fork-tender, 40 to 45 minutes. Remove the squash from the oven and let it cool. When it is cool enough to handle, scoop the flesh into a wide, shallow bowl and mash it until it is smooth.

2. Place the remaining olive oil in a large skillet and warm over medium heat. When the oil starts to shimmer, add the garlic and sauté for 1 minute. Remove the pan from heat, and transfer the garlic and oil to the bowl with the mashed squash. Add the cheeses, half of the sage, the nutmeg, season the mixture with salt and pepper, and stir to combine.

3. To begin preparations for the cannelloni, run the dough through a pasta maker until the sheets are about ¹⁄₁₆ inch thick. Lay the sheets on lightly floured, parchment paper–lined baking sheets. Working with one sheet at a time, place it on a flour-dusted work surface in front of you. Using a pastry cutter, cut each sheet into as many 4½- to 5-inch squares as possible. Place the finished squares on another flour-dusted, parchment-lined baking sheet so they don't touch. As you run out of room, lightly dust them with flour, cover with another sheet of parchment, and arrange more squares on top of that. Repeat with all the pasta sheets. Gather any scraps together into a ball, put it through the pasta maker to create additional pasta sheets, and cut those as well.

Continued...

4. Bring a large pot of water to a boil. Once it's boiling, add salt and stir to dissolve. Add the squares and cook until they are just tender, about 2 minutes. Drain, rinse under cold water, and toss with a teaspoon of olive oil to keep them from sticking together.

5. Generously coat a baking dish large enough to fit all the filled cannelloni in a single layer with olive oil. To fill the cannelloni, place a pasta square in front of you. Place ¼ cup of the squash mixture in the center of the square and shape

it into a rough cylinder. Roll the pasta square around the filling and transfer it to the prepared baking dish, seam side down. Repeat with remaining sheets and filling. When the baking dish is filled, brush the tops of the cannelloni with the remaining olive oil.

6. Preheat the oven to 375°F and place a rack in the center position. Put the baking dish in the oven and bake until the cannelloni are very hot and begin to turn golden brown, about 20 minutes. Top with the remaining sage and serve.

CLASSIC LASAGNA

YIELD: **6 SERVINGS**

ACTIVE TIME: **25 MINUTES**

TOTAL TIME: **1 HOUR AND 30 MINUTES**

INGREDIENTS

¾ LB. ALL-YOLK PASTA DOUGH (SEE PAGES 158–159)

1 TABLESPOON KOSHER SALT, PLUS MORE TO TASTE

1½ LBS. RICOTTA CHEESE

2 EGGS

1½ CUPS SHREDDED ITALIAN CHEESE BLEND (EQUAL PARTS ASIAGO, FONTINA, MOZZARELLA, PROVOLONE, PARMESAN, AND ROMANO), PLUS MORE FOR TOPPING

½ TEASPOON BLACK PEPPER

½ TEASPOON ONION POWDER

½ TEASPOON GARLIC POWDER

PINCH OF FRESHLY GRATED NUTMEG

1 TABLESPOON FINELY CHOPPED FRESH BASIL

1 TEASPOON DRIED OREGANO

½ CUP CHOPPED FRESH PARSLEY

2 CUPS BOLOGNESE SAUCE (SEE PAGE 101), PLUS MORE AS NEEDED

DIRECTIONS

1. Preheat the oven to 350°F. Divide the dough into four pieces and run them through a pasta maker until they are ⅟₁₆ inch thick. Cut the pieces into 14-inch-long sheets and place them on a flour-dusted, parchment-lined baking sheet. Gather any scraps into a ball, run this through the pasta maker, and cut into additional lasagna sheets.

2. Place all of the remaining ingredients in a mixing bowl and stir to combine.

3. Cover the bottom of a 9 x 13–inch baking dish with some sauce. Place a layer of lasagna noodles on top and cover them with one-third of the bolognese-and-cheese mixture. Alternate layers of the noodles and the mixture until all of the mixture has been used up. Top with another layer of noodles and spread a thin layer of sauce over them.

4. Place the dish in the oven and bake for 45 minutes. Remove from the oven, sprinkle more of the cheese blend on top, and return to the oven. Bake until the cheese has melted and is starting to brown, about 5 minutes. Remove the lasagna from the oven and let it stand for 20 minutes before slicing and serving.

PORCINI MUSHROOM & BÉCHAMEL LASAGNA

YIELD: **6 SERVINGS**

ACTIVE TIME: **1 HOUR**

TOTAL TIME: **2 HOURS**

INGREDIENTS

1 CUP DRY RED WINE

¾ LB. ALL-YOLK PASTA DOUGH (SEE PAGES 158–159)

2 TABLESPOONS UNSALTED BUTTER

3 SHALLOTS, MINCED

SALT AND PEPPER, TO TASTE

2 GARLIC CLOVES, PEELED AND MINCED

1 LB. CREMINI MUSHROOMS, STEMMED AND SLICED THIN

1 OZ. DRIED PORCINI MUSHROOMS, RECONSTITUTED AND CHOPPED, SOAKING LIQUID RESERVED

2 TABLESPOONS FINELY CHOPPED FRESH THYME, PLUS MORE FOR GARNISH

BÉCHAMEL SAUCE (SEE SIDEBAR)

½ LB. DRIED LASAGNA NOODLES

1½ CUPS FRESHLY GRATED PARMESAN CHEESE

DIRECTIONS

1. Place the wine in a small saucepan and bring it to a boil. Cook until it has reduced almost by half, about 5 minutes. Remove the pan from heat and set it aside.

2. Preheat the oven to 350°F. Divide the dough into four pieces and run them through a pasta maker until they are 1⁄16 inch thick. Cut the pieces into 14-inch-long sheets and place them on a flour-dusted, parchment-lined baking sheet. Gather any scraps into a ball, run this through the pasta maker, and cut into additional lasagna sheets.

3. Place the butter in a large, deep skillet and melt it over medium heat. Add the shallots and a pinch of salt and sauté until the shallots are translucent, about 3 minutes. Reduce the temperature to low, cover the pan, and cook, stirring occasionally, until the shallots have softened, about 10 minutes. Stir in the garlic and sauté for 30 seconds.

4. Raise the heat to medium-high, add the cremini and porcini mushrooms and the thyme, season with salt, and cook, while stirring frequently, until the mushrooms begin to release their liquid, about 5 minutes. Add the reduced wine and the porcini soaking liquid and bring to a gentle simmer. Cook, stirring occasionally, until the mushrooms are tender and the liquid has reduced by half, 12 to 15 minutes. Remove from the heat, season to taste, and then stir in the Béchamel Sauce.

Continued...

5. Cover the bottom of a deep 9 x 13–inch baking pan with some of the mushroom mixture. Cover with a layer of noodles, making sure they are slightly overlapping. Cover with a layer of the mushroom mixture and sprinkle ½ cup of the Parmesan on top. Repeat this layering two more times, concluding with a layer of the mushroom mixture topped with the remaining Parmesan.

Cover the pan loosely with aluminum foil, place in the oven, and bake for 35 minutes. Remove the foil and continue to bake until the edges of the lasagna sheets are lightly browned, about 12 minutes. For nice, clean slices, remove the lasagna from the oven and allow it to rest for at least 20 minutes before slicing.

PICI WITH CRISPY ANCHOVY BREADCRUMBS

YIELD: **4 SERVINGS**

ACTIVE TIME: **10 MINUTES**

TOTAL TIME: **25 MINUTES**

INGREDIENTS

⅓ CUP EXTRA-VIRGIN OLIVE OIL, PLUS 2½ TABLESPOONS

10 ANCHOVY FILLETS, BONED

2 CUPS BREAD CRUMBS

SALT AND PEPPER, TO TASTE

¾ LB. PICI (SEE PAGE 193)

2 HANDFULS OF FRESH PARSLEY, CHOPPED, FOR GARNISH

DIRECTIONS

1. Bring a large pot of water to a boil. Place the ⅓ cup of olive oil in a large skillet and warm over medium heat. When the oil starts to shimmer, add the anchovy fillets, mash them with a fork, and cook until they disintegrate, about 3 minutes.

2. Raise the heat to medium-high and stir in the bread crumbs. Cook until they are golden brown, about 3 minutes, and remove the skillet from heat. Season the mixture with salt and pepper and set it aside.

3. Add salt and the pasta to the boiling water and cook for 2 minutes less than the pasta's directed cooking time. Reserve ½ cup of the cooking water, drain, return the empty pot to the stove, and raise the heat to high. Add the remaining oil and reserved pasta water and stir to combine. Add the drained pasta and cook, tossing continuously, for 2 minutes. Transfer the pasta to a warm bowl. Top with the warm anchovy-and-breadcrumb mixture, toss to combine, and garnish with the parsley.

   TIP: For best results, use day-old bread that is not rock hard to make the bread crumbs, and consider using salt-packed anchovies.

FETTUCCINE ALFREDO

YIELD: **4 SERVINGS**

ACTIVE TIME: **15 MINUTES**

TOTAL TIME: **20 MINUTES**

INGREDIENTS

SALT AND PEPPER, TO TASTE

¾ LB. FETTUCCINE (SEE PAGES 156–157)

½ CUP HEAVY CREAM

2½ TABLESPOONS UNSALTED BUTTER, AT ROOM TEMPERATURE

1 CUP FRESHLY GRATED PARMESAN CHEESE, PLUS MORE FOR GARNISH

½ TEASPOON FRESHLY GRATED NUTMEG

DIRECTIONS

1. Bring a large pot of water to a boil. Once it's boiling, add salt and the fettuccine and cook for 2 minutes. Reserve ½ cup of pasta water and drain the pasta.

2. Place the reserved pasta water and heavy cream in a large skillet and bring it to a simmer. Add the butter and stir until it has been emulsified. Gradually incorporate the Parmesan, making sure each addition has melted before adding the next.

3. Add the fettuccine to the skillet and toss to combine. Sprinkle the nutmeg over the top before serving.

YIELD: **4 SERVINGS**

ACTIVE TIME: **45 MINUTES**

TOTAL TIME: **1 HOUR AND 30 MINUTES**

INGREDIENTS

1½ LBS. SARDINE FILLETS, BONED

½ CUP GOLDEN RAISINS

⅓ CUP PINE NUTS

SALT AND PEPPER, TO TASTE

1 HANDFUL OF FENNEL FRONDS

5 TABLESPOONS EXTRA-VIRGIN
OLIVE OIL, PLUS MORE AS NEEDED

1 SMALL YELLOW ONION, HALVED
AND SLICED THIN

5 ANCHOVY FILLETS IN OLIVE OIL,
BONED AND CHOPPED

½ TEASPOON FENNEL SEEDS

¾ LB. SPAGHETTI

PASTA CON LE SARDE

DIRECTIONS

1. Wash the sardine fillets under cold water and pat dry with paper towels. Chop half of the fillets into 1-inch pieces and leave the remainder whole.

2. Place the raisins in a small bowl, cover them with warm water, and soak for 10 minutes. Drain and transfer to a paper towel–lined plate to dry.

3. Warm a small skillet over medium-low heat for 2 minutes. Add the pine nuts and cook, stirring frequently, for 3 to 4 minutes. Remove the pan from heat and sprinkle the pine nuts with salt. Set them aside.

4. Bring a large pot of water to a boil. When it's boiling, add the fennel fronds and boil for 1 minute. Remove them from the water using a strainer, drain well, pat dry with paper towels, and chop. Keep the water at a low simmer.

5. Add 3 tablespoons of the olive oil to a large skillet and warm it over medium heat. When the oil begis to shimmer, add the onion and a couple pinches of salt and sauté until the onion is soft, about 10 minutes. Add the raisins and pine nuts, sauté for another 3 minutes, and then stir in the blanched fennel fronds and a pinch of salt. Reduce the heat to low, cover, and cook, stirring occasionally, until the onion becomes very tender, about 15 minutes. If the mixture begins to look too dry, add a tablespoon or two of the simmering water.

6. Preheat the oven to 400°F and grease a deep 9 x 13–inch baking dish with oil. Add the anchovies, chopped sardines, and fennel seeds to the skillet with the onion mixture and cook, stirring frequently, until the anchovies have completely dissolved, about 10 minutes.

7. Return the water to a boil. Once it's boiling, add salt and the spaghetti and cook 2 minutes less than the directed cooking time. Reserve ¼ cup of the pasta water and drain the spaghetti. Transfer the pasta to the skillet, add the reserved pasta water, and toss to combine. Transfer the mixture to the prepared baking dish, top it with the whole sardine fillets, drizzle the remaining 2 tablespoons of olive oil over it, and season with pepper. Place the dish in the oven and bake until the sardines start to brown, about 15 minutes. Remove from the oven and let cool slightly before serving.

BAKED SHELLS WITH ZUCCHINI, HAM & BÉCHAMEL SAUCE

YIELD: **6 SERVINGS**

ACTIVE TIME: **1 HOUR**

TOTAL TIME: **1 HOUR AND 45 MINUTES**

INGREDIENTS

2 TABLESPOONS EXTRA-VIRGIN OLIVE OIL

1 YELLOW ONION, CHOPPED

SALT AND PEPPER, TO TASTE

3 ZUCCHINI, MINCED

¾ LB. LARGE SHELL PASTA

¼ CUP BREAD CRUMBS

½ LB. FRESH MOZZARELLA CHEESE, GRATED

½ LB. HONEY HAM, MINCED

BÉCHAMEL SAUCE (SEE PAGE 373)

1½ CUPS FRESHLY GRATED PARMESAN CHEESE

DIRECTIONS

1. Place the olive oil in a large skillet and warm it over medium heat. When the oil begins to shimmer, add the onion and a couple pinches of salt and sauté until the onion is soft, about 10 minutes. Add the zucchini and sauté until it is cooked through, about 10 minutes. Remove the pan from heat and let the mixture cool.

2. Bring a large pot of water to a boil. Once it's boiling, add salt and the pasta and cook for three-quarters of the directed time. Drain, run the pasta under cold water, and place the shells on paper towels to dry.

3. Preheat the oven to 375°F. Combine the zucchini mixture, bread crumbs, mozzarella, ham, and 1 cup of the Béchamel Sauce in a large bowl, season to taste, and gently stir until combined. Divide the mixture between the cooked shells. Spread ¾ cup of the Béchamel Sauce over the bottom of a baking dish large enough to accommodate the pasta in a single layer. Add the filled shells and pour the remaining Béchamel Sauce over the top. Sprinkle the Parmesan over the top and cover the dish with aluminum foil.

4. Place the dish in the oven and reduce the temperature to 350°F. Bake for 20 minutes, remove the foil, and bake until the tops of the shells just start to turn golden brown, about 10 minutes. Remove from the oven and let cool briefly before serving.

BAKED ZITI

YIELD: **6 SERVINGS**

ACTIVE TIME: **40 MINUTES**

TOTAL TIME: **1 HOUR AND 30 MINUTES**

INGREDIENTS

2 TABLESPOONS EXTRA-VIRGIN
OLIVE OIL

½ CUP CHOPPED PANCETTA

1 LARGE YELLOW ONION, CHOPPED

SALT, TO TASTE

2 TEASPOONS RED PEPPER FLAKES

1 TABLESPOON TOMATO PASTE

1 TABLESPOON FISH SAUCE

3 (14 OZ.) CANS OF PEELED WHOLE
SAN MARZANO TOMATOES, WITH
THEIR LIQUID, PUREED

¼ TEASPOON SUGAR

1½ TABLESPOONS UNSALTED BUTTER

1 CUP BÉCHAMEL SAUCE
(SEE PAGE 373)

1 LB. FRESH MOZZARELLA CHEESE,
CHOPPED

1 LB. ZITI

2½ CUPS FRESHLY GRATED PARMESAN
CHEESE

1 HANDFUL OF FRESH BASIL,
CHOPPED, FOR GARNISH

DIRECTIONS

1. Place the olive oil in a large skillet and warm it over medium heat. When the oil begins to shimmer, add the pancetta and sauté until it is golden brown, 4 to 5 minutes. Raise the heat to medium-high and add the onion, a couple pinches of salt, and the red pepper flakes. Reduce the heat to low, cover the pan, and cook, stirring occasionally until the onion has become very soft, about 15 minutes.

2. Raise the heat to medium-high, stir in the tomato paste and fish sauce, and cook, stirring constantly, until the mixture has slightly darkened, about 2 minutes. Stir in the tomatoes, sugar, and a couple pinches of salt and bring the sauce to a gentle boil. Reduce the heat to low and cook, stirring frequently, until the sauce has reduced slightly, about 30 minutes. Season to taste with salt and pepper.

3. Preheat the oven to 350°F. Butter the sides and bottom of 9 x 13–inch baking dish. Combine the Béchamel Sauce and the mozzarella in a large bowl. Bring a large pot of water to a boil. Once it's boiling, add salt and the pasta and cook for half of the directed time. Drain and immediately add to the bowl containing the Béchamel Sauce-and-mozzarella mixture. Add 1 cup of the Parmesan and toss to combine.

4. Add all but 1½ cups of the tomato sauce to the bowl and gently fold to incorporate. Transfer the mixture to the baking dish and top with the remaining tomato sauce and Parmesan. Bake for 15 to 20 minutes and then turn the broiler on and broil the dish until the top starts to brown, about 4 minutes. Remove from the oven and let the dish rest for 15 minutes before serving. Garnish each portion with some of the basil.

RISOTTO WITH SAUSAGE, KALE & ROSEMARY

YIELD: **4 SERVINGS**

ACTIVE TIME: **45 MINUTES**

TOTAL TIME: **1 HOUR AND 30 MINUTES**

INGREDIENTS

4 CUPS VEGETABLE STOCK
(SEE PAGE 122)

1 TEASPOON EXTRA-VIRGIN OLIVE
OIL, PLUS MORE AS NEEDED

6 OZ. SWEET ITALIAN SAUSAGE,
CHOPPED

2 TABLESPOONS FINELY CHOPPED
SHALLOT

1 CUP ARBORIO RICE

½ CUP DRY WHITE WINE

3 LARGE KALE LEAVES, STEMMED
AND SLICED THIN

1 TEASPOON CHOPPED FRESH
ROSEMARY LEAVES

⅓ CUP FRESHLY GRATED PARMESAN
CHEESE, PLUS MORE FOR GARNISH

DIRECTIONS

1. Place the stock in a saucepan, bring it to a boil, and then turn off the heat. Cover the pan and set it aside.

2. Place a large skillet over medium heat and add the oil. When it starts to shimmer, add the sausage and cook until it is browned all over, about 6 minutes. Transfer the sausage to a bowl and set it aside.

3. If necessary, add a little more oil to the pan and add the shallot. Cook until it turns translucent, about 3 minutes, and add the rice. Toast the rice until it is fragrant, about 3 minutes, and then deglaze the pan with the white wine, scraping up any browned bits that have accumulated on the bottom of the pan. Add the sliced kale and continue to cook.

4. When the wine has reduced by half, add the warmed stock a little at a time. The tactic with risotto is to add enough liquid to just cover the rice and let it simmer and absorb the liquid slowly. Stir the contents of the pan occasionally so the rice does not stick to the bottom. Cook the rice, adding stock gradually, for another 8 to 10 minutes. Then, add the rosemary and return the sausage to the pan.

5. Continue adding the stock and stirring until the rice is just tender. Let the rice absorb all of the remaining liquid and remove the pan from heat.

6. Add the Parmesan cheese and gently stir. Spoon the risotto into bowls and top with additional Parmesan cheese.

SQUASH RISOTTO WITH BABY KALE, TOASTED WALNUTS & DRIED CRANBERRIES

YIELD: **6 SERVINGS**

ACTIVE TIME: **35 MINUTES**

TOTAL TIME: **1 HOUR AND 20 MINUTES**

INGREDIENTS

1 STICK OF UNSALTED BUTTER

2 YELLOW ONIONS, CHOPPED

1 SMALL BUTTERNUT SQUASH, PEELED AND CHOPPED

1 TABLESPOON KOSHER SALT, PLUS 2 TEASPOONS

3 CUPS WHOLE MILK

5 CUPS VEGETABLE STOCK (SEE PAGE 122)

2 CUPS ARBORIO RICE

2 CUPS WHITE WINE

3 CUPS BABY KALE, STEMMED AND CHOPPED

¾ CUP TOASTED WALNUTS

½ CUP DRIED CRANBERRIES

FRESH LEMON JUICE, TO TASTE

DIRECTIONS

1. Place 2 tablespoons of the butter in a saucepan and melt it over medium heat. Add one of the onions and cook until it is translucent, about 3 minutes. Add the squash, the tablespoon of salt, and the milk, reduce the heat to low, and cook until the squash is tender, about 20 minutes. Strain, discard the cooking liquid, and transfer the squash and onion to a blender. Puree until smooth and then set aside.

2. Place the stock in a saucepan, bring to a boil, and remove from heat.

3. Place the remaining butter in a large skillet with high sides and melt over medium heat. Add the remaining onion and sauté until translucent, about 3 minutes. Add the rice and remaining salt and cook, stirring constantly, until you can smell a toasted nutty aroma. Be careful not to brown the rice.

4. Deglaze the pan with the white wine and continue to stir until all the liquid has been absorbed. Add the stock in 1-cup increments and stir frequently until the rice is just tender.

5. Add the squash puree and kale, stir to incorporate, and season to taste. Stir in the walnuts, dried cranberries, and lemon juice and serve immediately.

SPRING RISOTTO

YIELD: **4 SERVINGS**

ACTIVE TIME: **45 MINUTES**

TOTAL TIME: **1 HOUR**

INGREDIENTS

½ CUP CHOPPED FRESH CHIVES

½ CUP EXTRA-VIRGIN OLIVE OIL, PLUS 2 TABLESPOONS

½ TEASPOON KOSHER SALT, PLUS MORE TO TASTE

½ LB. ASPARAGUS, TRIMMED

3 CUPS VEGETABLE STOCK (SEE PAGE 122)

1 TABLESPOON UNSALTED BUTTER

2 TABLESPOONS CHOPPED SHALLOT

½ CUP MINCED FENNEL

1 CUP ARBORIO RICE

¼ CUP DRY WHITE WINE

¼ CUP FRESHLY GRATED FONTINA CHEESE, PLUS MORE FOR GARNISH

BLACK PEPPER, TO TASTE

1 TABLESPOON FRESH LEMON JUICE

4 OZ. MUSHROOMS, SEPARATED AND TRIMMED

DIRECTIONS

1. Preheat the oven to 400°F. Place the chives, the ½ cup of olive oil, and salt in a blender and puree until smooth. Set aside.

2. Place the asparagus on a baking sheet, place it in the oven, and roast until tender, 15 to 20 minutes. Remove the asparagus from the oven and briefly let cool. Chop the asparagus into 1-inch pieces and set aside.

3. Place the stock in a small saucepan and bring to a simmer over medium heat. Turn off the heat and leave the pan on the stove. Place the butter and 1 tablespoon of the remaining olive oil in a large skillet and warm over medium heat. Add the shallot and fennel and sauté until they just start to brown, about 5 minutes. Add the rice and toast it until it starts to give off a nutty aroma, while stirring constantly.

4. Deglaze the pan with the white wine and scrape up any browned bits from the bottom. When the wine has been fully absorbed by the rice, add the warm stock a little at a time, stirring constantly to prevent sticking, and cook until the rice absorbs it. If the rice is still crunchy by the time you have used up all of the stock, incorporate water in 1-tablespoon increments until it reaches the desired tenderness.

5. When the rice is a few minutes from being done—still a little too firm—stir in the asparagus. When the rice is al dente, stir in the cheese, season with salt and pepper, and add the lemon juice. Stir to incorporate and turn off the heat.

Continued...

6. Place remaining oil in a large skillet, warm over medium-high heat, and then add the mushrooms in one layer. Add a pinch of salt and cook until the mushrooms start to brown, about 5 minutes. Turn the mushrooms over, add another pinch of salt, and cook for another 5 minutes. Divide the risotto between four warmed bowls and top each portion with a few mushrooms. Drizzle the chive-infused oil over the top and sprinkle additional fontina on top.

VEAL SCALLOPINI

YIELD: **4 SERVINGS**

ACTIVE TIME: **10 MINUTES**

TOTAL TIME: **15 MINUTES**

INGREDIENTS

½ CUP ALL-PURPOSE FLOUR

½ TEASPOON FRESHLY GRATED NUTMEG

SALT AND PEPPER, TO TASTE

2 TABLESPOONS UNSALTED BUTTER

1 LB. VEAL CUTLETS, POUNDED THIN

½ CUP CHICKEN STOCK
(SEE PAGE 118)

¼ CUP PITTED AND SLICED GREEN OLIVES

ZEST AND JUICE OF 1 LEMON

DIRECTIONS

1. Warm a large cast-iron skillet over medium heat for 5 minutes.

2. Place the flour, nutmeg, salt, and pepper on a large plate and stir to combine.

3. Place the butter in the pan. When it starts to sizzle, dredge the veal in the seasoned flour until it is coated lightly on both sides. Working in batches, place the veal in the skillet and cook for about 1 minute on each side, until browned and the juices run clear. Set the cooked veal aside.

4. Deglaze the pan with the stock. Add the olives, lemon zest, and lemon juice, stir to combine, and cook until heated through. To serve, plate the veal and pour the pan sauce over each cutlet.

   NOTE: If you are not a fan of veal, or are simply looking to switch things up, this same preparation will work just as well with chicken cutlets.

CAPRESE CHICKEN

YIELD: **6 SERVINGS**

ACTIVE TIME: **15 MINUTES**

TOTAL TIME: **45 MINUTES**

INGREDIENTS

1 GARLIC CLOVE, MINCED

1 TEASPOON DRIED OREGANO

1 TEASPOON GARLIC POWDER

SALT AND PEPPER, TO TASTE

2 TABLESPOONS EXTRA-VIRGIN OLIVE OIL

2 LBS. BONELESS, SKINLESS CHICKEN BREASTS, HALVED ALONG THEIR EQUATORS

1 LB. TOMATOES, SLICED

1 LB. FRESH MOZZARELLA CHEESE, DRAINED AND SLICED

LEAVES FROM 1 BUNCH OF FRESH BASIL

BALSAMIC GLAZE, FOR GARNISH

DIRECTIONS

1. Preheat the oven to 375°F. Place the minced garlic, oregano, garlic powder, salt, and pepper in a bowl and stir to combine. Place 1 tablespoon of the olive oil and the chicken breasts in a bowl and toss to coat. Dredge the chicken breasts in the garlic-and-spice mixture and set them aside.

2. Coat the bottom of a large cast-iron skillet with the remaining oil and warm it over medium-high heat. When the oil starts to shimmer, add the chicken in batches and sear for 1 minute on each side.

3. When all of the chicken has been seared, place half of the breasts in an even layer on the bottom of the skillet. Top with two-thirds of the tomatoes and mozzarella and half of the basil leaves. Place the remaining chicken breasts on top in an even layer and cover it with the remaining tomatoes, mozzarella, and basil.

4. Place the skillet in the oven and cook until the interior temperature of the chicken breasts is 165°F, about 15 minutes. Remove the skillet from the oven and let rest for 10 minutes. Drizzle the balsamic glaze over the top and serve.

SLOW-COOKER CHICKEN & SAUSAGE CACCIATORE

INGREDIENTS

6 BONELESS, SKINLESS CHICKEN THIGHS

1 (28 OZ.) CAN OF PEELED WHOLE SAN MARZANO TOMATOES, DRAINED

1 (28 OZ.) CAN OF DICED TOMATOES, WITH THEIR JUICE

⅔ CUP DRY RED WINE

4 SHALLOTS, CHOPPED

3 GARLIC CLOVES, MINCED

1 GREEN BELL PEPPER, STEMMED, SEEDS AND RIBS REMOVED, AND CHOPPED

1 YELLOW BELL PEPPER, STEMMED, SEEDS AND RIBS REMOVED, AND DICED

1 CUP BUTTON MUSHROOM CAPS, CHOPPED

1½ TEASPOONS DRIED OREGANO

1 TABLESPOON GARLIC POWDER

1 TABLESPOON SUGAR

2 TABLESPOONS KOSHER SALT, PLUS MORE TO TASTE

½ TEASPOON RED PEPPER FLAKES

BLACK PEPPER, TO TASTE

PARMESAN CHEESE, FRESHLY GRATED, FOR GARNISH

FRESH PARSLEY, FINELY CHOPPED, FOR GARNISH

DIRECTIONS

1. Place all of the ingredients, save the Parmesan and parsley, in a slow cooker and cook on low until the chicken is very tender, about 5½ hours. The cooking time may vary depending on your slow cooker, so be sure to check after about 4½ hours to avoid overcooking.

2. To serve, top each portion with a generous amount of Parmesan cheese and parsley.

PESTO CHICKEN WITH CHARRED TOMATOES

YIELD: **4 SERVINGS**

ACTIVE TIME: **5 MINUTES**

TOTAL TIME: **3 HOURS**

INGREDIENTS

2 LBS. CHICKEN PIECES

SALT AND PEPPER, TO TASTE

2 BATCHES OF BASIL PESTO
(SEE PAGE 78)

4 PLUM TOMATOES, HALVED

DIRECTIONS

1. Season the chicken with salt and pepper. Place the pesto in a bowl, add the chicken pieces, and stir until they are evenly coated. Cover the bowl and let the chicken marinate in the refrigerator for 2 hours.

2. Preheat the oven to 400°F. Remove the chicken from the refrigerator and let it come to room temperature.

3. Place the chicken in a baking dish. Season the tomatoes with salt and pepper and place them in the baking dish. Cover the dish with foil, place it in the oven, and roast for 25 minutes. Remove the foil and continue roasting until the chicken is cooked through, about 25 minutes. Remove from the oven and let the chicken rest for 10 minutes before serving.

CHAPTER 7

DESSERTS

Gelato and Granita in the warmer months. Cannoli and Zeppole for festive occasions. Biscotti and Torcetti di Saint Vincent when you need just a bit of sweetness to keep your eyes on all the good fortune that visited you today. Great with a cup of coffee or a digestif, these confections provide the day with a sweet conclusion while your mind starts to muse on the delicious dish you're going to make tomorrow.

LEMON GELATO

YIELD: **1 PINT**

ACTIVE TIME: **40 MINUTES**

TOTAL TIME: **6 HOURS**

INGREDIENTS

2 CUPS WHOLE MILK

ZEST OF ½ LEMON

5 LARGE EGG YOLKS

½ CUP SUGAR

DIRECTIONS

1. In a small saucepan, combine the milk and lemon zest and warm over medium-low heat until the mixture starts to steam. Remove the pan from heat, cover it, and let the mixture steep for about 20 minutes.

2. Put a few inches of ice water in a large bowl. In a mixing bowl, whisk together the egg yolks and sugar. Strain the infused milk into a pitcher, then whisk it into the yolk mixture.

3. Pour the mixture into a clean saucepan and place it over medium-low heat. While stirring constantly with a wooden spoon, warm until it is thick enough to coat back of the spoon, about 10 minutes. Take care not to overheat the mixture; it will curdle.

4. Place the pan in the ice water bath and stir until cool. Transfer to a bowl, cover it, and refrigerate for about 1 hour.

5. Pour the mixture into an ice cream maker and churn until it has the desired consistency, about 15 minutes. Transfer to an airtight container and freeze for 4 hours before serving.

STRAWBERRY GELATO

YIELD: **1 QUART**

ACTIVE TIME: **40 MINUTES**

TOTAL TIME: **6 HOURS**

INGREDIENTS

1 LB. RIPE, SWEET STRAWBERRIES, HULLED

½ CUP SUGAR

¼ CUP WATER

2 CUPS WHOLE MILK

2 TEASPOONS FRESH LEMON JUICE

PINCH OF FINE SEA SALT

DIRECTIONS

1. Place the strawberries, sugar, and water in a medium saucepan and bring the mixture to a simmer. Cook until the strawberries become very soft, about 15 minutes.

2. Remove from heat and transfer half of the mixture to a blender. Puree until smooth, add half of the milk, and puree to incorporate. Repeat with the remaining strawberry mixture and milk. Transfer the puree to a bowl and chill in the refrigerator for 1 hour.

3. Stir the lemon juice and salt into the gelato base. Pour the mixture into an ice cream maker and churn until it has the desired consistency, about 15 minutes. Transfer to an airtight container and freeze for 4 hours before serving.

CANNOLI

YIELD: **10 CANNOLI**

ACTIVE TIME: **45 MINUTES**

TOTAL TIME: **4 HOURS**

INGREDIENTS

¾ LB. WHOLE-MILK RICOTTA CHEESE

¾ LB. MASCARPONE CHEESE

4 OZ. GRATED CHOCOLATE

¾ CUP CONFECTIONERS' SUGAR

1½ TEASPOONS PURE VANILLA
EXTRACT

PINCH OF FINE SEA SALT

10 CANNOLI SHELLS

DIRECTIONS

1. Line a colander with three pieces of cheesecloth and place it in sink. Place the ricotta in the colander, form the cheesecloth into a pouch, and twist to extract as much liquid as possible from the ricotta. Keep the pouch taut and twisted, place it in a baking dish, and place a cast-iron skillet on top. Weight the skillet down with 2 large, heavy cans and place in the refrigerator for 1 hour.

2. Discard the drained liquid and transfer the ricotta to a mixing bowl. Add the mascarpone, half of the grated chocolate, the confectioners' sugar, vanilla, and salt and stir until well combined. Cover the bowl and refrigerate for at least 1 hour. The mixture will keep for up to 24 hours.

3. Line an 18 x 13-inch baking sheet with parchment paper. Fill a small saucepan halfway with water and bring it to a gentle simmer. Place the remaining chocolate in a heatproof mixing bowl, place it over the simmering water, and stir until it is melted.

4. Dip the ends of the cannoli shells in the melted chocolate, let the excess drip off, and transfer them to the baking sheet. Let the shells sit until chocolate is firm, about 1 hour.

5. Place the cannoli filling in a piping bag and cut a ½-inch slit in it. Pipe the filling into the shells, working from both ends in order to ensure they are filled evenly.

ZABAGLIONE

YIELD: **6 SERVINGS**

ACTIVE TIME: **20 MINUTES**

TOTAL TIME: **20 MINUTES**

INGREDIENTS

4 EGG YOLKS

¼ CUP SUGAR

½ CUP DRY MARSALA WINE

FRESH RASPBERRIES, FOR GARNISH

DIRECTIONS

1. Fill a small saucepan halfway with water and bring it to a gentle simmer. Combine the egg yolks and sugar in a heatproof bowl and place it over the simmering water. Whisk the mixture until it is pale yellow and creamy.

2. While whisking continually, slowly add the Marsala. The mixture will begin to foam and then it will swell. Whisk until it is very soft with a number of gentle peaks and valleys. Ladle into the serving glasses and garnish with fresh raspberries.

LEMON RICOTTA CHEESECAKE

YIELD: **1 CHEESECAKE**

ACTIVE TIME: **1 HOUR**

TOTAL TIME: **8 HOURS**

INGREDIENTS

½ LB. WHOLE-MILK RICOTTA CHEESE

½ LB. CREAM CHEESE, SOFTENED

6 OZ. SUGAR

1 EGG

ZEST AND JUICE OF 1 LEMON

¼ TEASPOON PURE VANILLA EXTRACT

1 TABLESPOON CORNSTARCH, PLUS 1½ TEASPOONS

1½ TABLESPOONS ALL-PURPOSE FLOUR

1 OZ. UNSALTED BUTTER, MELTED

1 CUP SOUR CREAM

1 GRAHAM CRACKER CRUST, IN A SPRINGFORM PAN

WHIPPED CREAM, FOR SERVING

DIRECTIONS

1. Preheat the oven to 350°F. Bring 8 cups of water to a boil in a medium saucepan.

2. In the work bowl of a stand mixer fitted with the paddle attachment, cream the ricotta, cream cheese, sugar, and lemon zest on high until the mixture is soft and airy, about 10 minutes. Scrape down the work bowl with a rubber spatula as needed. Reduce the speed of the mixer to medium and incorporate the egg, scraping the bowl as needed. Add the lemon juice and mix until incorporated. Add the cornstarch and flour and beat until incorporated. Reduce the speed to low, add the butter and sour cream, and beat until the mixture is very smooth.

3. Pour the mixture into the crust, place the cheesecake in a large baking pan with high sides, and gently pour the boiling water into the baking pan until it reaches halfway up the sides of the springform pan.

4. Cover the baking pan with aluminum foil, place it in the oven, and bake until the cheesecake is set and only slightly jiggly in the center, 50 minutes to 1 hour.

5. Turn off the oven and leave the oven door cracked. Allow the cheesecake to rest in the cooling oven for 45 minutes.

6. Remove the cheesecake from the oven and transfer to a cooling rack. Let it sit at room temperature for 1 hour.

7. Transfer the cheesecake to the refrigerator and let it cool for at least 4 hours before serving and slicing. To serve, top each slice with a dollop of whipped cream.

OLIVE OIL CAKE

YIELD: **1 CAKE**

ACTIVE TIME: **30 MINUTES**

TOTAL TIME: **2 HOURS**

INGREDIENTS

ZEST AND JUICE OF 3 LEMONS

½ CUP SUGAR, PLUS 7 OZ.

7 OZ. ALL-PURPOSE FLOUR

1 TEASPOON BAKING SODA

1 TEASPOON BAKING POWDER

½ TEASPOON KOSHER SALT

¾ CUP FULL-FAT PLAIN YOGURT

¾ CUP EXTRA-VIRGIN OLIVE OIL

3 EGGS

CONFECTIONERS' SUGAR, FOR DUSTING

DIRECTIONS

1. Preheat the oven to 325°F. Coat a round, 9-inch cake pan with nonstick cooking spray.

2. Place the lemon juice and the ½ cup of sugar in a small saucepan and bring the mixture to a boil, stirring to dissolve the sugar. Remove from heat and let the mixture cool.

3. Sift the flour, baking soda, and baking powder into a small bowl and set the mixture aside.

4. In a medium bowl, whisk the lemon zest, remaining sugar, salt, yogurt, olive oil, and eggs until the mixture smooth and combined. Add the dry mixture and whisk until a smooth batter forms.

5. Pour the batter into the prepared cake pan, place it in the oven, and bake until the cake is lightly golden brown and baked through, 45 minutes to 1 hour. Insert a cake tester in the center of each cake to check for doneness.

6. Remove the cake from the oven, transfer to a cooling rack, and gently pour the lemon syrup over the hot cake. Let the cake cool completely.

7. Carefully remove the cake from the pan, transfer to a serving plate, dust with confectioners' sugar, and serve.

FLORENTINES

YIELD: **30 COOKIES**

ACTIVE TIME: **10 MINUTES**

TOTAL TIME: **45 MINUTES**

INGREDIENTS

¾ CUP SUGAR

1 TEASPOON PURE VANILLA EXTRACT

7 TABLESPOONS HEAVY CREAM

1.5 OZ. UNSALTED BUTTER

1½ CUPS SLIVERED ALMONDS

⅓ CUP CANDIED CITRUS PEELS

⅓ CUP DRIED CHERRIES OR PLUMS, CHOPPED

⅓ CUP RAISINS

4 OZ. DARK CHOCOLATE

DIRECTIONS

1. Place the sugar, vanilla extract, and cream in a saucepan and bring to a boil. Remove from heat, add the butter, and let it melt. Stir in the almonds, candied citrus peels, dried cherries or plums, and the raisins.

2. Preheat the oven to 400°F and line two baking sheets with parchment paper. Place teaspoons of the mixture on the baking sheets, place the cookies in the oven, and bake for 5 to 10 minutes, until golden brown. Remove from the oven and let the cookies cool on the baking sheets for 5 minutes before transferring to wire racks to cool completely.

3. Fill a small saucepan halfway with water and bring it to a gentle simmer. Place the chocolate in a heatproof mixing bowl, place it over the simmering water, and stir until it is melted. Spread the melted chocolate on the undersides of the cookies and leave to set before serving.

ALMOND GRANITA

YIELD: **4 SERVINGS**

ACTIVE TIME: **30 MINUTES**

TOTAL TIME: **2 HOURS AND 30 MINUTES**

INGREDIENTS

1¼ CUPS WHOLE MILK

1¼ CUPS WATER

3 OZ. SLIVERED ALMONDS (ABOUT ½ CUP), TOASTED, COOLED, CHOPPED

2.7 OZ. SUGAR (ABOUT ⅓ CUP)

2.5 OZ. ALMOND PASTE (ABOUT ¼ CUP)

1 TEASPOON ALMOND EXTRACT

DIRECTIONS

1. Place all of the ingredients in a blender and puree until smooth.

2. Place a fine-mesh strainer over a square, metal 9-inch baking pan. Strain the puree into the pan, pressing down on the solids to extract as much liquid as possible. Discard the solids.

3. Cover the pan with plastic wrap and freeze until the mixture is firm, about 2 hours.

4. Using a fork, vigorously scrape the mixture until it is a collection of icy flakes. Cover with aluminum foil and store in freezer. Scrape again with a fork before enjoying.

   NOTE: Make sure you use almond paste, and not marzipan, which sweetened.

PIGNOLI

YIELD: **36 COOKIES**

ACTIVE TIME: **15 MINUTES**

TOTAL TIME: **40 MINUTES**

INGREDIENTS

1¾ CUPS UNSWEETENED ALMOND
PASTE, PLUS 1 TEASPOON

1½ CUPS CONFECTIONERS' SUGAR

2 TABLESPOONS HONEY

PINCH OF CINNAMON

PINCH OF FINE SEA SALT

2 LARGE EGG WHITES, AT ROOM
TEMPERATURE

ZEST OF 1 LEMON

¾ CUP PINE NUTS

DIRECTIONS

1. Preheat the oven to 350°F and line two baking sheets with parchment paper. In the work bowl of a stand mixer fitted with the paddle attachment, beat the almond paste until it is thoroughly broken up. Add the confectioners' sugar and beat the mixture on low until combined.

2. Add the honey, cinnamon, salt, egg whites, and lemon zest, raise the speed to medium, and beat until the mixture is very thick, about 5 minutes.

3. Drop tablespoons of dough onto the prepared baking sheets and gently pat pine nuts into each of the cookies. Place the cookies in the oven and bake until golden brown, 12 to 14 minutes. Remove from the oven and let the cookies cool on the baking sheets before enjoying.

ORANGE PISTACHIO BISCOTTI

YIELD: **24 BISCOTTI**

ACTIVE TIME: **1 HOUR**

TOTAL TIME: **4 HOURS AND 30 MINUTES**

INGREDIENTS

4 OZ. UNSALTED BUTTER, SOFTENED

ZEST OF 1 ORANGE

7 OZ. SUGAR

¾ TEASPOON PURE VANILLA EXTRACT

2 EGGS

10 OZ. ALL-PURPOSE FLOUR

½ TEASPOON BAKING SODA

½ TEASPOON BAKING POWDER

½ TEASPOON FINE SEA SALT

4 OZ. SHELLED PISTACHIOS, TOASTED

1 CUP DRIED CRANBERRIES

DIRECTIONS

1. Line a baking sheet with parchment paper. In the work bowl of a stand mixer fitted with the paddle attachment, cream the butter, orange zest, sugar, and vanilla extract on medium until the mixture is very light and fluffy, about 5 minutes. Scrape down the work bowl and then beat the mixture for another 5 minutes.

2. Add the eggs one at a time and beat on low until incorporated, again scraping the work bowl as needed. When both eggs have been incorporated, scrape down the work bowl and beat on medium for 1 minute.

3. Add the remaining ingredients, reduce the speed to low, and beat until the mixture comes together as a dough.

4. Place the dough on the baking sheet and form it into a log that is the length of the pan and anywhere from 3 to 4 inches wide. Place the dough in the refrigerator for 1 hour.

5. Preheat the oven to 350°F.

6. Place the biscotti dough in the oven and bake until golden brown and a cake tester comes out clean when inserted into the center, 25 to 30 minutes. Remove the biscotti from the oven, transfer it to a cooling rack, and let it cool completely before chilling in the refrigerator for 2 hours.

7. Preheat the oven to 250°F. Cut the biscotti to the desired size, place them on their sides, place in the oven, and bake for 10 minutes. Remove from the oven, turn them over, and bake for another 6 minutes. Remove from the oven and let them cool completely before enjoying.

LEMON & ALMOND BISCOTTI

YIELD: **24 BISCOTTI**

ACTIVE TIME: **1 HOUR**

TOTAL TIME: **4 HOURS AND 30 MINUTES**

INGREDIENTS

8 OZ. UNSALTED BUTTER, SOFTENED

ZEST OF 1 LEMON

7 OZ. SUGAR

¾ TEASPOON VANILLA EXTRACT

2 EGGS

10 OZ. ALL-PURPOSE FLOUR

½ TEASPOON BAKING SODA

½ TEASPOON BAKING POWDER

½ TEASPOON FINE SEA SALT

8 OZ. SLIVERED ALMOND, TOASTED

DIRECTIONS

1. Line a baking sheet with parchment paper. In the work bowl of a stand mixer fitted with the paddle attachment, cream the butter, lemon zest, sugar, and vanilla extract on medium until the mixture is very light and fluffy, about 5 minutes. Scrape down the work bowl and then beat the mixture for another 5 minutes.

2. Add the eggs one at a time and beat on low until incorporated, again scraping the work bowl as needed. When both eggs have been incorporated, scrape down the work bowl and beat on medium for 1 minute.

3. Add the remaining ingredients, reduce the speed to low, and beat until the mixture comes together as a dough.

4. Place the dough on the baking sheet and form it into a log that is the length of the pan and anywhere from 3 to 4 inches wide. Place the dough in the refrigerator for 1 hour.

5. Preheat the oven to 350°F.

6. Place the biscotti dough in the oven and bake until golden brown and a cake tester comes out clean when inserted into the center, 25 to 30 minutes. Remove the biscotti from the oven, transfer it to a cooling rack, and let it cool completely before chilling in the refrigerator for 2 hours.

7. Preheat the oven to 250°F. Cut the biscotti to the desired size, place them on their sides, place in the oven, and bake for 10 minutes. Remove from the oven, turn them over, and bake for another 6 minutes. Remove from the oven and let them cool completely before enjoying.

ZEPPOLE

YIELD: **18 ZEPPOLE**

ACTIVE TIME: **30 MINUTES**

TOTAL TIME: **1 HOUR**

INGREDIENTS

6.7 OZ. ALL-PURPOSE FLOUR

1 TABLESPOON SUGAR

2 TEASPOONS INSTANT YEAST

1 TEASPOON BAKING POWDER

½ TEASPOON FINE SEA SALT

1 CUP WARM WATER (105°F)

½ TEASPOON PURE VANILLA
EXTRACT

CANOLA OIL, AS NEEDED

CONFECTIONERS' SUGAR, FOR
DUSTING (OPTIONAL)

DIRECTIONS

1. Combine the flour, sugar, yeast, baking powder, and salt in
    large bowl and whisk in the water and vanilla. Cover the bowl
    with plastic wrap and let the batter rise at room temperature
    until it doubles in size, 15 to 25 minutes.

2. Add oil to a Dutch oven until it is about 1½ inches deep and
    warm to 350°F over medium heat.

3. Using a greased tablespoon, add six heaping tablespoons of
    the batter to the oil and fry until golden brown and cooked
    through, 2 to 3 minutes, turning halfway through. Make sure
    the oil remains around 350°F while frying the zeppole.

4. Transfer the cooked zeppole to a paper towel–lined plate.
    When all of the zeppole have been cooked, dust them with
    confectioners' sugar (if desired) and serve.

TORCETTI DI SAINT VINCENT

YIELD: **24 COOKIES**

ACTIVE TIME: **45 MINUTES**

TOTAL TIME: **3 HOURS**

INGREDIENTS

½ CUP WARM WATER (105°F)

1¼ TEASPOONS ACTIVE DRY YEAST

7.5 OZ. ALL-PURPOSE FLOUR, PLUS MORE AS NEEDED

¼ TEASPOON FINE SEA SALT

1.25 OZ. UNSALTED BUTTER, CHILLED

¼ CUP SUGAR

DIRECTIONS

1. Place the water and yeast in a mixing bowl and gently stir to combine. Let the mixture sit until it becomes foamy, about 10 minutes.

2. In mixing bowl, combine the flour and salt. Add the butter and work the mixture with your hands until it is incorporated and the mixture is fine and crumbly. Stir in the yeast mixture and work the mixture until it comes together as a dough. Place the dough in a greased bowl and roll it around until it is well coated. Cover the bowl with plastic wrap and let the dough rise for 1 hour.

3. Line two baking sheets with parchment paper. Place the dough on a flour-dusted work surface and pat it into a square that is about 3 inches thick. Cut the dough into smaller squares and roll each one until 5 inches long and as thin as a pencil.

4. Place the sugar on a plate and roll the pieces of dough in it until completely coated. Form the pieces of dough into loops, place them on the baking sheets, leaving 1½ inches between them, and let them rest for 20 minutes.

5. Preheat the oven to 325°F.

6. Place the cookies in the oven and bake until golden brown, 20 to 25 minutes. Remove from the oven and let cool completely before serving.

LADYFINGERS

YIELD: **30 LADYFINGERS**

ACTIVE TIME: **30 MINUTES**

TOTAL TIME: **1 HOUR AND 15 MINUTES**

INGREDIENTS

3.3 OZ. SIFTED ALL-PURPOSE FLOUR,
PLUS MORE AS NEEDED

3 EGGS, SEPARATED

3.5 OZ. SUGAR, PLUS 1 TABLESPOON

1 TEASPOON PURE VANILLA EXTRACT

PINCH OF SALT

3 OZ. CONFECTIONERS' SUGAR

DIRECTIONS

1. Preheat the oven to 300°F. Line two baking sheets with parchment paper and dust them with flour. Shake to remove any excess.

2. Place the egg yolks in a mixing bowl and gradually incorporate the sugar, beat with a handheld mixer at high speed. When the mixture is thick and a pale yellow, whisk in the vanilla.

3. In the work bowl of a stand mixer fitted with the whisk attachment, beat the egg whites and salt until the mixture holds soft peaks. Scoop one-quarter of the egg whites into the egg yolk mixture and sift one-quarter of the flour on top. Fold to combine and repeat until all of the egg whites and flour have been incorporated and the mixture is light and airy.

4. Spread the batter in 4-inch-long strips on the baking sheets, leaving 1 inch between them. Sprinkle the confectioners' sugar over the top and place them in the oven.

5. Bake until lightly golden brown and just crispy, about 20 minutes. Remove from the oven and transfer the ladyfingers to a wire rack to cool completely before enjoying.

TIRAMISU

YIELD: **8 TO 10 SERVINGS**

ACTIVE TIME: **20 MINUTES**

TOTAL TIME: **3 HOURS AND 30 MINUTES**

INGREDIENTS

2 CUPS FRESHLY BREWED ESPRESSO

½ CUP GRANULATED SUGAR, PLUS 1 TABLESPOON

3 TABLESPOONS KAHLÚA

4 LARGE EGG YOLKS

2 CUPS MASCARPONE CHEESE

1 CUP HEAVY CREAM

30 LADYFINGERS (SEE PAGE 428)

2 TABLESPOONS COCOA POWDER

DIRECTIONS

1. Place the espresso, 1 tablespoon of sugar, and Kahlúa in a bowl and stir to combine. Set the mixture aside.

2. Place two inches of water in a saucepan and bring to a simmer. Place the remaining sugar and egg yolks in a heatproof mixing bowl and set the bowl over the simmering water. Whisk the mixture continually until it has nearly tripled in size, approximately 10 minutes. Remove from heat, add the mascarpone, and fold to incorporate.

3. Pour the heavy cream into a separate bowl and whisk until soft peaks start to form. Gently fold the whipped cream into the mascarpone mixture.

4. Place the Ladyfingers in the espresso mixture and briefly submerge them. Place an even layer of the soaked Ladyfingers on the bottom of a 9 x 13-inch baking dish. This will use up approximately half of the Ladyfingers. Spread half of the mascarpone mixture on top of the Ladyfingers and then repeat until the Ladyfingers and mascarpone have been used up.

5. Cover with plastic and place in the refrigerator for 3 hours. Sprinkle the cocoa powder over the top before serving.

RUSTICO WITH HONEY GLAZE

YIELD: **8 SERVINGS**

ACTIVE TIME: **15 MINUTES**

TOTAL TIME: **30 MINUTES**

INGREDIENTS

CANOLA OIL, AS NEEDED

4 SHEETS OF FROZEN PUFF PASTRY, THAWED

½ LB. FRESH MOZZARELLA CHEESE, SLICED

1 CUP HONEY

DIRECTIONS

1. Add canola oil to a Dutch oven until it is 2 inches deep and warm it to 350°F. Cut eight 5-inch circles and eight 4-inch circles from the sheets of puff pastry. Place a slice of cheese in the center of each 5-inch circle. Place a 4-inch circle over the cheese, fold the bottom circle over the edge, and pinch to seal.

2. Place one or two rustico in the oil and fry until the dough is a light golden brown and crispy, about 2 to 3 minutes. Remove from the oil and transfer to a paper towel–lined wire rack. Repeat until all eight wraps have been fried. To serve, drizzle honey over the top of each rustico.

AFFOGATO

YIELD: **4 SERVINGS**

ACTIVE TIME: **5 MINUTES**

TOTAL TIME: **5 MINUTES**

INGREDIENTS

1 PINT OF VANILLA ICE CREAM

¼ CUP SAMBUCA

1 TEASPOON FRESHLY GRATED NUTMEG

1¼ CUPS FRESHLY BREWED ESPRESSO OR VERY STRONG COFFEE

WHIPPED CREAM, FOR SERVING

DIRECTIONS

1. Scoop ice cream into five small glasses. Pour some of the Sambuca over each scoop and sprinkle a bit of nutmeg on top.

2. Pour the espresso or coffee over the ice cream. Top each portion with whipped cream and serve.

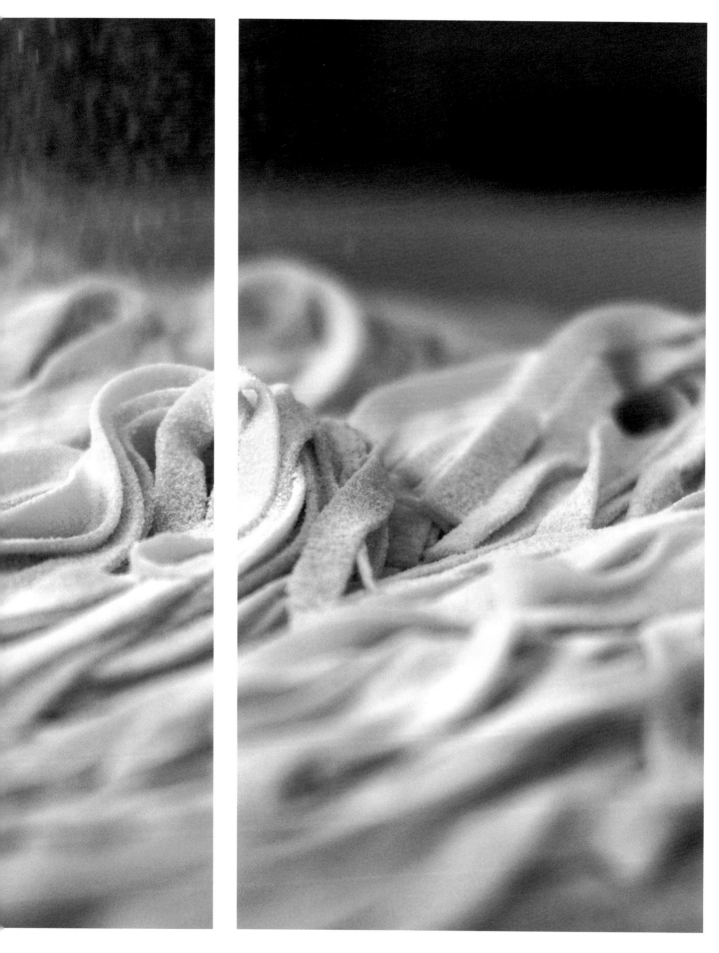

METRIC CONVERSIONS

U.S. Measurement	Approximate Metric Liquid Measurement	Approximate Metric Dry Measurement
1 teaspoon	5 ml	5 g
1 tablespoon or ½ ounce	15 ml	14 g
1 ounce or ⅛ cup	30 ml	29 g
¼ cup or 2 ounces	60 ml	57 g
⅓ cup	80 ml	76 g
½ cup or 4 ounces	120 ml	113 g
⅔ cup	160 ml	151 g
¾ cup or 6 ounces	180 ml	170 g
1 cup or 8 ounces or ½ pint	240 ml	227 g
1½ cups or 12 ounces	350 ml	340 g
2 cups or 1 pint or 16 ounces	475 ml	454 g
3 cups or 1½ pints	700 ml	680 g
4 cups or 2 pints or 1 quart	950 ml	908 g

INDEX

ABOUT CIDER MILL PRESS
BOOK PUBLISHERS

⁕ ⁕ ⁕

Good ideas ripen with time. From seed to harvest,
Cider Mill Press brings fine reading, information,
and entertainment together between the covers of its
creatively crafted books. Our Cider Mill bears fruit twice
a year, publishing a new crop of titles each spring and fall.

BOOK
PUBLISHERS
KENNEBUNKPORT, MAINE

"Where Good Books Are Ready for Press"

Visit us online at
cidermillpress.com
or write to us at
PO Box 454
12 Spring St.
Kennebunkport, Maine 04046